La Nostra Costa
(Our Coast)

A Family's Journey to and From the
North Coast of Santa Cruz, California
(1923-1983)

Ivano Franco Comelli

authorHOUSE

1663 Liberty Drive, Suite 200
Bloomington, Indiana 47403
(800) 839-8640
www.AuthorHouse.com

This book is a work of non-fiction. Unless otherwise noted, the author and the publisher make no explicit guarantees as to the accuracy of the information contained in this book and in some cases, names of people and places have been altered to protect their privacy.

© 2006 Ivano Franco Comelli. All rights reserved.

No part of this book may be reproduced, stored in a retrieval system, or transmitted by any means without the written permission of the author.

First published by AuthorHouse 2/23/2006

ISBN: 1-4208-7976-6 (sc)
ISBN: 1-4208-8192-2 (dj)

Library of Congress Control Number: 2005908243

Printed in the United States of America
Bloomington, Indiana

This book is printed on acid-free paper.

Dedication

I dedicated this book to the children:

Christopher Fritter
Andrew Fritter
Michael Fritter
Willie Fritter
Kristian Knowles
Cole Rydstrom
Wyatt Rydstrom

Shaina Reid
Mathew Reid
Andrew Roubal
Ryan Roubal

May the spirit of the Coast be with you always.

- Ivano

Table of Contents

A Rancere's Lament	1
1. Introduzione (Introduction)	3
2. La Costa (The Coast)	15
3. La Costa E La Guerra (The Coast And The War)	25
4. Il Golce (The Gulch)	35
5. Uomini Al Lavoro (Men At Work)	47
6. Donne Al Lavoro (Women At Work)	57
7. Ranceri (Ranchers)	63
8. La Cuoca (The Cook)	81
9. Finito Con Il Golce (Finished With The Gulch)	95
10. Davenport	105
11. Pino Brovia	119
12. La Strada Per Pescadero (The Road To Pescadereo)	129
13. Tre Famiglie Friulani (Three Friulian Families)	139
14. Famiglie Insieme (Families Together)	149
15. Il Mare (The Ocean)	161
16. Figli Di Ferro (Sons Of Iron)	175
17. Lina	187
18. Il Rancio Di Rodoni (The Rodoni Ranch)	201

19. Giochi (Games)	209
20. Sesso E Altri Divertimenti (Sex & Other Amusements)	215
21. Serafina's	221
22. Laguna	231
23. Il Rancio Di Lorenzi (The Lorenzi Ranch)	245
24. Il Carrettone Vecchio (The Old Carriage)	253
25. La Scuola (The School)	269
26. La Costa Spaventousa (The Scary Coast)	289
27. Rancio D' Bronco - Casa D' Valentina (Bronco's Ranch - Valentina's House)	303
28. Il Ponte E La Polizia (The Bridge And The Police)	319
29. Si Ritorna A La Costa (Let Us Return To The Coast)	343
30. Da Solo (Alone)	361
31. Dopo La Costa (After The Coast)	369
Il Ultimo Ponte (The Last Bridge)	375
Riconoscimenti (Acknowledgements)	379

A Rancere's Lament

(*circa* 1937)

On a particularly foggy morning, a *rancere* was in the field, dutifully irrigating the crops. He was deeply depressed. Leaning on his *shavola*, he looked up into the obscured sky. With sadness in his voice, and as though expecting something or someone to be *up there*, he began his lament:

"I work everyday in these fields, I am ankle-deep in mud, all I smell is *pattume*, and in a couple of hours *il vento* will blow dirt and debris in my face. Next month the rains will come; they will soak me through, and I will have to carry those wet sprout sacks up and down these muddy rows. I work ten to twelve hours every day for very little money. My young son is sick and I cannot pay the doctor. My young wife is pregnant and our second baby is on its way. Where will I get the money to feed another mouth? I promised my beautiful wife an easy life in America; all she got was hard work and desperate times. If there is a God up there, why doesn't he show himself? Why doesn't he make my son well? Why doesn't he help me? I need more money! O God, if you are up there, why don't you wave your hand, and make things better for me?"

Not really expecting an answer, the *rancere* lowered his head and with his *shavola* slowly returned to working the soil. Then from out of the thick, eerie mist, he thought he heard someone, perhaps a woman, say in a soft and gentle voice:

"O rancere mi. Don't you know? You live *su per la costa*—not Heaven."

1. Introduzione (Introduction)

The relatively small coastal town of Santa Cruz, California is located, in all its serenity, at the northern tip of Monterey Bay, about 75 miles south of San Francisco. I was born Ivano Franco Comelli on April 19, 1937, at the old Santa Cruz Hospital on Soquel Avenue. (Presently, this is the site of the Branciforte Plaza.) Dr. Norman R. Sullivan was the doctor in charge, and it was he who suggested the name Ivano [ee **vah** no] to my mother.[1] In 1942, because of circumstances that I will describe in this book, my name was unceremoniously changed to Ivan Frank Comelli.

My father, Gervasio [jerr **vah** zee-oh] Comelli, was born in 1900, in Nimis [**nee** meez], Provincia di Udine, Italia. Nimis, a small agricultural village, is located in the Friuli [**free** ou-lee] region, in the northeastern section of Italy, not too far from Trieste and what used to be the Yugoslavian border. The inhabitants, as they still do today, commonly spoke the Friulian dialect.[2] As a boy, Gervasio was known by the villagers as "Vasin" [**vah** zeen].

My mother, Valentina Bressani, was also born in Nimis, in 1913. As far as I know my grandfathers, Giovanni Comelli and Gianni Bressani were also born in Nimis. My grandmothers, Carolina (Cuciz) Comelli (paternal) and Angelina (Ronchi) Bressani (maternal), were born in the Friuli region. Like all others born in this region, they were known as *Friulanos* [**free** ou-lanos], or *Furlanos*. I never met my grandfathers or my paternal grandmother. My maternal grandmother, Angelina Bressani, came to the United States in 1955 and died in Santa Cruz in 1980, at the age of ninety-four.

My father immigrated to the United States at the age of twenty-three. Italy, after World War I, was in desperate straits both economically and politically. Times were so bad that his father (my grandfather) was steadily accumulating debt in order to sustain his family of seven. In 1922, the black shirted Fascists, under the leadership of Benito Mussolini, "marched" on Rome to seize power and ostensibly save the country from a plethora of government excesses caused by communism, socialism, and liberalism. In 1923, in order to consolidate his authority, Mussolini authorized his "black shirts" to commit certain violent acts, including murder, against his political opponents. It was during this period of political turmoil and upheaval, that Gervasio, my father, decided to make contact with villagers who had previously immigrated (for economic reasons) to the United States. As Providence would have it, some, like Antonio "Tony" Micossi, had settled in Santa Cruz County, *circa* 1920.[3] I am sure that my father's original intent was to come to the United States, make some money in order to help his family in Nimis, and then perhaps return to Italy to live.

The Ellis Island website has no records of a Gervasio Comelli.[4] However, they do indicate that a Garrasio Comelli, age twenty-three, and listing Kinis, Italy as his hometown, disembarked from the passenger ship America on December 3, 1923.[5] (I could find no information indicating that a Kinis, Italy even exists.) Probing further, I discovered that the ship's passenger manifest (for steerage) did in fact have Garrasio's hometown listed correctly as Nimis, Italy. On that manifest, Garrasio gave a final destination of Davenport, California, naming an Attilio Tomada as a friend. According to my father's goddaughter, Thelma (Micossi) Gill, Attilio Tomada was better known in Davenport as Massimo (mah **see** mo). Massimo, one of those earlier immigrants from Nimis, was later (1934) to become my brother's godfather. This final piece of information provides sufficient evidence, at least in my mind, that "Garrasio" Comelli was indeed my father, Gervasio Comelli.

La Nostra Costa (Our Coast)

Gervasio's journey by ship from Italy and then by train across the United States to the coast of California, was typical of the Italian immigrants who settled on the West Coast. Indeed, they must have been brave souls. Many came alone, unable to speak a word of English. My father often told the story of not even understanding the words "Women" and "Men" on bathroom doors. Astutely, he confused the Italian word for men, *uomini* [oh **meh** nee], with the word "women"—"men" being obviously too short—and quickly stepped into the wrong bathroom. Despite this misadventure, my father *was* eventually successful in reaching his destination.

Gervasio settled in Santa Cruz County and subsequently found work on the local ranches. *Italiani della costa,* (or "coastal Italians") called these *rancios* [**ron** chos] and the ranch hands were known as *ranceri* [**ron** cherr-ee]. Displaying very little knowledge of farming, and his first name being perhaps hard to pronounce, the *ranceri* gave him the nickname "Bronco." Like the young horse that bears the same name, he was gradually broken into his new role. To further distinguish my father from another Bronco who lived in Davenport, he was later given the descriptive moniker *Bronco della Costa* (Bronco of the Coast). Except for the Friulani, who continued to call him "Vasin," most *Italiani della costa* simply knew my father as Bronco.

In America, this was the post World War I era of Model T and Model A Fords, of Prohibition, giddy girl "flappers," and "bootlegged booze."[6] Besides Henry Ford, luminaries of the time also included U. S. Presidents Warren Harding and Calvin Coolidge, aviator Charles Lindberg, silent film stars Rudolph Valentino and Charlie Chaplin, boxer Jack Dempsey, baseball great "Babe" Ruth, and mobster Al Capone. *Ranceri* were not paid very much during what was later to become known as the Roaring Twenties. However, Bronco, being unencumbered by a wife and family, managed to save $5,000, a good sum of money in those days. This money enabled Bronco to return to Italy in 1931.

Indications are that, now back in Italy, he was keeping his options open about remaining there or returning to the United States. On the one hand, Thelma Micossi's baptism was postponed in order to wait for "Vasin" to return from Italy; on the other hand, once in Italy he had proceeded to build a second-floor addition to his father's house. Indeed, what is known (he having written to one of his younger brothers, Ruggero, "to find him a suitable woman for a wife") is that Bronco had definitely gone back to Italy to get married.

Arriving in Nimis, he soon discovered, much to his brother's consternation, that he did not much like the girl that Ruggero had picked for him. He decided to go out on the town, on his own, to search for the girl of his dreams. Much to his delight, he found that girl—a beautiful seventeen-year-old maiden, living and working in the Bressani household, not too far from his father's home. The smitten Bronco eagerly threw his hat into the ring with several other eligible suitors, and proceeded to court the young and vivacious Valentina, my future mother.

Fortunately, Bronco had several advantages over other would-be Romeos. My father-to-be was good looking, he had money (seemingly) and a terrific singing voice, and he had in his possession a portable Victrola phonograph. Using this phonograph, which he had bought in America, he romanced my mother by playing (and probably singing along with) Italian love songs popular at the time. I can not imagine my father dancing (I only saw him once, and he wasn't very good.); however, given the competition, he may have attempted a "whirl" or two with the young Valentina. After several months of having her mind filled with Italian love songs and wondrous tales of unlimited opportunities and "easy money" in America, Valentina agreed to marry Bronco.

Having spent a large portion of his savings, most of which was used to build the upstairs addition to his father's house and to pay off his father's accumulated debts, Bronco decided to return to the United States. The newly wed Valentina, not having the proper immigration papers, was to be left behind to live with Bronco's family. He comforted his disappointed bride by convincing her that he could not live without her and that he would make arrangements for her to join him in America, as soon as possible.

La Nostra Costa (Our Coast)

I recall my father saying that he was delayed in keeping his promise to Valentina because of the Republicans. President Herbert Hoover, who at the time occupied the White House, was attempting to come to grips with the ever-widening Depression in the United States. One of the things Hoover tried to do, probably because of the desperate employment situation here, was to restrict immigration from abroad.[7] It wasn't until President Franklin Roosevelt took office in 1933, that Bronco was able to bring my mother to the United States. (Understandably, Bronco and Valentina became instant fans of the new President and strong supporters of the Democratic Party.)

My mother departed Italy on August 23, 1933. Her exit visa bears a stamp indicating that it was the eleventh year of the Fascist era. Booking her passage as SECONDA CLASSE ECONOMICA on the Italian liner *Vulcania*, Valentina arrived in America on September 7, 1933. By that time, the world-wide Depression had really set in. Although President Roosevelt promised that his new programs would lift the Country out of its misery, it wouldn't be until the onset of World War II in the early 1940s, that the United States would start to become economically viable again. For the *ranceri*, the 1930s were particularly hard times. Valentina was soon to find out that the promised easy money was nothing but her new husband's "blagga" (i.e. "bull"). The only things that greeted her upon her arrival (besides Bronco) were hard work and the infernal coastal wind. The Italians called the wind *il vento*.[8]

Despite this dose of reality, Bronco and Valentina soon decided to start their own family. My only brother, Giovanni Primo Comelli (or John), was born in Santa Cruz on June 4, 1934. Although Bronco and Valentina had very little money, they still had hope—not for themselves, but for their newborn son. They believed that if they worked hard and saved their money, America, unlike their native Italy, would provide a better life for their son. In 1937, the hard times continued; however, they still had enough confidence in the American dream to share it with me. Thus did I begin my journey through life, in the rugged northern coast of Santa Cruz County.

From 1937 through 1953 my family lived on the Coast Road (U.S. Highway 1), about three miles north of Santa Cruz. In 1954 we moved to the city of Santa Cruz itself. I continued to live there with my family from 1954 until 1959. These were my formative years. In 1959 I joined the San Jose Police Force. (San Jose, California is located inland, approximately forty miles east of Santa Cruz.)I now realize that, although my life was to change drastically thereafter, my values and ways of coping with life changed little from what I had learned from my parents and the people who lived and worked on the coast.

There are hundreds of stories about the coast and the families that worked and lived there. For members of those families who do not get mentioned in this book, I sincerely apologize. Not being mentioned is not intended in any way to diminish their importance as *amici* [ah **mee** chee] *della costa* (coastal friends). Although I do describe places and locations along the coast, this book is mostly about the people who lived and worked there, and about some of the events that impacted my family.

As years pass, memories fade; events tend to get intertwined with one another. Whenever possible, I have attempted to authenticate the events that I mention in this book. These are boyhood memories that have stuck in my mind all these years. I sincerely hope that they are good enough to accurately portray the people and the way they lived.

There are no villains in this book (except for those who thought it necessary, for whatever reason, to murder another human being). Most interactions between my family and the other *ranceri* and *amici della costa* were positive. A very few were negative. Yet I never believed that even those interactions deemed negative by my family (or by me) were done with malice. It was all part of life "up/on the coast." Everyone, as we often would say, played "the hand that was dealt to him or her." Finally, this is the story of Bronco and Valentina and their family (that is to say, my family) as they chased after the "American Dream," on the rugged coastline of Santa Cruz County. I am fully aware that non-Italian families also worked and lived "up the coast." Many of these families had been established on the coast long before the arrival of the Italians. Surely, their contribution to coastal history is no less important. However, because of the many events and interactions that took place between my family and the other Italian families during this particular time period, I, as a boy growing up, came to believe that this was indeed *La Nostra Costa*—Our Coast.

Endnotes

[1] So that the non-Italian speaking reader might get a sense of how the Italian words are pronounced, I have used my own method of phonetically spelling some of the words and phrases. As in my name above, the pronunciation is displayed in [brackets]. The syllable shown in bold type is accentuated.

[2] *Circa* 181 BC, the Latin speaking Romans occupied the Friuli region, which was then inhabited by a Celtic speaking population. The Romans proceeded to colonize the region, mainly using it for defensive military purposes. The original inhabitants of the region subsequently learned to speak the Friulian dialect, which initially had its origin in a fractured version of Latin. It is currently referred to as Eastern Laden. A historical background on Friulian in Italy, may be found on the website: www.Euromosaic-Friulian in Italy.htm

[3] In the early 1920s, Tony, along with his wife Rosie, managed the old Swiss Hotel, on Water Street in Santa Cruz. According to what my father told me, he spent his first year living with the Micossis at that hotel. Later, in 1937, Tony Micossi would become my godfather.

[4] Ellis Island website: www.ellisisland.org

[5] After the Americans entered World War I in 1917, the U.S. government had a difficult time finding enough ships to transport troops to Europe. Interesting enough to me, author Gary Mead in his book, *The Doughboys*, mentions that the "America" was one of the passenger ships used to transport U.S. soldiers overseas during that time. *The Doughboys; America and the First World War*, by Gary Mead, The Overlook Press, Peter Mayer Publishers, Inc., 2000.

[6] *The Santa Cruz Sentinel Extra Century Edition*, reported that the wharfs at Santa Cruz and Capitola, as well as the beaches in Davenport, Rio Del Mar and La Selva were often used for the "off-loading" of illegal "booze." Website: www.santacruzsentinel.com/extra/century/25/

[7] In his book *The Shattered Dream*, published by William Morrow & Company, Inc. in 1970, author Gene Smith states that in 1930 Hoover went before Congress asking that we "close America's shores to foreigners."

[8] Evelina Cantarutti, a dear friend of my mother, often laments in Italian about those early days. "We had nothing then. Nothing. No money, no property. All we had was the clothes on our backs and *il vento* in our faces."

SOLDATO

BRONCO IN ITALY – C. 1922

VALENTINA

C. 1934

PADRINI

STANDING: PINA AND TONY MICOSSI, MASSIMO, CAROLINA AND THELMA MICOSSI

SEATED: GIOVANNI PRIMO, BRONCO, VALENTINA, IVANO FRANCO

C. 1938

2. La Costa (The Coast)

My first memories of *la costa* [**coh** stah] are of the time when my family lived on the Gulch Ranch, about three miles north of Santa Cruz. Our house, along with one other house, was situated on the east side of US Highway 1, commonly known as the Coast Road. (This section of the Coast Road is now part of the Cabrillo Highway, which stretches from Las Cruces, near Lompac, in the south, to San Francisco in the north.)

Italians, who lived on or near the Coast Road, would often say that they lived *su per la costa,* up the coast. The old Coast Road, like the new one today, ran parallel to, and, for the most part, within a mile or two of the Pacific Ocean. At times *la costa* could be almost paradisiacal. This was and is especially true during the months of September and October. There is far less fog during these two months, and by this time the coast's main crop—brussel sprouts—is ready for harvest. At this time, the golden rays of the late afternoon sun will shine off the Pacific Ocean at just the right angle, making it sparkle with the brilliance of a bluish green diamond, in sharp contrast with the white and brown terrain of the neighboring bluffs. Embroidered with varying hues of yellow and green foliage arranged in intermittent patterns, the rugged coastal plain is resplendent in its coat of "green gold." These are the words that come to mind when describing this panorama of splendid beauty that lavishes the countryside. Today, the many colors of this magnificent canvas remain virtually the same as they were when I was a boy. If the reader is ever fortunate enough to be *su per la costa* during one of these magical times of the year, he or she can still revel in the wonders of its natural bliss.

At other times, living *su per la costa* could be depressing because of all the fog and low-hovering gray skies. Just about every morning, my brother John and I woke up to gray overcast skies. By ten or eleven o'clock in the morning, however, *il vento* started to blow and the skies began to clear. This was not a gentle wind. It was quite strong and on the cool side. As the wind blew, we could see giant white caps, moving like little boats across the ocean surface. In a heroic attempt to shield us from the elements, Valentina, my mother, dressed John and me in tight-fitting caps, long-sleeve wool shirts, and stiff Levi pants and jackets. We seldom discarded the jackets. They were our constant companions and they did give us pretty good protection against *il vento*.[9]

On the other hand, we could not protect ourselves against the smell of manure. The coastal Italians called it *pattume* [pah **two** meh]. Every spring, prior to the planting season, chicken, horse, and/or cow manure was spread over the barren fields. The manure was then disked into the ground, thus preparing and fertilizing the soil for the new crop.

As the wind blew, the pungent smell of *pattume* intensified. Dust containing tiny manure particles blew into our eyes and onto our clothes. This double attack of wind-blown particles and smell continued until the fields were fully planted. The daily certainty of this wind blown pollution kept Valentina constantly on guard, especially when she was doing the washing. She had to hang our sheets and clothes out to dry in the early morning hours when the wind was nice and quiet, and then rush out to take them down just before *il vento* kicked up again.

As if to add insult to injury, the inviting aroma of the *pattume* brought the *mosce* [**moe** skeh]. My brother and I were constantly going around the house with giant fly swatters and/or hand held metal sprayers (the ones that look like manual air pumps used to inflate

La Nostra Costa (Our Coast)

footballs and basketballs), their attached reservoir cans fully loaded with liquid "anti-fly" spray. Our mission was to either swat or spray all uninvited houseflies into oblivion. Sometimes we did both, first spraying the flies to slow them down and then giving them the *coupe de grace* with the big old swatter. Valentina deemed our "mission" a success when no *mosce* were seen diving down kamikaze-style into our plate of minestrone soup or other food during dinnertime.

I think we did our job pretty well. Yet no matter how hard we tried, my brother and I could not keep new "recruits" from infiltrating through our screen doors. It was a never-ending battle. I don't blame Valentina for wanting to move to Santa Cruz. She reasoned that it was the only way she could get away from that infernal wind, that pungent smell of *pattume*, and those ever so bothersome *mosce*.

I certainly would be negligent here if I didn't tell the reader the following woeful tale of double trouble. This rather "filthy" story had its origin when my brother John, then about four years old, and his childhood friend Reno Cantarutti, mistakenly took a big old mound of manure to be a safe place to play. As little kids often do, they had a merry old time, first climbing to the top and then tumbling down the pile. *Che puzza!* [**poot** zah] I'm sure the reader can readily imagine how badly they stank. Not only did the two boys come home smelling like a couple of refugees from a subterranean mushroom factory, they also came home loaded with nasty fleas from head to toe. Needless to say, my mother had a real job on her hands. Getting them all cleaned up was not going to be an easy task.

As the story goes, Valentina had the two boys stand outside and remove all their clothes. Then in a firm and very agitated voice, she instructed them to close their eyes, to hold their noses, and above all, not to breath. After making sure that the two knuckleheads knew how to follow her directions, Valentina grabbed her trusty "anti-fly" (soon to be, "anti-flea") sprayer, and sprayed copious amounts of "anti-spray" onto their flea-covered bodies. Then and only then, did she allow them to breathe. Next, she escorted them inside the house and plunged their naked bodies into a bathtub filled with very warm and soapy water. These two numbskulls did survive their ordeal; however, it is unknown whether they learned much from their experience. They still seem a little slow on the uptake. (I'm sure that their clothes were salvaged in a similar manner, first being sprayed with copious amounts of "anti-flea" spray and then tumbled into my mother's old tank washing machine. In those days nothing, short of an item being on the verge of complete destruction, was to be thrown away.)[10]

Wishing to probe a bit further, the reader might now want to ask, "Did little Ivano ever play in a manure pile?" Certainly not! Never mind that I benefited from the older boys' experience. I think that I was just plain smarter than they were. Playing in it or not, this story made a very lasting impression on me. To this day, any time I drive pass a field freshly laden with manure, I take in a deep breath and inhale the surrounding sweet, pungent smell with all of its natural attributes. *Pattume!* My exclamation is directed at no one in particular; however, it elicits a sharp retort from my startled wife, who just happens to be riding along with me. "How can you do that? It smells awful," Mildred says as she cringes in the front seat. Little does she know that I have suddenly been whisked back in time, and I am experiencing, once again, Reno and my brother's misadventure and all those other wind blown days *su per la costa*.

In this diversified setting, more than fifty years ago, two houses stood side by side, situated no more than 100 feet from the eastern edge of the Coast Road. (Both houses shared the common address of Route 3, Box 961, Santa Cruz). My parents, Gervasio (Bronco) and Valentina, along with my brother John and myself, lived in one house, and the Gemignani [jeh mee **nyah** nee] family—Argentina and Aladino with their three sons Constantino (Augie), Lido, and Giovanni Giuseppe (Joe)—lived in the other house. Although we interacted quite frequently, still unknown to us at the time was the very important part that the Gemignani Family was to play in the future of the Comelli family.

In order to convey a better sense of how we lived during this time period, I will try to acquaint the reader with the actual physical habitat of the Comelli family. Our single-story batten-and boardhouse had only about 1,200 square feet of actual living space and was separated from the Coast Road by a small patch of lawn, which in turn was surrounded on three sides by a hedge of tall juniper plants. These thick, woody plants shielded the house, somewhat, from the dusty wind, but did little to mitigate the constant noise that was generated by passing vehicles.

The interior of the house consisted of a kitchen with small dining area, a living room, and two bedrooms with an inner-connecting bathroom. There was also a small utility room at the back entrance where my mother washed clothes. The utility room contained a small pantry where most of our canned and other non-perishable food was stored. We had no refrigerator or icebox, no telephone and, of course, no television. Radio and an old Victrola phonograph served as our home entertainment center. (I recently referred to our refrigerator as an icebox. My four-year-old grandson, Cole, asked me, "Why do they call it an icebox, Papa?" His eyes grew wide with amazement when I explained to him that in the "olden days," they put a big chunk of ice in a box to "keep stuff from rotting.")

Thinking this over, the inquisitive reader might now ask, "Without a refrigerator or an icebox, how in the world did you preserve your food?" Well, luckily, we raised our own rabbits, chickens and vegetables. By controlling the weekly "killings" and "pickings" our parents pretty well guaranteed us a fresh supply of meats and vegetables. A man called Don Santos, who owned a dairy near Yellow Bank Curve on the Coast Road, delivered milk on a weekly basis.[11] Of course, the best way to preserve food, including fish and meat purchased or delivered from the store, was to consume it as quickly as possible. My brother and I tried the best we could to cooperate. However, since Valentina prided herself in providing us with *piatti* [pee **yah** tee] filled with more than ample food, I must admit that we often failed to clear her plates. Some leftovers were usually the order of the day. Fortunately, we had a ventilated cupboard, conveniently located in the kitchen, which was attached to an exterior-facing wall. Outside air coming through screens caused the interior of the cupboard to be cooled (*sans* electric fans) by natural ventilation. Most perishable food was put in this cupboard which we called a cooler—or "coola" as my father preferred to pronounce it. Bronco, seeing a plate of uneaten food on the table, would often direct John or me to "metelo en coola"—meaning, of course, "put it in the cooler." As we grew older, John and I adopted Bronco's innocuous saying, and used it in a somewhat more disparaging fashion when directing one another (or someone else) to "put it where the sun don't shine."

Since *la costa* more often than not cooperated with cool weather, the "coola" kept most of our foods and milk reasonably fresh for two or three days. Actually, our tastes and stomachs grew accustomed to tolerating some foods for periods a lot longer than that. For instance, my brother and I soon learned that the taste of milk starting to go sour was just a signal to drink it faster. We also learned that food starting to display strange green speckles on top, could easily be salvaged by simply using a spoon to discard the offending material and then reheating at a high temperature. No use wasting perfectly good food. Shortly after the war, my mother bought a second hand Norge refrigerator. My brother and I were in seventh heaven. We now could keep foods for days on end. To this day, I can not understand why my lovely and diligent wife, Mildred, insists on discarding food left in the refrigerator after only a couple of days. Such a waste.

Originally, the kitchen had a wood-burning stove. Not only was most of the cooking done on this stove, but it was also our only source of heat for the entire house. I can remember Bronco getting up very early in the morning, rekindling the fire in the stove, and then just before he left for work, opening the doors wide to our bedrooms, allowing the heat to come in. Standing separate from the main stove was a very small butane stove, having only two burners. These burners were used mainly to boil water, to reheat foods, or to fry eggs in the morning. A brand new butane stove with four burners and an oven came much later.

I must not forget to mention, that at the front of the house and strategically located underneath the living room floor, was a small dirt "dugout." This dugout was used by my parents as a cellar, to store wine and vinegar as well as a few other bulk foods. As I grew

La Nostra Costa (Our Coast)

older, I learned to take full advantage of the dugout. It was here that I hid from my parents, or listened in, surreptitiously, to their conversations. At times, I seated myself on the dugout steps, and there—accompanied only by the musty, sweet and sour effusions derived from an ensemble of uncovered soil, stored wine, vinegar, onions, potatoes, and garlic —I experimented with smoking some of my parents "borrowed" cigarettes.

One of my favorite pastimes was flipping through pages of popular magazines such as the Saturday Evening Post, Look, or Life—searching for those pictures of smiling movie stars smoking, with obvious enjoyment, their favorite brand of cigarette. As I turned the pages, I attempted to emulate them by taking a few puffs on a swiped Camel or Lucky Strike cigarette. I wasn't very good at it. I kept coughing and getting smoke in my eyes, which proved to be a great hindrance to my seeing the pictures clearly. Somewhere along the line, I must have lost patience and just plain gave up. I never did get hooked, although in college I did try to impress the girls, on more than one occasion, by dangling a white "coffin nail" from my lips. Just like that tough guy, Robert Mitchum.

This brings me to the Coast Road itself, or at least to that portion with which I was most familiar. As today, it was then a major roadway for automobile traffic going to and from Santa Cruz, Davenport, Pescadero, San Gregorio, Half Moon Bay, and San Francisco. (No, Cucamonga was not and is not on the Coast Road.)[12] The road had only two lanes: that is, one northbound and one southbound. (As best as I can remember, there were no passing lanes.) There were far fewer vehicles on the road in those days; however, as I will describe below, it still had a significant amount of traffic.

My first memories regarding that traffic were of the flatbed trucks with their attached trailers, hauling sacks of cement. These trucks started their journey at the Portland Cement Plant, located in Davenport, about five and a half miles north of where we lived. Not only were these trucks big, they were also very noisy. The noise varied greatly, depending on the size of the load and the skills and proficiency of the driver at the wheel. Going south towards Santa

Cruz, the trucks were loaded with bags of cement, securely tied to their trailers. Before passing our house, the trucks had to descend into a gulch and then climb a steep grade on the other side. The drivers, in their efforts to sustain enough speed to climb the grade, accelerated their trucks coming down into the gulch and then downshifted their gears going up the grade. Our house was located right at the top of the grade where the trucks completed their climb. If the load was not too great and/or the driver had coordinated his accelerating and shifting correctly, the truck passed by making somewhat less noise. If the load was very heavy or if the driver was off his mark with pedal and lever, the truck's motor, with accompanying stacked exhaust pipes, would burst out with a deep gurgling sound, and then emit angry snarls as it struggled up the hill. Many times, a truck going by was so noisy that our single wall house literally shook on its foundation. This could happen any time, day or night, because the trucks ran up and down the Coast Road, "24/7," or at least it seemed so to me.

Going the other way (up from Santa Cruz), the trucks also made noises, but they sounded very different. With their trailers usually empty, the trucks had a "head of steam" when approaching the gulch, causing their trailers to rattle like runaway roller coasters as they rushed past our house and down into the gulch. The loudness of their clanking depended on how much of a hurry the driver was in to get back home.

Mercifully, when the highway was rebuilt in the latter part of the 1950s, this particular portion of the gulch was mostly filled in with rock and sand. The present roadway has a slight dip, but no longer does it have that steep descent. Upon completion, much of the noise caused by the grade would be gone; however, by that time Bronco and Valentina's family would also be gone.

It would not have been so bad, if we only had to worry about the noise, but the traffic situation was also very dangerous for my brother and me. This was because our house was located on the eastern side of the highway. It seemed to me that anything and everything of interest was located across the highway on its western side, including the major portion of the ranch, which was approximately 100 acres in size. Also, the Pacific Ocean, with its big sandy beach, was about one half mile directly to the west of our house. The Rodoni Ranch, where my brother and I could play with children our own age, was located nearby—but was also on the western side of the highway. So, the only way to get to these points of interest was to cross the highway by foot, bike, or car. This of course exposed us to the steady stream of traffic on the road.

Did this traffic situation have an impact on my psyche? You bet it did! I can best illustrate the magnitude of this impact by recounting to the reader, the following frightening and recurring mental vision which every once in a while rears its ugly head from way back within the recesses of my mind. At times, when I am alone, I stare off into deep space: I see myself as a child, hiding along the side of those bushy junipers plants, growing tall and very near the Coast Road. I can hear myself saying, "get ready, set, go!" Then without looking for oncoming traffic, I bolt across the road. All of a sudden, out of the corner of my eye, I spot a black car speeding towards me! I hear a loud blast from the horn! Brakes screech and squeal! I attempt to get away, but I fall down, tumbling headfirst to the other side of the road! That's when the bristles on the back of my neck become stiff and erect as if electrified. Shivers run up and down my spine. I close my eyes and quickly try to shake these thoughts from my mind. So real are these episodes that I often wonder: "Did I really commit such a foolish and dangerous act?" I probably will never find out for sure that I did, but I take solace in the fact that I never see myself being hit by that car. Brrr!

Endnotes

[9] My boyhood friend, Jim Ceragioli, remembers using a fishing pole with heavy line to "master" the coastal wind when flying his homemade kites. In recent visits to *la costa*, I haven't noticed *il vento* being quite that strong anymore. Maybe the "restless spirits" of the coast have calmed themselves over these many years.

[10] Even today my wife, Mildred, finds socks in my drawers, years old, many with holes in them. "What are you doing keeping all these old socks," she yells at me in exasperation. Implying that something ominous is about to happen, I sheepishly answer back, "The Depression my dear, the Depression."

[11] I remember Don Santos as being extremely polite. He always addressed my mother as Mrs. Comelli. This really impressed me because the use of "Mr."and/or "Mrs." was rare *su per la costa*. Later, Don Santos, who had acquired property in Scotts Valley, a small town just east of Santa Cruz, played an instrumental part in that city's early development.

[12] Mel Blanc, who for many years was the voice of Bugs Bunny, Porky Pig, Tweety Bird, Sylvester the Cat, Daffy Duck and other cartoon characters, had a regular stint on the Jack Benny Radio Show, during the 1940s and early 1950s. On it, he often played the part of a "railroad conductor," shouting out the names of several Southern California Cities along his "route," such as Los Angeles, Santa Ana, Azusa, and Anaheim—and always ending by uttering a long and deliberate "**Kook**- ahhh-monga!"

3. La Costa E La Guerra
(The Coast And The War)

Living on the eastern side of the road was not only dangerous—it also had its economic disadvantages. This was clearly demonstrated during World War II. Bronco and Valentina, being immigrants from Italy without U.S. citizenship—and Italy having allied itself with Nazi Germany—were declared to be enemy aliens. Soon after the United States had entered the war, enemy aliens *su per la costa* were restricted from going on the western side of U.S. Highway 1. Conveniently, the white line in the middle of the road was used to separate east from west.

It was apparent that the United States government did not want enemy aliens to get too close to the Pacific Ocean. The fear was that these aliens could signal to hostile boats off the coast or help enemy soldiers to land on the rough coastline. According to Lawrence Distasi, Project Director of the traveling exhibit *Una Storia Segreta* and editor of the book by the same name the entire coast from the Oregon border to just below Santa Barbara was declared off-limits to enemy aliens effective February 24, 1942.[13] An article dated Feb. 3, 1942, appearing in the Santa Cruz Sentinel-News, warned that all the area west of the Coast Road and the Watsonville Highway (U.S. Highway 1) and south of Laguna Creek (Santa Cruz County) to the Carmel River (in Monterey County), was to be a restricted area, and had to be cleared of enemy aliens, supposedly by that date. Other articles in the Sentinel-News, (Feb-Mar 1942) pointed out that the courthouse in downtown Santa Cruz (as well as the downtown shopping area) was in the restricted zone. Consequently, Italian aliens who were in the pipeline for naturalization could not go there to get their citizen papers. One article stated that a Mrs. Teresa Bertacca, of Davenport, had to be given a special permit in order to appear at the courthouse as the Plaintiff in her civil suit against the Cement Plant.

A much more recent article, appearing in the Monterey Herald on July 12, 2000, reported that a series of U.S. Army proclamations, with regard to that same time period, forbade enemy aliens from traveling beyond a five-mile radius of home without an application for a travel permit, and from possessing any firearms, short-wave radios, cameras, or "signaling devices," including flashlights. Enemy aliens were also confined to their homes between 8:00 p.m. and 6:00 a.m.

Being classified as an enemy alien, Bronco could not work anywhere west of the highway. Since the major portion of the Gulch Ranch was on the western side of the road, it left my father with very little to do. He had to go out and find himself another job.

With some luck he was able to get work at the A. K. Salz Tannery, located on River Street (just east of Highway 1) in Santa Cruz. I can remember that when he returned from work, my mother forbade him entry into the house. The combination of chemicals used to clean and preserve the hides of many a slaughtered cow, and to transform these into usable commercial leather and other products, produced a foul-smelling odor that clung to my father's body and clothes with grim determination.[14] Bronco had to remove all his clothes before gaining entry. (No, Valentina didn't spray him.) Mercifully, the Attorney General of the United States finally lifted the restrictions against Italians on October 12, 1942. This made Bronco very happy. He could now return to his normal line of work on the rancio. I was just happy that my father smelled better and could now enter the house without taking his clothes off.[15]

Theoretically, my brother and I, having been born in the United States, could have walked to the beach with impunity, while our adult parents were restricted. However, Valentina never allowed us to go to the beach alone. Thus I am sure that we were also restricted from going to the other side of the ranch. I have some memories of playing at the Rodoni Ranch (on the west side of the road) during this time period; I know that my mother was with me while I did. This may have been after the restrictions were lifted. (Dante Rodoni, although of Italian ancestry, was a Swiss citizen; thus his family was exempt from the law because Switzerland remained neutral during the War.) Later, in 1943, Italy surrendered and, in turn, became an ally of the United States. Then Bronco and Valentina were accepted as friendly aliens. Although they never even thought about being involved in subversive activities, they felt very fortunate that they had survived this part of the war without going to jail.

Bronco and Valentina never forgot this scary experience. However, I don't remember ever hearing my father or mother complain about the restrictions placed on them. Because the United States was at war against Italy, they accepted the fact that certain restrictions against Italian aliens were necessary. Bronco, being a realist, always theorized that if the shoe were on the other foot, Benito Mussolini, Italy's wartime dictator, would have done the same or even worse to American aliens. Then again, surely, they must have realized it was more prudent for them to remain silent during these turbulent times. Subsequently, having been taught such a hard lesson, Bronco and Valentina made sure that they did not have to relive these unpleasant events, ever again. They quickly applied for naturalization, and eventually became American Citizens.

Lest the doubting reader think that things were not as serious as I have described them above, please read on. According to an article appearing in the Monterey Herald, dated July 12, 2000, the American Italian Historical Association estimated that "approximately 700,000 Italian Americans across the country were effected by the war, either by home searches, relocation or internment." According to the article, more than 250 were interned; about 90 were from California.

The paranoid thinking prevalent at the time is exemplified in a story as told by Ezio Pinza, the famous Italian singer, in his autobiography.[16] Mr. Pinza, who was later to star in the 1950s Broadway musical "South Pacific", was incarcerated for two months at Ellis Island in New York, in 1942. The United States government suspected Mr. Pinza of changing the tempo of his singing voice in an attempt to send messages to the Fascist Italian government via his Saturday morning Metropolitan Opera radio broadcasts. (Ironically, while working in the fields, it was indeed common practice for Friulian husbands, wives and other workers in Italy to communicate by singing to one another.) I never thought about it then, but, given the thinking at the time, all those Italian singers *su per la costa*— including Bronco—could have been silenced for the duration of the war.

I have vivid memories of the military using the Coast Road during the war. From time to time, we saw long rows of tanks and other military vehicles moving north along the highway. I distinctly remember once seeing a cavalry troop, horses and all, traveling on the road. It seemed to me that the troops, with their equipment, always traveled northward. Bronco thought that they were enroute to San Francisco to embark by ship for overseas duty. There was also an Army detachment stationed in Davenport during the war. Thelma (Micossi) Gill, who lived in Davenport during the early 1940s, recalled that the Army set up camp along the San Vicente Creek in Davenport. Their defenses included placing cannons on the cliffs overlooking the Pacific Ocean. Some of the men and equipment might have gone to that destination.[17]

It probably was not much fun for the soldiers traveling north to embark for war duty, but it was really fun for my brother and me to watch them parade by. I remember one night being awakened by the loud rumble of machinery passing our house. Bronco was already awake and looking out the window. "Come here and see this," he called in Italian. I went to the window and saw what seemed to be an endless row of tanks and armored vehicles, all traveling without lights. (This, of course, was to prevent enemy planes that might be flying above or submarines lurking off the coast from spotting the armored vehicles as they proceeded to their destination.) As the tanks rumbled and clanked past our house, going down into the gulch, I could see soldiers, wearing brown leather helmets, standing in their turrets, heads exposed, eyes straining, as they peered into the darkness that lay before them. This was a lot of fun to watch, but it was also a bit scary for a five-year-old kid. I think I had to sleep with my mother after that parade.

Another fun thing for my brother and I to do, was to wait and watch for a U.S. Coast Guard truck, which stopped in front of our house every evening just before dusk. As we stood by watching with great anticipation, two Coast Guardsmen and one German Shepherd dog dismounted from the vehicle. The men were outfitted in navy-blue uniforms with white sailor caps. They wore web belts and leggings, and were armed with rifles and pistols. The two men, with their dog held tightly on a leash, proceeded to walk down a dirt road which led them westward towards the Pacific Ocean. On a bluff overlooking the ocean and the beach, the military had built a small one-room shed. (Numerous one room sheds were placed up and down the coast at various intervals.) There, as one man slept, the other stood watch for enemy ships, submarines and/or spies. (One can reasonably assume that during the first two years of the war, my parents, as well as many other coastal Italians, were considered to be potential spies.) The shed, or "lookout house" as my brother and I called it, also offered shelter for the men during inclement weather. Coast Guardsmen with their dogs kept watch for the duration of the war. I even remember that, at least one time, I saw two Coast Guardsmen sitting at the boarding-room table in the Gulch Ranch cookhouse, eating food and drinking wine. Surely, this must have been during the latter stages of the war, when tensions between the Italians and Americans had eased.

I also remember airplanes engaging in practice maneuvers over the Pacific Ocean. While one plane towed a white oblong, sleeve target, other planes dove down from the sky and shot at it with their machine guns. Sometimes, when we went exploring, my brother and I found spent machine gun cartridges that had drifted down on to the beach or over the ranch. I would imagine that each one of these large cartridges had several little bullets inside. This would explain why so many shots were heard and so few cartridges were found. After all didn't those movie cowboys—Roy Rogers, Gene Autry, Johnny Mack Brown and Charles "The Durango Kid" Starrett—keep shooting throughout the show without reloading? They must have had the same type of ammunition—don't you think?[18]

Blackouts were scary, but also great fun. Valentina covered all the windows with blankets, and then turned off the lights, except for one very small light bulb located in the kitchen. This light bulb barely emitted any light at all; we called it the "dim light." The "dim light" hung from the ceiling on an electrical cord and emitted its eerie glow directly over the dining table. Bronco, Valentina, John and I sat around the table listening to the radio or just talking, while we waited for the Air Raid Warden's car to come pass our house, sounding the "all clear" with its siren.

During one particularly eventful blackout, Bronco, who was still considered to be an "enemy" alien at the time, was almost arrested as a spy. As I have previously mentioned, we raised our own chickens and rabbits. The chicken house and the rabbit hutches were located in our back yard. Bronco apparently came home late from work and arrived after the imposition of the blackout. Well, the poor rabbits and chickens hadn't been fed all day. My father decided that he would take his flashlight and go and feed the animals. The next thing we knew the Air Raid Warden drove up into our yard, and demanded that my father turn off the flashlight and give himself up. Or so I thought at the time.

This spurious espionage caper developed as follows. Feeding the chickens was simple enough. Dig into a sack of feed and throw it on the ground, a fistful at a time. No need of much light here. Feeding the rabbits proved to be more complicated. Bronco needed light to find and open each door on several individual hutches. Each time he opened a hutch door, he put the flashlight under his arm or on top of the hutch, thus freeing his hands to feed the rabbits. In doing so, the light from the flashlight shot into the sky at all different angles. Seeing this, the Warden, who just happened to be driving by at the

La Nostra Costa (Our Coast)

time, apparently thought that he had just spotted a clandestine spy signaling to enemy airplanes.

Bronco had to do some fast explaining. Using his broken English and pointing excitedly to the rabbit hutches he was able to make the Warden understand what he was doing. The Warden actually turned out to be a nice guy. Not only did he accept my father's explanation, he also showed us how we could properly use a flashlight during a blackout. The Warden placed a red bandana type handkerchief over the lens of the flashlight making a "dim light" out of the flashlight. Thus, the following valuable lesson was learned. If you are going to feed animals during wartime, best feed them in the morning.

It was during this period of wartime paranoia that my name was changed forever. It was my first week at Laurel Elementary School (1942). I can still remember our kindergarten teacher teaching us the Pledge of Allegiance. This was before the "One nation under God," phrasing was added. If I remember correctly, she had the kids place their right hands over their hearts and then, as the words "to the flag of the United States of America" were recited, she instructed all of us to point towards the flag. She demonstrated this by extending her right arm (the one holding her hand over the heart), in one horizontal motion, keeping the palm of the hand open to the inside, ending with the five fingers pointing directly towards the flag. Not wishing to disappoint, we all dutifully followed her example. This was kind of fun. When the words "to the flag" were recited, we all tried to be the first to point to the flag. Inevitably, there were always one or two of us that lagged far behind.

A short time later we were told to disregard her previous instructions, and to just keep our right hand over the heart throughout the recital. At first I thought that we might have been too slow in extending our right arm; however, later I figured out that someone in authority (maybe President Roosevelt), must have gotten the idea that this symbolic gesture was too similar to the Nazi salute. Probably so as not to associate us with any Hitler Youth movements, it was thought best we not extend our right arm. That was all right with me. I didn't mind changing the salute to the flag; however, I wasn't quite happy when they changed my name.

It was probably during this same week when my kindergarten teacher came over to where I was sitting, and asked me what my name was. I responded in a very soft voice, "Mi chiamo [kee **yah** mo] Ivano." The teacher, not being able to associate my face with the name, gave me a puzzled look and again asked, "What is your name?" I once again responded in an even softer voice, "Mi chiamo, Ivano." (I am called Ivano.) The teacher, now being even more confused, turned and went back to her desk to check the roll. After making sure that I was indeed one of her students, she returned and, as if I had done something wrong, she said to me in a very firm manner, "Your name is Ivan."

Really! That was news to me. Later, I figured it out. Someone in authority (maybe President Roosevelt), must have thought it more prudent that I be called Ivan [**eye** van]. After all, the Russians were our allies and Italy was our enemy. However, I remember at the time going home to my mother and telling her that I had been given a new name. Surely, she would tell the teacher that she had made a big mistake. Much to my surprise, Valentina rationalized this intrusion on my person by saying, in Italian, "It must be your American name." I think what she really wanted to say was, "I know that you don't like it, but we are in no position to make trouble." Ever since that time, "it" has been my name and I have been known as Ivan Frank Comelli. I guess the only name they couldn't Americanize was my last name. I don't think my parents would have gone along with that one.

The reader may now want to ask, "If this was such a big deal to you, why didn't you simply change your name back after the war?" I could have. However, by then, every kid in the school knew me as Ivan. Besides, I really thought it was my American name. However, years later I did make a feeble attempt to reclaim my true identity.

In 1974 I joined the Santa Cruz Elk's Club, and I registered as Ivano. When visiting other Lodges, I would always listen, with great consternation, as I was being introduced as "Eye-vano." My fellow Brothers at the Lodge picked up on this, and quickly made sport of it. I decided to let things go and reverted back to just being Ivan; however, my picture does hang on their wall, along with other Past Exalted Rulers, with the name "Ivano."

Probably as a consequence of all the above, the following story unfolded years later. In 1993, when my grandson Michael was born, my daughter Madeline wanted to give her newborn baby my name as his middle name. She asked me if she should name him Ivan or Ivano. Without hesitation, and admittedly without much thought as to how the child might feel, I requested that she name him Ivano. Thus did she honor me. Now, I often console the young lad by saying that Michael Ivano is a great name for a "pop" singer or an actor. Much to my chagrin, Michael answers back that his current classmates prefer to call him Michael Eye-vano. They think he is French. Arrrgh!

Endnotes

[13] *Una Storia Segreta: The Secret History of Italian American Evacuation and Internment during World War II.* Edited with an introduction by Lawrence Distasi. Forward by Sandra M. Gilbert, published by Heyday Books, Berkeley, California, 2001.

[14] In an article appearing in the *Santa Cruz Sentinel*, dated April 21, 2003, reporter Dan White states that the Salz's buildings were now being considered for the housing of an arts complex. (Can "stink" be captured on canvas?)

[15] A shorter version of Bronco's story, as written by the author, has been previously published in a piece entitled, "Wrong Side of the Highway." It appears in the book, *Una Storia Segreta*, cited above.

[16] *Ezio Pinza: An Autobiography*: Ezio Pinza with Robert Magidoff, Rinehat & Co., New York 1958. Also cited in an article by Lawrence Distasi entitled, "Dis-enchanted Evenings: Ezio Pinza's Wartime Ordeal", appearing in the Summer 1999 issue of *The Ambassador Magazine*, published quarterly by NIAF (National Italian American Foundation).

[17] *The Santa Cruz Sentinel* in its special edition, "Santa Cruz County—A Century," reported that the 54th Coast Artillery Battalion, a segregated all-Black group of soldiers, was given the assignment to protect the coast. Camps were also set up at Lighthouse Point in Santa Cruz, at Moss Landing, and at Point Pinos on the Monterey Peninsula.

[18] In his biography of the Confederate officer William Clarke Quantrill, author Edward E. Leslie reveals that many of the "bushwhackers" that rode with Quantrill often carried eight or more fully loaded revolvers on their persons and horses, during their Civil War raids. See there. No need to reload. Those old cowboy movies got it right. *The Devil Knows How to Ride:* Random House, New York, 1996.

4. Il Golce (The Gulch)

The Gulch Ranch, where we lived, derives its name from the deep ravine that runs through it vertically and in an irregular fashion, beginning in foothills in the east and ending at the Pacific Ocean in the west. Coastal Italians called the ranch Il Golce [eel **goal** che], their Italianization of gulch. As I have previously mentioned, the old Coast Road intersected and, after taking that big up-and-down dip, crossed the gulch, leaving approximately seventy-five per cent of the ranch acreage on the western side of the road. It was in the latter part of 1937 (the year I was born), that Bronco bought a half share in the Gulch Ranch Partnership, thus bringing his young family to live on the ranch.[19]

The Gulch Ranch compound was located at the bottom of the gulch, immediately east of the Coast Road. The *ranceri* called this portion of the gulch *il buco* [**boo** koh], which simply means "the hole." It was to here that Bronco went every morning for sixteen years, to have his meals at the cookhouse and to start his day of work. It was here where Valentina cleaned sprouts in the barn and it was here where my brother and I started our first jobs.

The Gulch Ranch compound consisted of a white two-story cookhouse with living quarters for three or four ranceri, a separate living residence, usually lived in by the foreman or one of the partners, a barn with outside horse corral, and several sheds and garages. Directly to the front of the cookhouse was a covered shed with several wash basins and sinks. Here the men washed up before meals. Nearby, there was a bigger shed that covered a dugout serving as a cellar where wine was stored in big vats. For a long time, the Gulch Ranch made its own wine, buying grapes and then crushing them in a giant wooden tun a few feet east of the cookhouse.

Further east of these buildings and the wine tun was another cookhouse and living quarters for several Filipino ranch hands. At times, the role of the Filipinos *su per la costa* has been forgotten. However, I will never forget how hard-working and friendly they were. Before the arrival of the Mexican laborers in the 1940s, their work as brussel sprout and artichoke pickers was indispensable.[20]

I can remember going into the fields to watch them harvest the crop. Seeing me, a particularly dark skinned Filipino named Vittorio would often shout out in broken English, "Hey, young Bronco! You come here pic 'em some sprouts with me!" Seeing me hesitate, he would get me off the hook by saying, "Ahh—neber-u-mine." He would then smile, showing his white teeth, before breaking out with a cackling laugh. His fellow Filipino workers, thus having been alerted to my presence, would follow suit, smiling and laughing, before stooping down to continue their labor.

Italian and Filipino ranch hands did work together in the fields, but seldom if ever did they eat or bunk together. The Filipinos had their own Filipino field boss. Although subordinate to the ranch foreman, he did all the hiring and firing of the Filipino workers and ran their camp with an iron fist. The Filipinos also had their own cook, who prepared the preferred Filipino ethnic cuisine. By today's standards, the physical and social separation of the Filipino and Italian workers probably smacks of segregation at its worst. During this time period it was the general practice, although the Filipinos probably only went along with it in order to get work on the *rancios*.

Personally, I never did observe any fights or other acts of violence between the Filipino workers and the *ranceri*. However, in their book about Santa Cruz County, authors Jennie Dennis Verardo and

Denzil Verardo, Ph. D. , state that during the Depression, Filipinos suffered abuses which whites often instigated. According to the authors, some of the most violent physical attacks against Filipinos occurred in Watsonville in January 1930. The authors attribute the death of at least one Filipino to the violence that occurred during this time.[21]

The Filipinos for the most part had their own entertainment, which included various games of chance and, at times, the staging of cock fights. I only remember attending one of these. I must have been eleven or twelve at the time. The event was scheduled to go off on a Saturday afternoon, and was held in *il buco*, just outside the Filipinos' living quarters. This was one of the few times I saw *ranceri* and Filipino workers actually mingling and socializing together after work.

There was an air of great excitement hanging over the gathering. The Filipinos were chattering excitedly in their native language, as they formed a circle around two roosters and their Filipino handlers. The two handlers were holding on to their birds at opposite ends of the circle. The two roosters, attired in plumage of bright reddish brown and black feathers and sporting orange red crowns on their heads, flapped their wings wildly, while flashing leg-attached metal knives. Every once in a while, one would lunge forward in attack mode, only to be pulled back by its handler. It was obvious that the two birds were ready to fight.

The Filipinos in the crowd quickly became impatient, shouting and yelling at the two handlers. Although I did not understand what they were saying, it was clear from their gestures and tone of speech that they wanted the show to get started. Then, unexpectedly, one of the Filipino handlers pulled his rooster out of the match. It appeared to me that this particular handler had a great sentimental attachment to his prize rooster. I don't think that he could bear to see his bird killed or seriously injured. This display of compassion on the handler's part greatly impressed me. After much arguing between the two handlers and also among the spectators, the match was called off. I breathed a sigh of relief. I didn't want to see the roosters get hurt either.

When my father bought into *Il Golce*, there were six or seven other partners, including Amerigo (Piccino) Presepi, the foreman. Coastal Italians often called the foreman *il bosso* [**boh** so], the boss. Piccino [pee **chee** no] was married to Louisa, a fine-looking and very amicable Italian woman. The one thing I selfishly regretted about Piccino and Louisa was that they had no children for my brother and me to play with. That was to come later when the Fambrini Family came to live on the ranch.

Under Piccino's assertive leadership, the Gulch Ranch became known as *Il Rancio di Pompieri* [pohm **pyerr** ee], The Ranch of the Firemen. From what my father told us, I learned this name was given to the *ranceri* because Piccino always wanted everything done in a hurry. He had the workers in the field earlier than anyone else and made them work harder and faster than other ranch hands. He was a stern boss who would not tolerate anyone who wasted time or displayed signs of laziness. Because of these aggressive tendencies, some *ranceri* did not like Piccino. My father respected him because Piccino was a very hard worker himself; however, he often stood up to him when he thought that Piccino was pushing too hard. Bronco and Piccino, both possessed volatile personalities, thus they had some epic arguments. A few, according to Bronco, even bordered on physical confrontation.

The Italian word *piccino* means "small or little one." Piccino, a Toscano, might have been small as a child, but he certainly was not small as an adult. He was a well-built, muscular man, standing about six feet tall. Most of the time he had this very stern look on his face, and he had this tendency of squinting with one eye when he became angry or annoyed. This was usually his persona when he was working, except when he saw my brother or me in the vicinity. Then his face would light up. Displaying a big, broad smile, he would come forward to greet us. It was clear that Piccino liked us. This was also true of Louisa, who always made us feel welcome when we were around. I was never afraid of Piccino and I liked him a lot. I could

La Nostra Costa (Our Coast)

not understand why some of the *ranceri* didn't get along with him. Of course, I didn't have to work for him.

Piccino, sold his share and left the Gulch Ranch in the early 1940s. About this time, John Fambrini became *il bosso*. John was married to Margaret (Dimeo) and, much to my delight, they had a son Raymond and a daughter Nadine. This was very fortunate because Raymond was about my brother's age and Nadine was close to my age. Since they lived in the foreman's residence in *il buco*, we could play with them while my mother worked cleaning sprouts in the barn. During the time they lived there, our family and the Fambrini family visited each other quite often. Though he didn't get along with Piccino, Bronco got along very well with John. John and Margaret were very friendly people and of course my brother and I had great fun playing with Raymond and Nadine.

I particularly remember one glorious afternoon when Nadine and I (we must have been four or five years old) were playing hide-and-seek in the barn. Nadine hid herself in an old empty wine barrel. I quickly found her and then, on the spur of the moment, I climbed in the wine barrel with her. We started to laugh and giggle. I think we were having a very good time. All of sudden John, Nadine's father, shows up and starts yelling at us to get out of the barrel. We quickly climbed out and I could see that John was very angry. He yelled at me, "Don't do that ever again!" I never could figure out what "that" was. As far as I can remember Nadine and I hadn't done anything wrong. Or had we?

I quickly ran to where my mother was working. I had to tell her what had happened because I was really scared that John was going to do something bad to me. Valentina listened closely, as I, in my best Italian stammer, told her my story. She tried to calm me down by saying that she would not let John hurt me. She said that she would go look for John and have a talk with him. After doing so, she came back and told me that John was afraid that I was hurting Nadine, however, he now knew that I wasn't. She then added in firm Italian, "Bada, Ivano. No fa quello, mai piu." You guessed it.

Valentina's warning was clear. "Beware, Ivano. Don't do that ever again."

End of story. John never mentioned the episode to me again and he returned to being his friendly self again. I was glad he did, because he sure scared me. Consequently, because of this misadventure, I never did do "that" again. At least not with Nadine.

Unfortunately the Fambrinis' stay at the Gulch Ranch was too short. They departed to run their own farm, which was located off what now is Dimeo Lane. Their leaving left the door open for Pietro (Pete) Rinaldi to eventually become *il bosso* of the Gulch Ranch. The reader will learn later, as our story continues to unfold, that this happening will have unexpected and unsettling consequences for the Comelli Family.

Endnotes

[19] The *ranceri* commonly formed partnerships to work and manage the rancios. The land being farmed was usually owned outside of the partnerships. Thus, ranceri most commonly would lease the land for a specific period of time, usually three to seven years.

[20] The Santa Cruz Sentinel in its special edition, "Santa Cruz County: A Century" reported that the "Bracero Program" with Mexico was implemented in 1942, to help alleviate the loss of field workers due to war. The full impact of this program was not realized until the late 1940s or early 1950s. At that time, some saw the importation of Mexican laborers as a threat to American jobs. Therefore, they successfully lobbied to have the program eliminated. Ironically, I knew of very few, if any, Anglo-American workers who wanted to be "pickers."

[21] Their book produced in cooperation with the Santa Cruz Chamber of Commerce is entitled, *Restless Paradise, Santa Cruz County; An Illustrated History* and was published by Windsor Publications, Inc. , in 1987.

FAMIGLIA COMELLI

C. 1945

TERRI DOES A HAT TRICK

C. 1946

THIS OLD HOUSE

C. 1947

THE AUTHOR AND THE COAST ROAD

C. 1949

5. Uomini Al Lavoro (Men At Work)

Probably, the best way in which I can describe to the reader how *uomini* [oh **meh** nee] *al lavoro* worked the *rancios*, is by describing my father's own daily routine. Each morning, like clockwork, Bronco got up at 5:30 a.m. After washing up, he usually dressed himself in a tan or blue work shirt, rolling up the sleeves to just above his elbows; an old pair of Levi jeans, and ankle-high heavy leather work shoes. When dressed, he pulled the end of his pant legs down and over the top of his shoes, twisting the front of each pant leg into a knot; thereby tightening them on the shoe itself. Using the ends of the long leather shoelaces more or less like tourniquets, he proceeded to tie down the twisted knots, interlacing the pant legs with the fronts of his shoes. With the remaining loose ends of his shoelaces, he secured the pant legs to his high-tops by going once or twice (depending on the length of the lace) over the pants and tying them off at the sides and on the outside the shoes. This made nice tight seals over the shoes, preventing dirt and debris from seeping in.

Sealing off the top of my work shoe was one of the first things my father taught me when I went to work on the Gulch Ranch. Thanks to Bronco, I seldom got dirt inside of my shoe. My brother, on the other hand, liked to wear engineer's boots. These looked better and had a higher top than the shoes that I wore; however, they do not have shoelaces. Consequently, John could not seal off the top of his boots; he was always getting his socks and feet dirty. John never did get it. Style won over cleanliness. His hard-headedness may have had something to do with that *pattume* incident. Maybe he hadn't held his breath long enough when my mother was applying the "anti-flea" spray.

Once he had tied off his pant legs, Bronco, favoring a well-worn brown or gray fedora-style work hat, placed the *cappello* [kah **pel** oh] on his head, slightly tilting the brim at an angle over his right eye. Using a dirt path that ran parallel to the Coast Road, he proceeded to walk north towards the edge of the gulch, and then descended into *il buco*. Once at the bottom of the incline, he walked to the "cookahousa" and seated himself at a long table and proceeded to have breakfast with nine or ten other *ranceri*. (The distance from our house to the cookhouse was no more than a quarter of a mile.) After breakfast he and the other men picked up their tools and equipment and readied themselves for the work of the day. At about 6:50 a.m. trucks took them to the fields to commence work.

At about 11:50 a.m. the noonday meal was ready to be served back at the cookhouse. In the early days, the cook, using a metal pipe, banged on a gong (usually an old broken disk or cultivator blade that hung on a post), and raised a white flag (probably an old dish towel) that could be seen at the top of the gulch, blowing in the wind. This alerted the men that it was time to eat. *Ranceri* working close to the cookhouse started to walk in; those working in distant fields waited for a truck to pick them up. During the summer months, I remember my father going to lunch at 12:30 p.m., one half hour later than the other men. Thus, he often ate the noon meal alone. This probably had to do with the nature of the work he was doing at the time.

The *ranceri* had an hour for lunch and then returned to the field to resume their work. At 5:50 p.m., the men were once again picked up and returned to the cookhouse. There they had their evening meal. After the meal, Bronco slowly climbed back up the steep incline, and leaving *Il Buco* behind for another day, he retraced his steps back home. To wind down from his day's labor, he often worked in the family garden for about an hour. This, in itself, used to amaze me.

Here was a man who worked very hard for ten or twelve hours each day, but had enough energy left to work in the family garden for enjoyment.

Bronco was 5'11" tall and weighted 175 pounds. His weight never deviated from this by more than two or three pounds, except at the end of his life when he was very sick. His wiry, muscular body could endure long periods of hard physical labor. In his youth, Bronco had a crop of thick black hair, which started to turn gray in his late twenties. At the end of his life at age eighty-three, he still had all his hair, although it had now become completely white. Bronco's face was lean with the skin being taunt and well tempered by the wind and the rays of the coastal sun. He had deep-set, dark-brown eyes, which he often used to give intense stares when he was angry. He possessed a larger-than-normal nose, although I never thought of it as being disproportional to his head and face. In my mind, it enhanced the Italian in his facial features. Although a five o'clock shadow tended to appear on his face, even if he had just shaven, Bronco never grew a beard or mustache. But at various times in his life he did favor long sideburns. His long arms bore permanent dark sun tan marks, extending from the back of his hands up to just over his elbows. This, of course, was because he liked to roll up those shirtsleeves when working.

Bronco, during his youth, was quite handsome. I remember my mother showing some photographs of my father when he was in his early thirties to Andreina Rodoni, one of our neighbors. After viewing the photos, Andreina commented, with a touch of awe in her voice, that Bronco was "really good looking" when he was young. Using a pet name for her best friend and possibly remembering those earlier song-filled days at her father's "bar," Valentina responded in a very matter-of-fact manner, "Of course, Andrea. I wouldn't have married him if he hadn't been."

Like the other men on the ranch, Bronco did various tasks, including picking and/or packing sprouts, artichokes and broccoli, hand-loading manure on to trucks (the one job he really hated) and even cleaning sprouts. However, his main job during the spring and summer months was that of a *bagnatore* [bah nyah **torr** eh]. The Italian verb *bagnare* [bah **nyah** rreh] means "to wet." Bronco was an irrigator. Before the common usage of irrigation pipes with their attached whirlybird sprinklers, irrigation in the fields was done by the hand-and-shovel method. The job of the *bagnatore* was an invaluable one. They had to have a keenness for judging the make-up of the soil in the fields. Some fields, or different areas in the same field, required varying amounts of water to satisfy the crop. Not everyone had the skill to do this job. A poor *bagnatore* could drown the crop by flooding an area with too much water, or he could dry out the plants by not giving them enough water. Bronco had the reputation of being one of the best *bagnatore su per la costa*, and I know that he enjoyed this job the most.

As a young boy, I would go into the fields to watch my father work. Bronco used the *shavola* (shah **voh** lah) method of irrigation. Of course, *shavola* was a coastal Italianization of "shovel." With his *shavola* Bronco made *paratas* [pa **rah** tahs]. The word used in this context probably means to parry, which is exactly what Bronco did with the water flow, by creating dirt barricades. Relying solely on my memory, I will try to describe in some detail how the crops were irrigated using this method.

To prepare the field for irrigation, horse-drawn plows (tractors were used later on) made furrows through the middle of every three or four rows of brussel sprouts or artichokes. These were long furrows that ran vertically and parallel to the rows of plants. At the top of the rows, the plow dug a deeper ditch —the main ditch—which ran horizontally across the entire length of the field. When completed the main ditch, which would carry the water from the main water canals, met each successive furrow at its top end, thereby sealing off the ends with soil.

Once the main ditch was filled with water, Bronco used his trusty *shavola* to remove the dirt blocking the entrance to the furrow at farthest end of the field. This allowed the water to flow from the main ditch, into the furrow. He then walked or ran, depending on how fast the water was flowing, down to the very end of the row.

Once the water flow reached the end, he created breaks in the sides of the furrow causing the water to flow out and into the planted field. Then he parried the unleashed water between and among the plants by creating a series of divots and mounds in the dirt. Alternating quickly back and forth, Bronco irrigated plants on either side of the furrow almost simultaneously. Once he estimated that the plants had received sufficient water, Bronco selected a spot further up the furrow, and with his *shavola* built a dirt *parata* to intercept the water flow. He then opened the sides of the furrow and once again, manicuring the soil, diverted or parried the water to where he wanted it to go. This process continued all the way up to the top of the row where the main ditch was. At that point, Bronco re-directed the water flow, by creating an opening in the next successive furrow and then, just beyond that point, building a dirt *parata* in the main ditch. Thus the whole field was irrigated.

Irrigating the fields by the *shavola* method took close coordination between the *bagnatore* and the person (usually the foreman) who sent the water down to the fields from the reservoir via metal pipes, wooden canals, or ditches. Italianizing the English word "dam," the *ranceri* called these reservoirs *damas* [**dah** mahs]. The Gulch Ranch *dama*, which resembled a gigantic cement swimming pool, was located on the eastern side of the Coast Road at the intersection of what now is Dimeo Lane. (Presently, this giant swimming pool is located on the western side of the Coast Road.) The *dama* was usually filled during the evening hours, using both well water and county supplied water. Depending on the location of the field being irrigated, the flow of water from the *dama* to the *bagnatore* could take from five to thirty or more minutes.

The big problem would come when too much water was sent down the canal. When that happened, it became very difficult to direct the water with a *shavola* and dirt *paratas*. Excessive water, of course, caused the rate of the flow to increase. The rapid flow soon filled the ditches and furrows, causing the water to "jump" the banks and *paratas*. Directing its flow became virtually impossible. One could easily tell how things were going in the fields by the demeanor of the *bagnatore*. For example, when the water was normal, Bronco sang Italian songs. When things weren't going well, my father, with his volatile temper, yelled and swore, trying to get someone to slow down the flow of water. At the same time he would work his tail off trying to direct the flow of water away from flooding areas. If it got too bad he would have to abandon the field and find a way to shut down the water himself, or find a way to direct its flow completely away from the field. Although I cannot remember any blows being struck over any such incident, I know that there were many verbal arguments between the *bagnatore* and whoever was sending the water his way.

This was probably the major problem Bronco had with some of the *bossos*. The foremen perhaps wanting to get the work done faster, sent more and more water down the canals. Bronco would then work himself to exhaustion trying to manage all that water. Unable to do so, he would go into one of his famous tirades, probably shouting out, "Dio Cane! Ti mando al inferno!" ("God damn it! I'm going to send you to Hell!") As far as I know, the promised journey to Hell for some of the *bossos* did not materialize. However, Bronco's outbursts would not endear him to the person controlling the water.

The fact that Bronco had to eat his noon meal one half hour later than the rest of the men, probably was related to the fact that the foreman did not wish to completely shut down the flow of water to the fields. By keeping at least one irrigator in the field, while the other irrigator ate, the flow of water could continue, though at a reduced rate. When Bronco returned to the field there was no down time caused by having to wait for the water to start flowing down the ditches from the *dama*.

During the fall and early winter months, when rains made hand irrigation less of a factor, my father worked in the field with the other men, picking sprouts. The brussel sprout is a cabbage-like plant sporting floppy green leaves on its long stem. At maturity, the plant stands approximately four feet high. Small, edible round heads grow on the stem between the leaves. Before the advent of the electric sprout cutting and cleaning machines, these small heads (simply called sprouts) were picked, cleaned and sorted by hand. The Italian and Filipino field workers did the picking, stripping the mature sprouts off the stem and placing them in carry-along hampers. (These hampers were first made out of balsa wood; later they were made from aluminum.) To a large extent, Mexican nationals came later, in the late 1940s and early 1950s, supplanting the work done by the Filipinos.

The specific variety of the brussel sprout used during this time period required each plant to be picked seven to nine times during the harvest period. The small heads started to mature at the bottom of the stem first, then gradually matured up to the top of the plant. The first picking was the hardest because of the increased back strain it caused. The field hands had to stoop very low, to first strip the bottom leaves off the stem and then to pick the sprouts. The rest of the leaves and sprouts on the plant were left intact.

The first picking also produced the worst sprouts. They were leafier and not as hard as the sprouts that eventually matured higher on the stem. Being low on the stem also meant that some sprout heads came in contact with the ground. This caused above-average spoilage due to excessive moisture or the boring of ground insects. I can recall that even when there was no market for these low-grade sprouts, workers had to be sent into the field to clean off the bottom of the plant. Otherwise, the sprouts further up the plant could also become contaminated.

I must confess to the reader that later, as an amateur "sprout picker," I had my problems harvesting the crop. On occasions, I leaned or pressed on the top of the plant too hard, causing the head or the stem to break off. This was a no-no because it rendered the plant useless for further pickings. Also, I used to strip off all the leaves on the plant during one picking. I thought this made picking the sprouts off the stem easier. That may have been so, but it left the remaining sprout heads exposed to the elements without the benefit of leaf cover. I was cured of this bad habit while working on the Rodoni Ranch in 1953. Upon seeing what I was doing, Dante Rodoni, the foreman, took me aside and in a voice filled with exasperation, he told me the obvious. I was wrecking his sprout plants. He then patiently demonstrated how to properly "peel" the plant, one section at a time, starting from the bottom. This left the rest of the leaves on the plant intact, allowing the remaining sprouts to mature properly. Although I quickly learned the proper method, I never did like picking sprouts. Fortunately for me, the new school year commenced just about the time the harvest started. I was able to leave the majority of the pickings to the true professionals.

Every ten to twelve days (depending on how fast the sprout heads matured), workers passed through the fields, first stripping the leaves, then picking the mature sprout heads from the stem. This process was followed until the last viable sprout was taken from the top of the plant. During each picking, the leaves were discarded and left on the ground; the picked sprouts were thrown into the hampers. When a hamper was full, the sprouts were dumped into a burlap sack. In turn, when the sack was full, the ranch hand slung it over his shoulder (each sack weighted approximately 75 to 85 pounds) and then carried it to the end of the row. There the sack was stacked upright with other previously filled sacks. The workers' trek became more difficult when it rained. The wet sacks became heavier, and the mixture of mud and discarded leaves made the rows slushy and extremely slippery. (One particular Filipino named Louie took delight in navigating the course with a sack of sprouts squarely placed on his head.)

As one can see, this entire process was labor intensive, requiring many field hands in order to keep up with the timely stripping of the ever maturing sprout heads. Mr. John DeBenedetti, a much respected *rancere* and land owner *su per la costa*, stated in an oral interview for the University of California at Santa Cruz (UCSC) that at times he had 200 or more workers in his fields picking sprouts. Much later, a variety of brussel sprouts called Jade was introduced. This variety had the capability of having its entire sprout heads mature at the same time. The plant stem could be cut at the bottom and then placed through a stripping machine mounted on a cart. A tractor then towed the cart filled with collected sprouts to the packing shed. One machine picking is a much more efficient way of doing the job, requiring far fewer men than the old handpicking method. However, I didn't think that the Jade variety produced a better tasting sprout.[22]

Endnotes

[22] The entire text of Mr. DeBenedetti's interview for the UCSC Regional History Project may be seen on the UCSC web site, www.library.ucsc.edu/reg-hist/debendetti.pdf. Later, during the 1970s Mr. DeBenedetti and his family afforded my brother and I the opportunity to purchase our own piece of agricultural land.

6. Donne Al Lavoro
(Women At Work)

In the pre-machine picking days, the stacked sacks of sprouts placed at the end of the rows had to be loaded by hand onto a pickup or flatbed truck and then driven to the ranch compound for cleaning. At the compound, the sacks were taken to a *capannone* [ka pa **no** neh], the Italian for packing shed. The old barn in *il buco* at the Gulch Ranch served as the *capannone*. Once arrived, the sacks were hand-lifted off the back of the truck and taken inside, where the sprouts were dumped out onto long tables made of wood. These tables were usually attached with big metal hinges to the side of a wall inside the packing shed. (The hinges allowed these tables to be folded up against the wall when not in use.) At night or when visibility was made poor by inclement weather, the sprouts on the tables were illuminated (rather poorly) by oversized light bulbs attached to single strands of insulated wire hanging from the ceiling. Valentina along with several other women stood or sat in front of these tables and "cleaned" the sprouts by pulling off the yellow or loose leaves with their hands and cutting the stems with short, curved hand knives.

In preparing for her sprout cleaning duties, Valentina, who usually dressed in blue denim work pants, with a cotton shirt and warm sweater, placed two large wooden crates on her left side. The first crate she set on the floor, turning it upside down; the second crate, she placed upright and on top of the upside-down crate. Behind these two crates, she placed a third crate, set upright on the floor or on top of a second upside down crate. Then, facing the table before her, she pulled a small pile of sprouts toward her, using her hands or a wooden board. (The board, usually ripped from an old crate, increased Valentina's reach as she "cleaned" more deeply into the mound of sprouts on the table.) Then with her curved hand knife, she proceeded to clean the selected sprouts, flipping them backhanded into the top crate on her left when done. The oversized sprouts went in the upright crate at her rear. The *ranceri* referred to these sprouts as *faloppas*. (The Italian word *faloppa* actually means defective cocoon.) The yellow and loose leaves, along with damaged, malformed, or insect-ridden sprouts, went on the floor.

Once Valentina's crate was filled with cleaned sprouts, a *rancere* in attendance usually removed it and stacked it against the wall, away from where she was working. I can remember my mother on occasion lifting some of the crates and stacking them herself, to save time. According to Augie Gemignani, who used to work with my mother, a full crate of brussel sprouts weighed from 100 to 120 pounds. Eventually, the stacked crates were hand-loaded onto a flatbed truck and driven to Santa Cruz for shipping by rail to the East Coast.

As you can see, cleaning sprouts in the above-described manner was hard work. It became more difficult and uncomfortable during the fall and winter months, when the sprouts got wet from the rains or heavy dew. Valentina wore a rubber apron and boots to give her some semblance of protection from the water that came rolling off the sprouts; however, her surroundings quickly became damp and wet. To make matters worse, the packing sheds were usually drafty and without heat. (Some women used portable electric heaters to help warm their feet.) Yet, Valentina and numerous other Italian ladies living on the coast performed this work for eight or more hours per day, during each harvest season. This work was not for the weak, lame, or lazy.

As a young boy, it amazed me to see my mother *al lavoro*, cleaning sprouts. Valentina, who by then was known to many coastal Italians as "Vale" (**vah**-leh) and to some American co-workers as "Val," was simply a marvel at this job. She was extremely fast with her hands. The sprouts flew back out of her hands and into the crate like machine gun bullets. As a full crate was removed, Valentina replaced it with an empty one, quickly resuming her work. Gradually, the discarded sprouts and leaves started to pile up on the floor around her ankles. Once in awhile, much to her dismay (for time was money), Valentina had to stop her work and, using a large bristle broom, sweep the discards under the table.

Every couple of weeks, a dairy farmer came by and loaded the discarded leaves and sprouts onto a truck and hauled them away to feed his cows. At other times they were simply taken to a barren field and dumped into a pile. Later, after fermenting a while, and thus adding their putrid smell to the coastal winds, their mushy remains were disked under to enrich the soil. Sometimes, prior to their being disked under, my brother and I, wearing rubber boots, would go to the pile to romp and stomp in the soft gooey matter. On the down side, the smell was pretty bad; on the up side, there were no fleas.

Before being taken away, the leaves and discarded sprouts would pile up quite high under the tables. Taking advantage of this, I used to crawl under the tables to bury myself in sprout leaves. There, alone or with a companion, I would happily play peek-a-boo. This continued for quite some time, until one of the ladies accused me of looking up her dress. What a *faloppa* she was! Afterward, giving me another one of her *Bada! No fa quello, mia pui* speeches, Valentina put a stop to my activities.

If I remember correctly, during the late 1940s my mother made 40 cents for every crate she filled. I believe that at the height of the harvest season she made ten to twelve dollars a day. That was good money in those days. Unlike many of the women who were slower, Valentina never wanted to be put on an hourly scale. She made more money by doing piecework. I seem to remember that on some days she filled as many as forty crates. That certainly would have been an amazing feat.

Not only was Valentina a hard worker, she was also good looking. At the time, she was a full-bodied women, standing 5'5" tall and weighing in the neighborhood of 135 to 160 pounds, depending on whether she was dieting or not. My mother was an excellent cook. Much to her own consternation and disappointment, she often ate too much of her own cooking. She had brown eyes; her complexion was fair with a blush of red in her cheeks. She usually wore her brown hair cut short, although in the 1940s she did wear it long enough to be able to curl the sides and back around those spongy, felt rollers that were fashionable at the time. As the reader already knows from my earlier accounts, Valentina, when young, was a very beautiful girl. Bronco was very proud of the fact that he had captured such a prize, and a hard worker to boot.

Like many women *su per la costa,* Valentina supplemented the family income by taking in laundry. My mother's customers were mostly *ranceri* that worked on the Gulch and Rodoni ranches. Valentina owned a tank-type washing machine (top-loaded of course), with an electric-powered agitator. The rollers on the top of the machine were not powered by electricity and had to be operated by a hand crank. Next to the washing machine was an oversized wash basin where she hand-scrubbed some of the *ranceri's* dirtiest clothes, using one of those old wooden washboards with the metal ripples in front. Once finished, Valentina took the clothes and hung them on clotheslines conveniently located in our back yard. Keeping a close eye on the elements (remember *il vento* and the *pattume*), she waited until the sun had dried the clothes. Quickly, she then took them down from the clothesline and brought them back into the house. There she systematically sewed on buttons (as necessary), and ironed and neatly folded the clothes. Valentina then wrapped the clothes in separate packages, one each per customer, using old Italian-language newspapers, and tying them up with string. My brother and I were then given the task of delivering the clean laundry back to the *ranceri*. I don't remember ever receiving a tip from any of the *ranceri*. I believe that my mother initially charged one dollar per month per customer, and gradually increased the price to four dollars per month. Such a bargain for washing, ironing, sewing, delivery service, and, in addition to all that, reading material for the *rancere!* (As the reader will learn later, the *rancere* also used old newspapers for purposes other than reading.)

When I think about my mother washing clothes, it brings back memories of one of the most colorful characters that ever worked on the coastal ranches. He was known by his last name, Smerigli [Smerr **eel** yee], and his antics were legendary among the *ranceri*.

I can't remember ever hearing Smerigli called by his first name. I do remember that he was often referred to as "Mr. Brown", because for some unknown reason he often greeted people by calling out in English, "Hello, Mr. Brown. Ha ya doing today?" Smerigli was perhaps 5'10" tall, and his body weight of well over 200 pounds was supported by thick thighs and muscular legs. Although he had some fat, his body was composed mostly of bone and muscle. He had broad shoulders, powerful arms with oversized hands attached, a barrel-like chest, and a very short, thick neck. His large round head was completely bald and sported an indentation in the middle of the forehead. (Coastal lore has it that he received that indentation at the end of a policeman's nightstick.) When he smiled, which was quite often, his big, wide mouth displayed a series of shiny gold teeth. Smerigli loved to tell jokes and laugh. His laugh would start off from way back in his throat as a wheezy "heeh, heeh, heeh" and end up as a deep, raspy, "heh, heh, heh." When Smerigli was sober, he was the nicest guy and hardest worker on the ranch. When he was drunk, he became nasty and incorrigible.

One day Smerigli brought his clothes to my mother for washing. After washing the clothes, Valentina noticed that the bottom of the breast pockets, located on the flaps of Smerigli's overalls were torn. (When working, Smerigli, usually liked to wear blue overalls over his long, wool underwear. No shirt.) Being the dutiful laundress, she proceeded to sew the torn pockets. After receiving his laundry, Smerigli came back to the house and in a very nice manner (he had much respect for my mother), he told Valentina that he had intentionally cut open the bottom of the pockets and would she please not sew them again.

"Perche?" (Why?) she asked. Smerigli gave her a big wide smiled and also a very plausible explanation. He said that when he was working, he often shoveled dirt or manure over his head and shoulders. Because he worked so hard and fast, some of the debris often fell on top of him. Soon the top pockets in his overalls would fill up; then he would have to stop work to clean them out. If the pockets were cut open at the bottom, most of the manure and debris would filter through and he would not have to clean his pockets out.

Not wishing to interfere with Smerigli's work habits, Valentina obliged and ceased sewing his pockets. I suppose that made Smerigli perfectly happy. "Mr. Brown" didn't much care that he was covered with *pattume* from head to toe, he just didn't want to take time out from work to clean out his pockets. Makes sense to me. Doesn't it to you?

7. Ranceri (Ranchers)

The words *ranceri* (plural) and *rancere* (singular) were normally used to describe the Italian ranch worker. (Bronco would often say that the job of the *rancere* was "il ultimo mestiere" [mess **tyer-eh**], meaning that it was the least desirable job and that anyone could do it, if he had to. This, of course, was an overstatement on his part.) The term *ranceri* was also used to describe the Italian ranch family. When asked what we did up the coast, my mother often replied, "Siamo [**syah** moh] ranceri," meaning, of course, "We are ranchers." This was certainly apropos as far as our family was concerned, because we lived on the ranch, and we were either working or being directly impacted by the ranch work itself. In this chapter, I choose to use the word *ranceri* to mainly describe the mannerisms and adventures of some of the Italian ranch hands I knew and remembered. Although the word *ranceri* was not use to describe non-Italian workers—Filipino and Mexican labors were usually referred to by their nationality, i.e. *I Filipini* or *I Messicani*—the reader shall see at the end of this chapter, that I also use the word *ranceri* to describe two very special workers, who probably weren't Italian at all.

Maybe they weren't all as colorful as Smerigli. But most of the *ranceri* were rough-and-tumble guys. They didn't pay much attention to the manners and niceties of a more gentile society. Theirs was a man's world, ruled by those who could work the hardest and the fastest, often under the most adverse weather conditions. Rain and freezing conditions did not stop the men from going into the fields to harvest the crops. When it rained, these men simply put on their rain gear (raincoats, rain hats, rubber gloves and hip boots) and continued with the harvest. The weak and/or the lazy, were quickly cast aside or assigned lower rankings in the pecking order.

Ranceri came from various regions in Italy and Switzerland; however, most were Toscanos, claiming the Tuscany region of Italy as their place of birth. Their language was usually that of the Italian peasant, spoken in the familiar tense, with the sharpness of a Tuscan accent. They added coarseness to their language by frequently using swear words. They were especially fond of coupling the Italian word for the deity, *Dio,* with various derogatory adjectives or other demonstrative pronouns. *Dio Cane* ("dog God, or dog of a God"), its intended meaning being the equivalent of the American "God damn," was a common every day expression used by the ranchers. *Dio Bestia* ("Beast of a God") was also heard quite frequently. On the other hand, the more reverent *ranceri*, in order to get their feelings across, chose less profane words such as *accidenti* [ah chee **den** tee], most probably meaning "damn it," or the phrase, *porca la miseria* (**por** kah lah mee **zerr** yah), which when loosely translated probably meant "dirty (or lousy) misery," or perhaps even "darn/damn the misery."

As very young boys, my brother and I were exposed to the most vile curse words imaginable. The only time that I did not hear the *ranceri* swear (much) was when my mother was around. Valentina's presence seemed to have a civilizing affect on their coarse behavior. (Maybe they were afraid of her wrath.) Once in catechism class, I asked one of the nuns if she thought that all the ranchers would go to hell because they often took God's name in vain. She was nice enough to answer that they probably didn't mean what they were saying and so they would be forgiven. This relieved me greatly, since Bronco was one of the great champions of swearing and cursing, both in Italian and in Friulano.

My mother did not swear, and taught us to say "Dio Buono," which referred to a good and benevolent God, instead of using the

La Nostra Costa (Our Coast)

"other" swear words. I guess she didn't think that "Dio Buono" was a swear word except, maybe, when she was angry with me. On one occasion, Valentina caught me smoking in the dugout underneath the house. Actually, my boyhood friends, Mario and Elio Rodoni were with me during this clandestine session. Being novices at the game, Mario and Elio inhaled and began coughing. This gave away our position. *Porca la miseria!* I was immediately branded the instigator. As I tried to make my get-away, she grabbed a broom and started chasing me around the house yelling, "Dio Buono, Ivano! Aspetta quando ti piglio [**peel** yo]!" In effect she meant something like, "Good God, Ivano! Just wait until I catch you!" She sure wasn't calling on the good graces of God to bless me, on that particular day.

The *ranceri* also liked to pepper their speech with Italianized American words and phrases. Thus, gulch was pronounced "**goal**che," boss, "**boh**so," cookhouse, "**cook**-ahousa," drive was "**dry**vah"or **dry**-var, stop sign, "**stoppah**-sighnah," brakes, "**breh**-kee," push "**poosh**-ah," shovel, "**shah**-volah," box, **bohx**-ah, crate, **creh**-tah, and cowboy was "**cowa**boya" or "**capo**boy." The Caterpillar tractor became known as the "cara**pee**lah," the town of Half Moon Bay became "Haffa Moombay," and San Francisco, was always Sahn Frahn-**cheez**-co. The expression, "Oh sure" was "**ma** shua," and of course, bullshit became "**bulla**-shita" and son-of-a-bitch, became "sonnama **beecha**."

Interestingly enough, the *ranceri* referred to the automobile as "la macchina [mah **kee** nah]," meaning, of course, "the machine." This in itself brings to mind a very amusing story, as told to me by Police Officer Jim Emmons. One evening, while patrolling the streets of San Jose during the late 1960s, he came across a citizen waving frantically at him and shouting, "They stola my machine. They stola my machine." Not really being sure what the citizen, who obviously was of Italian decent, was referring to, Officer Emmons asked, "What machine? Your sewing machine?"

"No! No!" the Italian gentleman responded in exasperation. He then pointed excitedly to a parked car and exclaimed, "Da machine, da machine! Dem sonnama beechas stola my caro!"

As I was growing up, I thought that the above words and sayings were all part of the Italian language. In 1949 the Delgi Esposti boys, Roberto and Fabrizio, arrived from Italy to live on the Rodoni Ranch. I soon found out that they did not know what these words meant. Not being dense, the two boys quickly picked up on our language and were soon Italianizing American words on their own.

Some of the *ranceri* were known alcoholics. The coastal Italians called them *ciucos* [**chew** kohs]. (The Italian noun *ciuco* means donkey, ignorant ass and/or blockhead.) Valentina would say that it was important for men to marry, otherwise they would become *ciucos* and lose themselves in the world of drink. I am sure that this was not true in all cases, but it did seem to me that many of the ranch workers who were not married did drink quite heavily. Probably because red table wine was readily available on most all of the *rancios*, it seemed to be the *rancere*'s favorite drink. Bronco liked his red wine, but only drank it with his meals. He often said that a person who drank red wine without food was probably a *ciuco*.

One of the most famous *ciuco* stories circulating *su per la costa* was about Smerigli and his arrest by the police for drunk and disorderly conduct. As I have previously mentioned to the reader, Smerigli was a very nice person. But when drunk he became nasty. As the story goes, Smerigli went to town and got really drunk, causing him to want to fight anybody and everybody. The police were called to control this hunk of granite that walked like a man. It took several officers to accomplish this feat. Having finally subdued the struggling Smerigli, the officers handcuffed him. Apparently, they could not force Smerigli's hands behind his back. (Remember those big, powerful arms)

Contrary to proper police procedure, they handcuffed him hands-to-the-front. According to the way I was trained, this is a "no-no" unless you also strap down the prisoner's arms. The officers apparently did not do this. Once Smerigli got to his feet, he balanced himself on one leg while bending the other. Simultaneously, he raised his hands high above his head, and then, aiming for his bent leg, brought them down hard and fast. The metal handcuffs struck his thick, muscular thigh just above the knee. The force of the blow supposedly broke the link on the handcuffs. This being the case, Smerigli was on the loose again and the officers had to subdue him all over again. In the process, one of the officers struck Smerigli across the forehead with his nightstick, rendering him unconscious. Smerigli survived the blow to fight another day, however, he bore the indentation made by the nightstick for the rest of his life. At least that's how the story goes.

No one dared to call another *rancere*—named Jimmy—a *ciuco*. He was too fine of a man and worker to be called that. Generally speaking, he was a good-looking guy. He was about 5'10" tall with a stocky build, dark features, bushy eyebrows, and a "five o'clock" shadow constantly on his face. He reminded me a great deal of Steve Cochran, a popular movie actor of that time. Seeing Cochran, with helmet and goggles on his head, standing inside the turret of his tank in the movie "The Tanks Are Coming," brings back memories of Jimmy driving the "carapeela" on the Gulch Ranch.[23]

Jimmy was no slouch. He was entrusted with driving and maintaining all of the mechanized equipment on the Gulch Ranch. This was no small feat. To make sure he did his work properly, Jimmy would be the first at work in the morning and the last to come into the cookhouse in the evening. He spoke English well enough and seldom swore. His favorite expression was, "Oh boy!" By the inflection of Jimmy's "Oh boy!" a *rancere* could easily tell whether Jimmy was pleased or just plain disgusted. I never saw Jimmy drunk while on the ranch, but, I had heard about his reputation of going into town on the weekends and "blowing his money" at the local bars. I couldn't quite believe this about Jimmy, because he was such a sober and disciplined worker on the Gulch Ranch.

Thinking back, it must have been around 1960. I was home on leave from the Army. One evening, having some time on my hands,

I drove to the intersection of Market and Water Streets, the location of Adolph's, a popular restaurant and bar.[24]

There, for the first time in a long time, I saw Jimmy. He was sitting at the corner of the bar and it was obvious to me that he'd had too much to drink. As was his wont to do, he was buying drinks for friends and strangers alike. Having by this time some experience (because of my police background) in handling these kinds of problems, I went over to see if I could be of some assistance. He didn't recognize me. All he wanted to do was to buy me a drink. Smitty, the ever popular bartender at Adolf's, came over and informed me that he knew Jimmy and that he would take good care of him.[25] I got the distinct impression from Smitty that this was not an unusual situation for him. Jimmy liked to drink, and when he'd had too much to drink, he wanted everyone to drink with him. Unlike Smerigli, Jimmy did not become violent when drunk. He just wanted everybody to have a good time. Thus, the stories of Jimmy "blowing" his money on drink gained a measure of credibility with me. Still I could never quite reconcile the two images I had in my mind of this one *rancere*. Oh yes, Smitty was true to his word. Jimmy always seemed to make it back home safely.

Writing all this about drinking reminds me of my first real *ciuca* (drunkenness). I must have been four or five years old at the time. My mother had been hosting a couple of *ranceri* in our kitchen. They were all seated around the kitchen table smoking and conversing in Italian. Valentina then pulled out a big jug of white wine and poured the visitors a couple of glasses. (I guess it was all right to drink white wine without food.) Each time they drank the wine, they would raise their glasses and say, "Salute!" ("Health!")

Watching all this, I must have thought that this ceremony was the "adult thing" to do. When the visitors left they took their smokes with them; however, the jug of wine and glasses were left on the table. When Valentina went outside to see the *ranceri* off, I jumped at the opportunity to see for myself what this ceremony was all about. I poured a glass of wine, lifted the glass, said the obligatory "Salute!", and proceeded to drink. As I recall, the wine tasted sweet and not all that bad to me. I poured another glass, repeated the necessary ritual and drank the wine. I must have had at least three full glasses of wine before my mother came back. By that time my head was spinning and my stomach began to ache.

Seeing what had happened, Valentina went into a panic, shouting, "O Dio! Che cosa hai fatto?" ("Oh God! What have you done?") "Il vino," I answered, pointing at the jug of wine as I fell to the floor. Regaining her composure, Valentina picked me up and carried me into the bathroom. There she induced me to vomit by having me stick my finger down my throat. Fortunately, I was saved; however, I was sick for the next couple of days. For many years after this incident, the mere thought of white wine made me sick to my stomach. It wasn't until I was in my late twenties that I was able to drink white wine again. So much for ceremonial drinking!

Unfortunately, too many of the *ranceri* did die at a relatively young age, probably from alcohol-related diseases. In a couple of incidents that I can remember, they just dropped dead while working in the fields. I recall a *rancere* named Angelo, who was typical of the ranch hands who had succumbed to *la bibita del diavolo rosso*—"the drink of the red devil." At times, I thought that Angelo's face took on the color of the wine he drank. It was an unhealthy looking purplish-red. One day, as Angelo was working in the fields, he keeled over and died. I don't think anyone was really surprised or shocked by the incident, even though Angelo probably was only in his late fifties or early sixties at the time. At least he died with his proverbial boots on. Many other *ranceri*, drinkers and non-drinkers alike (my father included), were to die in hospital beds after suffering from various lingering illnesses. Given a choice, I think they would have liked to have gone out like Angelo did—an instant death, working in the fields that they loved.

Many *ranceri* were also heavy smokers, which no doubt contributed to their health problems. *Ranceri* seemed to favor Camel or Lucky Strike cigarettes. The few *ranceri* who smoked Pall Mall or Chesterfield cigarettes were for some reason thought to be a bit elitist. Some *ranceri* smoked small curved pipes or simply rolled their own cigarettes, using tobacco packed in "Prince Albert" tins. (As a three or four year old, I tried to emulate the *ranceri*, by rolling fresh dirt in a piece of old newspaper and sticking it my mouth. A bit too gritty for my taste.) Other *ranceri* preferred those small, dark brown and evil smelling Toscani cigars. Toscani cigars are about five inches long and resemble a tree twig when stuck in the corner of the mouth.

These woody looking cigars always remind me of one of my godfathers, Antonio "Tony" Marcucci. (He was my godfather at my Confirmation ceremony at Holy Cross Church in Santa Cruz. Italians call these honored persons *padrini*.) I can still visualize him working in the fields, all bent over, picking sprouts with a slow-burning Toscano firmly clenched between his teeth. Although this allowed him to work with both hands free, he had to stop frequently to relight his spent cigar. Cupping his two gnarled hands together to shield the flame of his lighted match from the wind, he hunched his shoulders and bent his head down real low, touching the end of the Toscano to the fire. With a few puffs on the cigar, smoke started to bellow from the palms of his hands, signaling that his Toscano was once again functional. Then, straightening up the best he could, he would continue with his work. It was amazing to me that the small gray mustache that he constantly sported on his upper lip never caught fire.

Tony Marcucci was a wonder, and he spent his entire life working on the *rancios*, mostly as a day laborer for Pfyffer Brothers.[26] He still was working on the ranches well into his seventies. He was a small, wiry Friulano with coarse, sandpaper-like hands, and fingernails all blackened and torn at the edges. When he took my small hands into his, I could actually feel my skin being scraped away. As he got older, he could not quite fully straighten his body. Walking, for Tony Marcucci, became an ordeal in itself. When he stepped forward, his small upper body remained bent over with a slight tilt to the left. All that hard work on the *rancios* had taken its toll.

Tony Marcucci liked to stick to the old ways of doing things. By doing so he sometimes appeared odd. For example, in the mid-1950s

Tony, and his wife Alvira, accompanied my aunt, Lina Gemignani, and her husband Joe, on a flight to Italy. Since my godfather had never flown on an airplane before, he made darn sure that they had plenty to eat and drink, to perhaps save a little money. He thought the flight would be similar to the long, arduous sea voyage by which he came to America in the early 1900s. He could not forget that dining accommodations in steerage were not the best. Consequently, he brought along a long stick of dry salami, a big wedge of dry Monterey cheese, a couple of loaves of fresh French bread, and two or three bottles of homemade red wine.[27] Lina and Joe laughed and felt a bit embarrassed as Tony passed his bottle of wine to them and cut into the food with his pocketknife. He continued this process, doling out morsels of food and pouring wine for the duration of the flight.

Joe and Lina, as well as the astonished airline stewardesses, thought that my godfather's behavior was a bit strange and certainly out-of-date for "modern" day travel. After all, as the stewardesses tried to inform him, the airline did provide ample food and drink. (With all due respect to my aunt and uncle, and with some deference to the airline personnel, I think my godfather was far ahead of his time, given the quality of airline food and the "no frills" approach to air travel these days.) My aunt and uncle might have been embarrassed then, by my godfather's unorthodox behavior; however, later Joe related to me that, because of Tony's antics during the trip, it turned out to be the most enjoyable and memorable flight they had ever taken. Unfortunately, Tony Marcucci's return to America was to be his last airplane flight. My godfather died in 1960. Cause of death—throat cancer.[28]

I can now attest to the reader that two of the hardest working *ranceri* on the Gulch Ranch never drank wine, never smoked cigarettes, and were never paid. They were named Charlie and Prince. These were the two *cavallos* (kah **vah** lows) who lived on the ranch. Charlie and Prince were work (i.e. plow) horses. They were worth their weight in gold. They worked hard, seldom complained, and hardly ever got sick. Before the common use of the tractor and other mechanized equipment, horses were used to do most of the plowing, cultivating and hauling. With a soft but firm "Gettie upah Chalee! Gettie upah Princ-eh!" or a simple *click-click* of the tongue from the handler, these two horses moved out at a slow, even pace, pulling whatever was attached to their harness. The trailing *rancere* guided them along with a pair of long leather reins, attached to bits in the horses' mouth. Charlie and Prince could work as a team or solo, depending on the weight of the equipment they were hauling. Sometimes the *rancere* got to ride on the equipment he was using; other times he had to walk behind the horses. Near the end of the day, when everyone was getting tired, the horses often became slow in responding to commands, and the *rancere* became impatient waiting for them to execute their maneuvers. Then the soft "Gettie upah Chalee!" or "Gettie upah Princ-eh!" became a loud and menacing, "Dio cane! Brutta bestia! Muoveti! Gettie upah ! Porca la miseria! Gettie upah!" Loosely translated, the impatient *rancere* was probably shouting, "God damn it! Move, you ugly beast! Get going! Damn the lousy misery! Get going!" Despite these irreverent words, I never did see any of the *ranceri* mistreat these two animals. Any handler that did would have been immediately fired. Such was the value of these two *ranceri*.

Charlie and Prince were housed in the rear portion of the barn where my mother cleaned sprouts. Immediately outside their stalls was a large, fenced-in corral. It was here that my brother and I spent a good deal of time getting acquainted with these two gentle creatures. We often sat on the corral fence, feeding them carrots and apples. These two *cavallos* were large animals with broad backs and big legs and hooves. Their build made them well suited for ranch work, but not for riding. Charlie was the better looking of the two horses. He was solid brown in color, with a white face. Prince was more of a chestnut color with many speckles of white showing throughout his coat. I think Charlie was the older horse; however, Prince's speckled coat made him look older.

One day (I must have been ten years old at the time) Charlie was working solo, pulling a cultivator in the field adjacent to our house. Smerigli was guiding the horse while walking behind the cultivator. Because I liked Smerigli a lot, I went into the field to watch "Mr.

La Nostra Costa (Our Coast)

Brown" work the big brown *cavallo*. As they came to the end of the row where I was standing, Smerigli saw me and quickly greeted me with a "Haya doing, Mr. Brown?" After allowing me to pet Charlie, he asked me if I would please get him a glass of water. Wanting to please him, I said that I would, but knowing how much he liked his wine I added, "Wouldn't you like a glass of wine better?" Smerigli's face lit up as it broke out in a big wide grin, showing a row of gold teeth. "Sure, Mr. Brown! Sure!" he answered gleefully.

I went back to the house to get the wine, knowing that no one was at home. I got a jug of red wine out of the "coola" and poured a water glass full of the alcoholic beverage. I then took the glass to the field and gave it to Smerigli. Smerigli gulped the wine down with enthusiasm. "Thank you, Mr. Brown," he said, returning the empty glass to me. He then turned Charlie around and proceeded to cultivate the next row of sprouts.

Seeing how much he enjoyed the wine, I ran back to the "coola" and re-filled the water glass with some more of the refreshing red liquid. I then returned to the field to await Charlie and Smerigli. After finishing the row, Smerigli took the glass from me and again gulped down the wine. When he returned the glass to me, he said, "Mr. Brown, maybe it's better that you bring me the bottle of *vino*—then you don't have to keep running back and forth."

Doesn't that make sense to you? It sure made sense to me. I went back to the house to get the wine. Knowing that I shouldn't give him the whole jug, I poured some of the wine into an empty whiskey quart bottle. I brought this bottle to the field and gave it to Smerigli. He took it from my hand and gulped some of the wine straight out of the bottle. Then he said, "Now, I will put this bottle in the shade, right here under this sprout plant. When I come back down I can have another drink and you won't have to run back to the house."

After watching Smerigli and Charlie for awhile, I must have gotten bored, because I left, forgetting about the whole incident. The next day, I was at home with my mother when we heard a knock on the door. It was *il bosso*. Much to my distress, he informed her that yesterday Charlie and Smerigli were all over the field, cultivating some of the sprout plants right out of their roots. Smerigli first blamed Charlie for not being able to keep a straight line, but "the boss" did not buy the story. After getting into a heated argument, the foreman was able to get Smerigli to admit that he had been drinking wine. Worse, he identified me as the "procurer of the grape." Needless to say, Valentina went into one of her "Bada, Ivano! No fa quello mia piu!" routines, with a few "Dio Buonos" thrown in for good measure. (For this episode, she may have given me a few whacks on the rump, too.) Thankfully, Charlie did not get the blame, and Smerigli did not lose his job; however, my short career as a "bootlegger" was over. *Porca la miseria!*

In all these years I have not forgotten Charlie and Prince. I am now telling their story to my grandsons, Kristian and Willie. As we drive by the many horses that reside in Carmel Valley, Willie and Kristian yell out, "There's Charlie! There's Prince!" If I am able to, I pull over to their corral, and with my best whinny I call the horses over to the fence. Although the horses are riding horses, rather than plow horses, I am still able to relive with my grandsons (just for a few moments) those days of old, when Charlie and Prince worked the fields on the Gulch Ranch.

As we get ready to leave, Kristian yells out, "Good-bye Charlie! Good-bye Prince! See ya tomorrow!" Oh, how I wish it could be so. With the advent of the Farmall and John Deere tractors, Charlie and Prince outlived their usefulness on the ranch. I never did learn what happened to these two majestic giants. Hopefully, they were sold to some horse ranch where they lived out the rest of their days on greener pastures. I hope the reader understands that I don't have the courage to dig into it any more than that.

Endnotes

[23] "The Tanks Are Coming" is presently available on Warner Home Video.

[24] According to a recent article by Karen Davis of the Santa Cruz Sentinel, the Camarlinghi family of Santa Cruz has owned Adolph's since 1938. Regrettably, the same article indicated that the restaurant was soon to close its doors for good. The article dated January 25, 2003, and titled, "Patrons bid farewell to Adolph's restaurant," also mentioned that during World War II, the restaurant, originally located elsewhere in downtown Santa Cruz, had its name changed from La Paloma Bar to Adolph's. Apparently, like "Ivano," other Italian-sounding names were not too popular during the early part of the war. No matter, many coastal Italians got around this intrusion by simply calling the restaurant *Adolfo*.

[25] Smitty's real name was Grover Smith. Sporting a crew cut and usually dressed in a short-sleeved white dress shirt with a brightly colored, sleeveless pullover sweater, Smitty would make the customers feel really good by listening intensely to their mundane jokes and then breaking out with a cackling laugh when the punch line was delivered.

[26] Fred Pfyffer and his brother Pino managed several rancios *su per la costa*, and also owned the Pfyffer Brothers Packing and Shipping Company, located on Mission Street (U.S. Highway 1), near the South Pacific Railroad tracks at the west end of Santa Cruz. An article appearing in the *Santa Cruz Sentinel*, dated January 3, 1989, reported that Fred Pfyffer came to Santa Cruz County in 1920 after graduating with a degree in Agricultural Economics from the University of Fribourg in Switzerland. Though he was only nineteen years old at the time, the owners of the Coast Dairies and Land Company had enough confidence in the young man to have him help them manage their company. In 1929, they made Fred Pfyffer the President of the Coast Dairies and Land Company.

[27] My godfather made the wine in his garage. "Assaggia di aceto," [ah **che** toh] my father would tell us. Bronco frequently complained of my godfather's wine as being too vinegary; however, he made sure to always compliment Tony on his ability to make good wine. Thus, he kept us all in good stead with my godfather.

[28] Joe Gemignani's own death from cancer was to occur some 38 years later. In one of those twists of fate, his burial vault at Holy Cross Cemetery would be almost directly across from one bearing the names of my godfather, Antonio Marcucci, and his wife, Alvira. Their voyage continues.

BAGNATORE BRONCO WITH VIRGINIA BROVIA

C. 1937

BRONCO IN HIS RANCERE OUTFIT

C. 1950

DANTE DINELLI AND TWO RANCERI

C. 1935

AL LAVORO, DIANE DINELLI, ANGELINA LORENZI

C. 1950

DANTE DINELLI AND VIVIAN FISTOLERA

C. 1935

8. La Cuoca (The Cook)

For a short period of time, *circa* 1949, Valentina was the *cuoca* [**quoh** kah] doing the cooking for the *ranceri* at the Gulch Ranch. During this period, my brother and I had ample opportunity to explore the old cookhouse. The *ranceri* pronounced the word "**cook**ahousa." The "cookahousa" had a large kitchen with a big black gas range stove where all the cooking was done. Next to the kitchen was a smaller storeroom where most non-perishable foods and cooking utensils were stored. Adjacent to the storeroom, shaped like a bank vault, was a large, walk-in refrigerator/freezer where all the perishable items were stored. Next to the kitchen on the opposite side of the building was a large dining room, containing two long tables, with benches on either side that could accommodate ten or twelve people. This was the room were the *ranceri* came to have all their meals.[29]

The cookhouse building also had three or four residential rooms where the Italian day laborers slept. At the southeast corner of the building was a shower with a small dressing area. Bronco loved that shower. Our house had only a small bathtub, and he never felt comfortable taking a bath in it. I remember that every Saturday afternoon, after finishing work, my father would go into that shower room and have himself a long, steamy shower. He then returned home clean and completely refreshed. After taking a short nap, he was ready to enjoy the weekend with his family.

The most interesting thing to me about the cookhouse was the walk-in refrigerator. I loved to go inside the "vault" and feel the coolness all around me. Once inside I took visual and olfactory inventory of all the items that were being preserved. Big slabs of beef and pork hung on hooks, while smaller cuts of meat, packages containing vegetables, eggs, butter, and cheese, and vats of milk were placed on icy shelves or on the floor. I remember thinking that we would never be short of food as long as this vault was around.

Just about then, Valentina would discover me in the vault. "Fuori, fuori!" [**foh** ree], "Out, out!" she would yell at me. My mother would then explain to me for the hundredth time that the door could not be opened from the inside. If the door should close and the outside latch accidentally become engaged, there would be no way that I could get out. Worse, the door was so thick and well insulated that no one would hear my yells for help. Naturally, Valentina's warnings didn't stop me from sneaking in when she wasn't looking. Fortunately for me the vault door never did close on me. On the other hand, I remember once or twice luring my brother inside and then slamming the door shut. I think the devil made me do it. I at least had the common sense to open it before he froze to death. I thought it was all in great fun; John thought otherwise.

The other thing in the cookhouse that fascinated me was the telephone that hung on the wall in the dinning room. We did not have a telephone at our home, so the working of this gadget really intrigued me. This telephone did not look anything like the phones of today. It was self-contained in a brown wooden box with a black metal speaker emitting straight out from its center. Situated just over the speaker were two separate bells clad in black metal covers. As those of today, these bells rang when there was an incoming call. A black, cone-like listening device (i.e. the receiver) hung upside-down from a forceps-style holder, which was located on the side of the box. The phone did not have a rotary or touch-tone dialing device. Instead, on the side opposite the receiver was a small, black-metal hand crank. To place a telephone call, the caller had to first wind the crank, which alerted the operator, and then remove the receiver from the holder. Removing the receiver allowed the holder to move upward, which in turn created an open connection with a party line. This method of operation caused an operator to diligently come on the line asking for a telephone number. When the telephone call was finished, the receiver was placed back on the holder. The weight of the receiver pressed the holder downward, causing the phone to "hang up."

Party lines could at times be exasperating , especially when a call could not be made because the line was occupied by a gabby party member. I remember Valentina getting into an argument with a female party-liner who kept on talking and would not relinquish the line. My mother ended the caller's conversation by calling the woman a *papagalla*. It was Valentina's way of letting the woman know, in no uncertain terms, that the woman's mindless, never-ending chatter, reminded her of a squawking, incoherent parrot. I just thought that this was hilarious; I rolled on the floor laughing uncontrollably. (After this incident, I kept reminding her not to be a *papagalla* herself when she made a telephone call.) Amazingly, Valentina had a pretty good idea who the other woman was. This was probably also true of the other woman; however, I noticed that the next time they actually met in person, they both went on talking to each other as if nothing had happened. Such was life on the party line.

As far as I was concerned, the party line was always fun and informative. It enabled me, as well as others, I suppose, to listen in on people's conversation without them knowing it. Even more conveniently, each telephone number on the line had its own signal, consisting of a combination of rings. (I believe that the Gulch Ranch phone signal was two long rings and one short ring.) Each person on the party line could phone another on the line by simply using the crank on their own phone to "crank out" the desired combination of long and short rings. In time, everyone got to know everyone else's signal. Thus, by just listening to the telephone ringing, one could tell who was being called. This would help me immensely when deciding whether or not I wanted to listen in. Of course that was much later, when I became more sophisticated with the use of this instrument.

For now, I was just content in waiting for the right opportunity to use the phone. When I was sure no one was around, I placed a chair below the phone and climbed on it, so I could position my mouth directly in front of the metal speaker. After turning the crank, I picked up the receiver and waited for the operator to answer. I still remember the static-sounding voice of the operator as she (I don't recall any male operators ever answering) came on the line and asked, "Number, please?" I replied, in a very polite tone of voice, "Time, please." The operator would dutifully respond with the correct time. After thanking her I hung up the phone and walked away with an inner feeling of great accomplishment. I had actually talked on the telephone.

Did I just hear the reader say, "Big deal! You talked on the telephone." Hold on. In this day of the cell phone and the internet, it is not such a big deal, but I venture to guess that during that time period, the majority of the *ranceri* never put their hands on that telephone, not to make a call, nor to answer one. I know that Bronco never spoke on a telephone until much later in his life. It certainly was an amazing instrument, and what really impressed me was that those operators never got tired of giving me the correct time. Or—did they?

Valentina certainly excelled as a cook and worked very hard to put a variety of wholesome savory meals on the table for the workers. I often watched her as she placed huge aluminum pots and iron frying pans on top of the big, black butane stove. Soon, with the pots boiling and the frying pans sizzling, with an assortment of meat, poultry and vegetables, amply flavored with home-grown garlic, onions, mushrooms, rosemary, parsley, basil and/or bell peppers—a consortium of flavorful aromas rose up from the stove and filled the surrounding air. Into my quivering nostrils I deliberately breathed these heavenly scents, which in turn caused my throat muscles to involuntarily tighten and my salivary glands to spew forth, soon filling my mouth with sweet, watery liquid. "Quando si mangia?" I would impatiently ask my mother. "When are we going to eat?" "Subito, subito," she would answer. "Soon, soon." *Subito* [sue **bee** toe] never came soon enough for chubby me. I was always ready to eat.

Breakfast for the *ranceri* was simple enough: bacon and eggs, toast, coffee, and a side dish of fruit. Infrequently, my mother would add French toast and hot cakes for variety. At times some of the *ranceri*, my father and brother included, concocted a cappuccino-like mixture of egg yolks, sugar, and coffee. Into an oversized coffee cup or small breakfast bowl they placed a raw egg yolk or two, along with two or three heaping spoonfuls of granulated sugar. They then blended the sugar and egg yolk together, vigorously beating the mixture with a large tablespoon until it formed a gritty white paste. Steaming hot coffee was then poured into the bowl and stirred into the mixture. When all was ready, the *ranceri* sat back and slowly drank their coffee drink, stopping often to dip their toast or bread into the syrupy brew. "Mmmm, buono!" It really tasted good. But I found that although this concoction did give you a quick burst of energy, it only satiated your hunger until about mid-morning. That left a long time to go before the noon meal. More substance was needed. I stuck with the eggs, bacon and toast.

The noon and evening meals were more elaborate and complex. The two long tables were often preset with dishes of *formaggio* (cheese) with salami or *presciutto*, and accompanied by baskets of French bread and bottles of red wine. The first course usually featured a soup (minestrone or chicken with vegetables) or a broth made with *bolito* (boiled beef shank), and/or a pasta dish (spaghetti, ravioli, or gnocchi), or *risotto con suggo* [**sue** go], usually a meat sauce. At some meals, a meat dish or dishes such as roast, beefsteaks, veal cutlets, or pork chops served as the entrée. At times, Valentina served *polpettas* (meat patties), made by hand-grinding leftover meats and vegetables together. Nothing much was ever wasted.

Since the Gulch Ranch raised its own chickens, poultry and egg dishes were quite common. Some of the savory dishes prepared by Valentina were chicken cacciatore, cooked with vegetables and served in a red wine and tomato sauce; baked or roasted chicken flavored with fresh rosemary and served with small, white baked potatoes; and giant *frittatas* made with eggs, cheese, vegetables and, at times, left-over meats.

Occasionally, Valentina made *polenta* by pouring coarse, dry corn meal into a big pot of boiling water and then constantly stirring for forty to fifty minutes. *Polenta* at this time was not yet a "yuppie" dish, and it certainly was not served out in little bitty squares as done today in some upscale restaurants or delicatessens. (My daughter, Rhonda, recently brought home a *polenta* sandwich for me to eat. It consisted of two thin slices of *polenta* with a mushroom and cheese concoction spread between. No matter how many times I asked, she would not tell me how much it had cost.)

In contrast, at the "cookahousa" a huge mound of the cooked, mush-like *polenta* was placed on the table in a large serving platter. The *ranceri* then spooned out the hot *polenta* from the platter, dumping several spoonfuls in the middles of their plates. They then engulfed the *polenta* with heaping spoonfuls of red tomato sauce accompanied by big hunks of beef, chicken, or rabbit. "Si mangia!" [see **mahn** jah], the *ranceri* would say before digging in—meaning "Let's eat!"

Polenta was always a real treat for me, but some workers did not like it. It seems they had eaten too much of it while growing up in Italy. Bronco, for one, recounted many times how he had to eat *polenta* three times a day during his youth. Of course, the *polenta* at that time had not been served in the manner described above. It was mainly used as a bread substitute by the less affluent families. According to Bronco, his *polenta* sandwich often consisted of a fistful of cold *polenta* with a slice of *formaggio* slapped in. I guess that having *polenta* on the menu three times a day would indeed get a bit tiring after a while.[30]

Fish would usually be served on Friday or Saturday evenings. A favorite fish dish with the ranch hands was *bacala* [bah **kah** lah], a dry, salted codfish which came in a wooden or cardboard box. After being soaked overnight in water, the codfish was boiled and then served cold, mixed with garbanzo beans in olive oil, garlic, and rosemary. On rare occasions, Valentina would serve *bacala* cooked in a red tomato sauce which, in turn, was then poured over a dish of steaming hot *polenta*. A word of caution to the more adventurous reader who might wish to try these dishes on his or her own. Make sure that you soak the *bacala* overnight in a bowl of cold water, changing the water at least once, in order to soften it and to get most of the salt out. Otherwise, the reader will be eating something that tastes like salt-laden cardboard. Also, when eating *bacala* watch out for the *spine* [**spee** neh], i.e. the fish's small bones. Many a hungry *rancere* has had an anxious moment or two—with a *spina* caught in his throat. To quickly clear the throat of a clinging *spina*, the *rancere* simply swallowed a crust of French bread, followed by a full glass of red wine. The alarmed reader is probably throwing his arms up and exclaiming, "Stop! That is not the recommended medical procedure for clearing one's throat!" Of course it isn't. However, it seemed to serve the purposes of the *rancere* quite nicely, saving him a trip to the doctor and, of course, giving him an excuse to drink an extra glass of wine.

The Gulch Ranch had its own vegetable garden. Fresh salads made with lettuce or radicchio were plentiful (and usually eaten at the end of the meal).[31] Other *verdura* (vegetable) dishes made with greens and vegetables such as zucchini, spinach, and rappini (wild mustard greens) picked from the fields when in season, tomatoes, cucumbers, peas, corn, green and dry beans, artichokes, and even brussel sprouts, were in abundance. I should note here that many of the *ranceri* thought that brussel sprouts should be grown, not eaten. I emphatically disagreed. Two of my favorite dishes which my mother prepared were brussel sprouts stir-fried in olive oil, with garlic and *salsiccia* [sausage], or boiled sprouts cut in half and served cold with olive oil and vinegar, sprinkled with grated cheese on top. "Molto bouno!" Very good! And as Valentina would add, "Ti fan bene." ("They'll do you good.")

Valentina also baked pies and cakes (usually on the weekend). A particular favorite that the workers simply called "La Torta" (the pie or cake), consisted of a filling containing a mixture of raisins, sugar and other cooked vegetables and/or fruits. Before serving ,the filling was baked in a round piecrust. The piecrust alone was scrumptious. Unlike a regular piecrust, it was thick and had a cake or cookie like taste.

My mother also made *biscotti* cookies, flavored with vanilla, almonds, lemon juice, or sesame seeds. These *biscotti* were wedge-shaped cookies, somewhat smaller than what the reader might see in the stores today. Also, "Valentina's Original Biscotti Cookies" were not augmented with chocolate or any other flavored coating. The *ranceri* preferred their *biscotti* very hard and very plain. The ranch hands loved to dip these cookies into their morning coffee mixed with milk *(caffe e latte),* or into their wine after the evening meal. Louie Scanoni, an old, grizzly ranch hand, loved his biscotti and red wine. After biting into a piece of wine soaked cookie, he would make a sizzling sound by sharply sucking in his breath between clenched teeth. "Buono, buono!" he would exclaim. (I recently bought a plastic jar containing 26 *biscotti,* made by Nonni's Food Company, for about $10. Good, but I don't think Louie would have enjoyed them as much as Valentina's homemade *biscotti*.)

I pause here, feeling compelled to warn the reader that the *biscotti* ritual must not be taken lightly. This fact is clearly demonstrated by the Hollywood film "Crazy Joe." [32] In one particular scene of this gangster movie, Don Vittorio, played by Eli Wallach, tries to persuade Crazy Joe, played by Peter Boyle, to discard his newly acquired ambitions and to stay within the parameters of Don Vittorio's own Mafia family. On the coffee table in front of Don Vittorio sits a tall glass of *caffe e latte,* with several well placed biscotti lying alongside. Although it isn't wine and Don Vittorio doesn't suck in his breath and exclaim, "Buono, buono!" as did Louie the *Rancere,* it is clear that he is enjoying his own particular ritual with the *biscotti*. First, he dips them into the *caffe e latte* and then he savors the tastes by delicately biting into the soaked cookie. A sure sign of Don Vittorio's irritation with Crazy Joe's personal ambitions becomes quite clear when he does not offer a single *biscotto* to his invited guest. Crazy Joe, certainly should have taken this to be a bad omen, because shortly thereafter he, along with his personal ambitions, are disposed of "gangland style." Now, I venture to guess

La Nostra Costa (Our Coast)

that the attentive reader, in a jocular vein, might have the temerity to ask, "Isn't that the way the cookie crumbles?" Perhaps, but it is not so funny for Crazy Joe, who ought to have been forewarned by that aberrant *biscotti* ritual.

Back at the "cookahousa," the ranch hands were not really big on desserts. *La Torta* and *biscotti* notwithstanding, they preferred to finish their meal with a fruit or *pane e formaggio* (bread and cheese). Dry Monterey cheese with sweet (not sour) French bread was a particular favorite. Of course, all of the above was washed down with ample glasses of red wine. Ranch hands may not have been paid much, but they sure didn't starve to death. At least not when my mother was cooking.

As the *ranceri* ate their meals at the table, they had discussions and/or arguments about many things, such as the day's work, local gossip, current events, politics, and even sports. Boxing was a particularly hot topic. The *ranceri* loved to talk about the Italian fighters that were popular at the time, such as Rocky Graziano, Jake LaMotta, Tami Murillo, Paolo Rossi, Willie Pastrano, Rocky Marciano, and even "Two-Ton" Tony Galento. On the other hand, my father loved to talk about the merits of Primo Carnera, a Friulano who had won the Heavyweight Championship of the World, way back in 1933. Known in boxing circles as "The Ambling Alp," Carnera stood 6'6" tall and weighed 260-plus pounds. Naturally, being Friulano himself, Carnera was a particular source of pride for my father, who loved to embellish upon the boxing prowess of this champion. (So much so that I believed Carnera was a *rancere*-turned-boxer.) Much to Bronco's disappointment, Carnera lost the Championship in 1934, when Max Baer knocked him out.

Although my father was devastated at Carnera's loss, my brother John (Giovanni Primo), later came to believe it had been a most fortunate occurrence. According to my father, if Carnera had won, he would have named my brother—who happened to be born in 1934—Primo Giovanni Comelli. My brother never did relish the thought of being called *Primo* [**pree** moh], which means "first" in Italian, for the rest of his life.

On the other hand, I thought it might have been kind of fun. I now invite the imaginative reader to come with me, back to the house on the Coast Road. Picture, if you will, a shadowy figure, like me, in the darkened bedroom, crouched down and hiding behind the bed. John unsuspectingly comes in, and as he passes by the bed, I suddenly jump up and mount a sneak attack from his backside, all the while screaming at the top of my lungs, "Cream Da Preem!" Whacko! Great fun—don't you think?

Actually, my brother was afforded the rare opportunity to see his namesake in action. After losing the Heavyweight Boxing Championship, Primo continued to box for a few more years and then returned to Italy (*circa* 1937), where he subsequently joined an anti-Fascist group. His efforts against the Fascists landed him in a forced labor camp. He survived the war and later returned to the United States where he (like Bronco) became an American citizen. And on June 20, 1949 (according to the Santa Cruz Sentinel) Primo, who by then had retired from boxing and become a professional wrestler, actually fought in Santa Cruz.

I remember my father proudly announcing to his fellow *ranceri*, during a "cookahousa" meal, that he had bought tickets for Primo's "historic" wrestling match in Santa Cruz. Thus, the three of us—Bronco, John and myself—did go to the Santa Cruz Civic Auditorium to see the "Ambling Alp" take on a local favorite, Pete Petersen.[33] The giant Carnera won the bout by throwing his opponent against the ring post. Petersen was unable to continue due to a serious (not faked) shoulder injury caused by the collision.

At breakfast the following morning, Bronco relished the opportunity to reconstruct for the *ranceri*—with some embellishment of course—how Carnera had won. He certainly was happy that Carnera had won. However, I remember him telling the *ranceri* that he was somewhat disappointed that the former Heavyweight Boxing Champion of the World, and a fellow Friulano, had to resort to such "fakery" to make a living. In truth, Primo, who died in 1967, probably made more money as a professional wrestler than as a boxer. At least, he got to keep more of it for himself.[34]

As things turned out, Valentina didn't last too long as a cook. Although she excelled as a *cuoca*, she did not have the patience to deal with all the intricacy of the job, especially the need to give variety to the unending continuum of meals. She also found it time-consuming, leaving too little for her family. Another negative aspect of the job was that she had to deal with all those *ranceri*. Each had his own opinion of what ought to be on the menu.

One of the partners, an irascible and rather eccentric *rancere* nicknamed Baffi [**bah** fee], would eat only minestrone soup and French bread. *Baffi* means whiskers in Italian. Although he did not have them during this time, he had apparently earned the nickname by sporting bushy sideburns and mustache during his youth. (Funny, I could never imagine Baffi being young.) According to Baffi's prescription, the minestrone soup had to be of a perfect texture and color, containing the right amounts of vegetables and beans. It also had to be served on time, and at the right temperature. If not, he would have a fit. No matter what Valentina was preparing, she always had to have a pot of minestrone warming on the stove for Baffi.

I think that Baffi—a wiry, rather short Toscano, who accentuated his walk by taking long strides—liked to make "fashion statements" of sorts. For instance, he often wore a rope around his waist instead of a belt. Baffi apparently found that a piece of well-worn rope cost far less than a leather belt, and it still effectively kept his pants up. All in all, I found Baffi to be a likable fellow. But he had a notorious habit (sometimes in jest, sometimes not) of calling others *Ignorante* (ee nyoh **rahn** teh), meaning, of course, "Ignorant One." This was especially true if they didn't agree with his views of the world or if they didn't go along with his daily whims. Often, after delivering a diatribe explaining his views on a particular subject, he would end by asking, in a very emphatic tone of voice, "Hai capito?" [eye kah **pee** toh], which means, "Do you understand?" Of course, Baffi's mannerisms and tone of voice often gave one the impression that he thought the listener a little slow, or perhaps lacking the mental capacity to grasp his full meaning. Thus, Baffi's "Hai capito?" was more usually taken to mean, "*Now*, do you understand?" Then, if he still believed that you did not quite grasp the subject, he would stride away, muttering under his breath, "Ignorante!"

I don't think Baffi ever called Valentina by the name of "Ignorante," but on occasion, by his mannerisms and tone of voice, he would let my mother know that he was not exactly pleased with her cooking efforts. If the wrong dish of food was placed near where he was seated (such as a gelatin dessert, or a squeamish-looking fish dish), he would emphatically exclaim, "Mi fa schiffo!" [Mee fah **skee** foe], which means, "This disgusts me!" He would then brusquely order the dish placed "via di qui" ("away from here"). In doing this in front of the other *ranceri,* he sometimes embarrassed Valentina.

The possession by a *rancio* of a good cook was of prime importance, not only for the morale and well being of the ranch hands, but also for prestige. Coastal Italians knew which of the *rancios* had the best cooks, and often extolled their virtues. Such a reputation made it easier to hire and to keep good workers. Knowing this, Pete Rinaldi—*il bosso* at the time—tried all means possible to keep my mother. However, Valentina had made up her mind. She was getting out of the ranch-house kitchen. As a consequence, she husbanded all her cooking skills and expertise for her family and, of course, for her *amici di la costa*. Unfortunately, her leaving opened the door a bit wider for some unsettling events that were to occur a few years later.

Endnotes

[29] It was also here, in 1945 that Bronco, eating his noonday meal, first learned of his mother's death, which had occurred during the war. At first it was reported to him that his entire family had been wiped out. He was completely devastated. Unable to finish his meal, he walked back home to read the letter bearing the ill-begotten news. Understandably, he felt somewhat relieved to read that, although indeed his mother had been killed, the rest of the family, including his father, were still alive. Still, receiving the news as it had been initially delivered was a crushing blow; he never quite forgave the cook who delivered the erroneous message.

[30] Friulian folklore has it that the Romans conquered the world with *polenta*. As the story goes, each soldier carried a small sack of dry polenta, tying it to his belt. During encampment at night, they would boil hot water over open fires, mixing in their *polenta*. Thus, they were guaranteed a hot meal even in the most isolated of places.

[31] Radicchio, a reddish-purple lettuce, has a somewhat bitter taste. A particular favorite among the Friulani is *radicchio e polenta*, accompanied by a glass of red wine. As the reader probably already knows, radicchio salad mixes are now very popular and are commonly served at some very upscale restaurants.

[32] "Crazy Joe," Columbia Pictures, 1974, directed by Carlo Lizzani, writing credits, Nicholas Gage.

[33] For many years the Santa Cruz Civic Auditorium, which is still located in downtown Santa Cruz, was the venue for the talent and swimsuit portions of the Miss California pageants. From time to time, as well, other stars and celebrities appeared there. According to the *Santa Cruz Sentinel*, even Lucille Ball, before the days of "I Love Lucy," appeared at the Auditorium on December 17, 1947, starring in the play "Dream Girls."

[34] A short but authentic biography of Primo Carnera has been written by Ralph Hick and appears on his website at hickoksports.hypermart.net.

9. Finito Con Il Golce
(Finished With The Gulch)

The *ranceri* suffered through hard times in the 1930s and early 1940s. Money was hard to come by. According to Louis Bettiol, who worked with Bronco on the Marina Ranch in late 1920s, *ranceri* were paid two dollars a day during the Great Depression. Later, the war came and more jobs became available: the nation slowly pulled out of the Depression. Still, when I started to work on the ranch in 1953 (I was sixteen at the time), the wage for a *rancere* was seventy-five cents an hour, with room and board included. In the mid 1950s, the salary rose to one dollar an hour, but board was eliminated. Bronco was a working partner, so he got a draw of one hundred fifty dollars a month, and he shared in the year-end profits, if there were any.

Louie Scanoni, that grizzly old *rancere* who loved his wine soaked-biscotti, retired *circa* 1953. Louie, who was one of the few *ranceri* that spoke English well, told me that he did not have to work any longer. He had his monthly social security check and $15,000 in the bank. (I seem to recall him saying that his social security check was around $100 per month—not much by today's standards. However, rents were low and the dollar bought a lot more in those days.) To save his money for retirement, Louie had chosen to live in a very miserly way. Louie the *Rancere* really benefited from the room-and-board system on the *rancios*. While others left the ranch on the weekends, he stayed put at the "cookahousa" listening to the radio or reading the newspaper. He did not own a car and seldom if ever went into town. To save money, he even sent away for a comb with a razor-blade attachment. With this instrument he was able to give himself haircuts, saving the cost of a barber. He was about sixty-five years old at the time he retired, and I think he did manage to out-live his money. Of course, he wasn't married and did not have any sons or daughters.

Immediately after the war there were still restrictions and price controls on consumer goods. By 1948, things seemed to get better. Restrictions and controls were lifted; the Gulch Ranch started to produce some steady profits. My parents were able to save enough money to replace our old 1934 Lafayette automobile, which we called the Old Carrettone (karreh **toe** neh). *Carrettone* in Italian refers to a large carriage or cart. The car was thus named by our family because of its inherent shakes, rattles, and rolls—which constantly reminded my parents of an old squeaky horse buggy or lumbering ox cart. The Old Carrettone had been our family car since 1937.

My father now wanted to buy a Chevrolet, but was told he had to wait several weeks before the local dealer, Eugene Prolo, could deliver the new-model (1949) car. Prolo tried to persuade my father to buy the 1948-model car, which he had in stock, but Valentina would have none of it. "We waited this long for a new car; we can wait a few more weeks for the new model," she told my father. I remember waiting seemingly forever for the new car to arrive. Apparently we weren't the only people waiting forever for their new Chevy. Advertisements for Chevrolets appearing in the Santa Cruz Sentinel in the summer of 1949 urged potential buyers to bide their time and to "hold everything" in order to get the "best" for their money. Well, for the Comelli family, the best was about to come.

One day in the late summer of 1949, Bronco was informed that the car had arrived. He hitched a ride with Pete Rinaldi, and went to Prolo's Chevrolet in Santa Cruz, to pick up the car. He was gone for hours, or so I thought at the time. My brother and I waited anxiously outside the house and constantly looked southward towards the Rodoni Ranch, anticipating that the very next car coming around the bend would be our new car. Finally, Bronco, driving our brand new gunmetal gray 1949 four-door Chevrolet, appeared on the Coast Road. Yahoo! This was quite an occasion. We had a brand new car. Unlike the old car, this one had a radio and a heater. So what if it didn't have power steering? No one had even heard of that. Who cared that the car had a standard shift lever, located just under the steering wheel? Everyone knew that the newfangled automatic transmissions caused nothing but trouble. We just loved this car.[35]

We weren't the only family who got a brand-new car in 1949. The Cantarutti family, now with their new baby girl, Norma, came visiting in their brand-new blue four-door 1949 Chevrolet. Although both our cars were Chevrolets, they were not similar. Ours was in the sleek new torpedo-style; the Cantaruttis' model maintained the more traditional look, with a hump in the back where the trunk was. We had endless discussions on who had the better model car. In the end, we all decided that they were both beautiful cars. However, I must now inform Lido and Reno that the torpedo-style Chevrolet is—of the two models—the one that I see at all the "Classic Car" shows in the Monterey area.

Things did seem to be going well for the Comelli family. My father had bought another half share and now was a full partner in the ranch. We had a new car and profits from the Gulch Ranch continue to rise making us reasonably comfortable money-wise. However, I think Bronco was becoming increasingly frustrated by not having his own ranch to manage—with an opportunity to bring my brother in as a partner. There were also a few minor quarrels with the foreman, Pete Rinaldi. Because of an existing heart condition, my father had requested not to be sent out to load manure. Yet on occasions, Pete, being short of ranch hands, would send my father out to load manure. This did not sit well with my father.

In the summer of 1953, our lives were to change forever. Things started off well enough, at least for me. I didn't want to spend the summer sitting around the house or just going to the beach. I wanted to earn some money. One day Pete Rinaldi, driving his pickup truck, stopped near our back yard. I had been thinking about something for a long time. Now, I garnered enough courage to approach him and to ask him for a summer job. In Italian, I told Pete that since I didn't know that much about ranching, I would be willing to work for fifty cents per hour. To my surprise, Pete, with a big smile on his face, said, "No. If you are going to work for me, I will pay you the going rate of seventy-five cents per hour." Pete hired me on the spot. No matter what came after that, I never forgot that it was Pete Rinaldi who had given me my first job. I guess I could have recruited my father to do the asking for me, but at the time I thought it was something I had to do for myself. I am glad I did and Pete certainly made me feel really good about myself. In my eyes that day, he was "Il Bosso".

Unfortunately, the job lasted only a couple of months. My father and mother got drawn into a major argument with Pete. Of all things, it involved the ranch house cook. After my mother left, Pete Rinaldi eventually settled on the wife of one of the partners to be the cook. Everything went well for quite some time, but then Bronco began to notice the quality of the cooking was no longer what it should have been. Whether it was because the cook was experiencing health problems or whether it was just a simple case of "burnout" was a matter of conjecture. The men grumbled and complained, but they never had the nerve to make a complaint to *il bosso*.

The proverbial straw that broke the camel's back came when the cook declared that she no longer wanted to prepare meals on Saturday evenings. Bronco, with my mother's approval, forced the issue with Pete Rinaldi. Bronco told Pete that since the *ranceri* worked a half-day on Saturday, they deserved a hot meal in the evening. Pete replied that the cook was going to quit unless he gave her more time off. My father countered back by saying that it had been customary for quite a long time that the cook prepare a hot meal on Saturday night for the *ranceri*. (Sunday was normally the day off for the cook.) If she did not want to do it, then she should be replaced. The argument escalated to the point of irrevocable decision. Pete, against my father's wishes, backed the cook.

In those days, when partners could not resolve their problems amicably, they often sought a buy-out. "Si fa le parti" [**pahrr** tee] was the phrase used to initiate this rather rudimentary process. It literally means, "Let's make the parts." *Parti* probably was *rancere* legalese for "partition." My family's experience with the "si fa le parti" scheme of things was by no means the first, nor the last, such transaction that had or would take place *su per la costa*. Some breakups ended on friendly terms; others ended on not-so-friendly terms. Resentments still tend to linger on with surviving *ranceri* family members, who were run through the process on what they considered less than friendly terms. At times, unfortunately, the "si fa le parti" method of doing business not only broke up entire partnerships, but also caused havoc among disagreeing family members who may have been working together on the *rancios*.

I was present when Bronco and Pete decided to have their "si fa le parti" meeting. It was a Saturday, just after the noonday meal at the old "cookahousa." I saw my father and Rinaldi talking in the yard just outside of the building. All of sudden, they retreated to the old barn to have it out in private. I remained standing just outside the cookhouse, waiting anxiously for the meeting to end. It seemed to me that Bronco and Pete were in that old barn for hours. Finally, Bronco came out. I still remember quite clearly my feeling of disbelief when my father told me that he had "just bought Pete out." I had been certain that it would be the other way around. So I was elated, but somewhat subdued, thinking that something bad was going to happen. Apparently Valentina felt the same way, as she wanted to keep things quiet for awhile.

Attempting to reassure us, my father recounted what had occurred in the barn. According to Bronco, Pete had offered to buy my father's share for $13,000. My father had replied that for that price he would not sell, and had countered by offering to buy out Pete, for the same price. Unexpectedly, Rinaldi had agreed. Bronco left that confrontation thinking that he had in fact just bought Pete out of the Gulch Ranch Partnership. In the ensuing days, Pete said nothing to my family to dispel that notion.

Unfortunately, Valentina's and my forebodings were proven to be correct. The bearer of ill tidings turned out to be Joe Antonetti, who at the time was one of the landowners of the Gulch Ranch and also a non-working partner in the Gulch Ranch Partnership. I should note here, for the reader's information, that Joe Antonetti also was one of the owners of the Lucca Lunch Bar and Grill. (Lucca is a city in the Tuscany region of Italy.) Situated on Front Street in downtown Santa Cruz, the Lucca Lunch was a favorite gathering place for the *ranceri*; it was common for deals to be worked out over a *poncino* (poun **chee** no) or two. The term *poncino* was probably derived from the Italian noun *ponce* (punch) and was used most often by the *ranceri* to describe "coffee royals," made with strong black coffee, whisky, sugar, and a twist of lemon. (It also was used, from time to time, to describe various other mixed drinks.) As it turned out, Bronco probably should have stopped more often at that watering hole for a *poncino* or two.

As Antonetti entered our home, I immediately headed for the "dugout" underneath the house to listen in. I heard Antonetti begin his conversation by agreeing with my father that Pete had in fact accepted Bronco's offer to buy his share for $13,000. However, much to my disappointment, I also heard Antonetti inform my father and mother that he did not have much faith in having Bronco run the Gulch. He wanted Pete Rinaldi to stay and to continue in his role as *il bosso*. The problem was, according to Antonetti, Pete would not stay on if Bronco remained a partner. Then I heard Antonetti drop the hammer. He informed my mother and father that the other partners were in agreement with his decision to keep Rinaldi. He and his fellow landowners would not lease the Gulch Ranch to Bronco. Antonetti then told Bronco that there was no other choice. He had to leave. From that moment on, Bronco and Valentina would blame Pete Rinaldi for this reversal of fortune. To their dying day, they believed that Pete had inexplicably changed his mind about his original offer to sell, and then forced them out by refusing to stay on with Bronco. This may have been true; however, even at my young age, I could see that Antonetti was the person who called the shots. Because of his dual role as landowner and partner, he had a great deal of influence. I'm sure that if he had wanted to retain my father, the other partners would have followed his lead.

In retrospect, I think that if the whole incident had been handled a bit differently and in a calmer fashion, things could have been worked out. However, I don't think that Pete ever got along that well with Bronco, and vice versa. Emotions had taken over, and in the heat of the argument the "si fa le parti" decision had been made. Unfortunately, after that was said and done, neither party wished to back down. Legally, Bronco, probably could not so easily have been made to leave; however, he no longer desired to stay when it became obvious that he was not wanted.

My father and mother eventually agreed to sell for the sum of $15,000. Although it was a crushing blow, they took this money and, with additional funds from their savings, set out on a new life away from *Il Golce*. As the reader shall see later, out of this unsettling episode, Bronco was eventually to realize his dream of having his own ranch with my brother as a partner (G. Comelli & Son), and Valentina was to realize her dream of having her own home in Santa Cruz (at 729 Seaside Street). No more wind, no more smell of *pattume*, and no more *mosce*.

I am compelled to tell the reader, before closing this section, the amazing story of two houses that once stood side-by-side on the Gulch Ranch. In 1948, our next door neighbor Joe Gemignani married my mother's sister, Lina. They continued to live in the house next door for a short time. As my family did, the Gemignanis owned their own house, but not the land beneath it. They eventually bought an oversized lot in an unincorporated area near Capitola, a small coastal tourist town just south of Santa Cruz. They then had their family home moved to that location (1505 Bulb Avenue). When my father and mother sold their interest in the Gulch Ranch, Valentina offered to sell our house to the Gulch Ranch Partnership. Joe Antonetti subsequently informed my mother that the Partnership had agreed to buy the house for $500. Valentina, still bristling over the Rinaldi affair, responded in a voice filled with irritation, "For that price, I will sell it to my sister and Joe, if they want it."

Lina and Joe jumped at the chance. They bought the house from my family, and for $1,000 contracted the Landino Moving Company to move it to Bulb Avenue. Shortly thereafter, our house was cut into halves and taken south via the Coast Road to its new location, where it was reassembled right next to their existing house. As part of the sales agreement, we, the Comelli family, were allowed to live in this reassembled ranch house until our new house was constructed. Thus for about six months the Comelli and Gemignani families once again lived next door to each other just like they had for so many years on the Gulch Ranch.

Joe and Lina eventually remodeled the two houses, selling both in the early 1990s for approximately $300,000. This, of course, was after Bulb Avenue had been incorporated into the City of Capitola, and the Capitola Shopping Mall built nearby. The amazing part of this story, is that the two houses still stand there today, side by side, much as they did *su per la costa*. Ranceri have passed on or gone their separate ways. But these two houses seem destined to stay together as a reminiscence of a past life. At least it seems so, to the Comelli and Gemignani families. *Finito con il Golce.*

Endnotes

[35] According to a 1949 advertisement in the *Santa Cruz Sentinel*, factory-delivery price for the four-door model was approximately $1,500. I believe that my father paid around $2,000 for the new car.

10. Davenport

On many occasions, while living on the Gulch Ranch, my family took the five plus mile trip north to Davenport. According to Margaret Koch's excellent book, *Santa Cruz County, Parade of the Past,* the town of Davenport was founded in the mid-1800s by Captain John Pope Davenport, who had "sailed around the Horn" from Tiverton, Rhode Island.[36]

In a cove located about one mile north of the future town's site, Davenport constructed a 450-foot wharf. El Jarro Point, as it had been known, became Davenport Landing and was used for the export of lumber, fuel, and lime. It also became one of the most important whaling stations on the West Coast. Farmers often spotted whales while working their fields along the coast, and some became whaler-farmers, actually hunting the whales, and launching their long boats from the Landing.

In the early 1900s, the Portland Cement Company established its business of excavating limestone (the main ingredient in cement) from the hills just east of Davenport. (Those trucks that later were to rattle our house, as they transported bags of cement south on Highway 1, would begin their trips here.) As its operations grew, so did the town of Davenport. Two hotels were built to accommodate plant workers. The Hotel D'Italia with 48 rooms was opened in 1906, and the Ocean View Hotel with 29 rooms opened in 1907.

Immediately to the north, and upwind from the Cement Plant, which constantly and insidiously spewed cement dust over the town, new houses were constructed to accommodate officials and other "higher" workers of the Company. This area became known as New Town.

Davenport during the time of my childhood was home to a large number of Italian emigrants, who worked either on the *rancios* or for the Portland Cement Company.[37] This being the case, my mother and father had many friends who lived in Davenport. I remember that every Saturday afternoon my mother gave my father a grocery list. Bronco only worked a half-day on Saturday, so he had free time on his hands to drive the Old Carrettone, with my brother and I tagging along, to the Cash Store/Post Office in Davenport. The Cash Store, which I shall now describe to the reader, was built *circa* 1905, and eventually burned down in March 1954. (A New Cash Store, opened in 1978 on the same site, is now a cafe/boutique which caters mainly to whale watchers and other tourists.)

Upon entering The Cash Store, we would be greeted by a blend of savory smells emitted by the various staples such as cheeses, salamis, hams and coffee beans, prominently displayed at the front counter. As in the "cookahousa" my mouth would begin to fill with that *quando si mangia*, sweet-flavored water. Once inside, Bronco waited patiently to hand over Valentina's list to the proprietor, who would in turn fetch us our groceries. (Recently, Thelma [Micossi] Gill informed me that the proprietor's name was G. Morelli, he being assisted by his son Tillman and daughters Irene and Candina. Also assisting the Morellis was Rose Domenichelli, who would often take the list from my father.)

While Bronco waited for the groceries, he chatted and exchanged coastal *chiacchiera* [kyah **kah** rah] with the proprietors and patrons. Getting bored with listening to the local gossip, I used to wander to the front end of the store, where there was a prominent display of hunting rifles and other guns. My eyes inevitably came to rest on a "Red Ryder Daisy BB Gun" displayed on the wall. Oh, how I wanted to own that BB gun! I begged my father to buy it for me,

La Nostra Costa (Our Coast)

but Bronco always put me off by saying, "You will have to ask your mother." Similarly to the dialogue in the movie "A Christmas Story," Valentina always denied my request by saying, "No, Ivano. You will probably shoot your brother's eye out."[38] (It was not until much later that I purchased a BB Gun. I bought it from our boyhood friend Phil Taurian, who had brought it down from San Francisco. I think I paid five dollars for it. Guess what? I didn't shoot my brother's eye out, but I did "whack" him in the leg once or twice. That "devil" guy again, you know.)

After loading all the groceries in the Old Carrettone, Bronco drove us down the hill to visit my godmother, Giuseppina (Pina) Micossi, who at the time owned and managed the Hotel D'Italia. Pina, originally from the Friuli region of Italy, had purchased the hotel *circa* 1920 with Frank Micossi, her husband, and with partners Francesco Bragazzi and Giuseppe Ferlizza. (Giuseppe "Bepo" Ferlizza died in 1936 and Mary Ferlizza inherited his share in the hotel.) Frank and Pina, along with their daughter Thelma, actually lived at the hotel. When Frank Micossi died in May 1944, Pina and Francesco Bragazzi continued to manage the Hotel on their own.

I can still remember being impressed by the presence of a big man who seemed to be constantly at the hotel. The coastal Italians knew him as "Carabiniere" [kah rah bee **nier**- eh]. I have a lasting vision in my mind of Carabiniere—also from the Friuli region—sitting in the kitchen at the Hotel D'Italia, slurping coffee from a rather large cup, while talking very softly to my father in Friulano. He was a huge man. (Now, comparing photographs of Carabiniere and Primo Carnera, I would estimate that Carabiniere's height and weight were somewhat greater than 6'6" tall and 260 pounds.) He had big hands and, from what I remember, a long, unpleasant-looking face with a large nose and big ears. Some Italians thought him *tanto brutto* (really ugly). I think that his physical appearance and his stern demeanor reminded most Italians of a person who might have served in the Carabinieri, Italy's National Police Force. This and the fact that he "kept the peace" at the hotel probably earned him his nickname. (Thelma recently informed me that Carabiniere was in fact Francesco Bragazzi, part owner of the hotel. She also informed me that because of his immense size and menacing facial features, Hollywood had offered to hire Carabiniere to play the "heavy" in some of their films. True to his down-to-earth nature, Carabiniere never accepted.)

I only knew him briefly because, having a serious heart problem, he died in April 1945. Bronco, however, told some great stories about him. According to my father, Carabiniere was a gentle man and his *paisano* [pie **zah** no], a very good friend and countryman. Only on rare occasions did Carabiniere get angry, and usually only when provoked. When he did get angry, everyone got out of his way. I remember my father telling my brother and me of one such incident that occurred in his presence at the Hotel D'Italia.

Bronco was sitting at the bar minding his own business, when a worker from the cement plant, who apparently had had too much to drink, began directing derogatory remarks at him. Being insulted, Bronco got up from his stool in anticipation of a fight. Carabiniere, seeing what was about to happen, quickly stepped in. Just as in those old cowboy movies, he picked up the other guy by grabbing him by the back of his shirt collar and the seat of his pants, and then giving him the "bum's rush," threw him head-over-heels right out the front door. After being so unceremoniously thrown out the door, the cement plant worker quickly regained his footing and prepared himself for a fight. After seeing Carabiniere's huge, menacing frame standing in the doorway, he quickly changed his mind and decided that discretion was the better part of valor. He wisely retreated into the night.

After the incident was over, Bronco went up to Carabiniere and asked him why he had stepped in. After all he could have taken care of the man himself. Carabiniere, in a calm and soft voice, responded by saying that it was his job, and that as long as he didn't get hit in the nose, he could take care of anybody. (Unknown to many of his adversaries, his nose must have been his Achilles' heel.) Carabiniere, according to my father, was very protective of his *paisanos*. He made sure they didn't get hurt.

La Nostra Costa (Our Coast)

I must confess to the reader, that the above story really impressed me because many years later, I used a version of Carabiniere's "bum's rush" technique. As a rookie police officer, I was assigned to patrol the downtown area of San Jose with Joe Vitto, a veteran cop. We were called to the old Tico-Tico Bar on North Market Street to quell a disturbance. Once inside the bar, we quickly located a drunk who was causing the disturbance. When asked, the drunk refused to leave. Not yet having developed the art of patience, I grabbed the drunk by the back of his collar and the seat of his pants. Then in one continuous motion, I lifted him off the barstool, "quick walked" him to the front door, and threw him outside.

After the incident was over, Joe asked me in amazement, "Geez! Where in the hell did you learn that? Police School?" "No," I responded, "Davenport!" This prompted Joe to shoot back a sharp, disapproving look at me, as if to say, "This is not Davenport, kid! Clean up your act!"[39]

I feel compelled to explain to the reader, with many deferences to Carabiniere, that such "flash and dash" technique is not proper police procedure. The object of an arrest is to subdue the suspect, rendering him incapable of fleeing or doing further harm. The key is to keep control over the suspect; not release him, as I did, by throwing him out the door. Fortunately, as in the Carabiniere incident, the arrested party took one look at Joe and me and decided that he too had had enough.

The Hotel D' Italia must have seen its best days in the 1920s and 1930s. When my brother John and I used to go there in the 1940s it seemed large and mostly empty. It did have a big kitchen in the back, where my godmother cooked the meals, and a big long bar near the front entrance. It also had a *bocce* ball court in the front yard where the Italian men played the game, usually on the weekends. One of the side rooms near the bar housed two slot machines. They were great fun. My godmother would give my brother and me a handful of nickels. We would then go into that room and play slots. Once in a while we would hit a small jackpot, but—as all slot players have experienced—the winnings usually went back into the machines.

Constantly lingering with us during our sojourns in the hotel was a musty, damp smell, typical of dry rot. One can only assume that a combination of damp fog mixed with hovering cement dust had taken its toll on the old wooden structure. The odor stayed with us, as my brother and I explored the backrooms of the hotel. One particular room there now reminds me of the ballroom depicted in the movie "The Shining."[40]

At the time, because I am small, the room seems large, and stands empty. What appears to be the dance floor abuts several red-curtained booths. Some of these curtains are drawn shut to obscure vision and ensure privacy. One can only imagine the clandestine activities they hide. All of sudden the room comes alive with music. Couples appear on the dance floor, while others appear sitting at the bar drinking and conversing with the bartender. Waiters clad in black pants, and white dinner jackets with black bow ties, scurry about the booths; they discreetly peek between drawn curtains asking permission to serve drinks, before they return to the bar with their orders. As my brother and I turn to step out of the room, it empties and falls silent.

Understandably, the wary reader is probably holding back, resisting the urge to exclaim, "Wait a minute! That's surreal! It only happened in the movie!" Perhaps the reader is right. This scene probably exists only in my mind. Nevertheless, just as in the movie, misfortune was about to strike the Hotel D'Italia.

According to Thelma, that frightful night occurred on December 15, 1945. I remember being awakened by the sound of sirens from fire engines, as they rushed past our house. At the time, we had no way of knowing what was happening. The next day, my father told us he had heard that the hotel had just burned down. Fortunately, no one was seriously hurt. Thelma recollects that the fire started at approximately 9:00 p.m. in a section of the hotel leased out to Mexican nationals. The cause of the fire was probably defective wiring. Thelma remembers that the fire burned so hot, that the coins in the hotel safe melted together into one chunk of metal.

La Nostra Costa (Our Coast)

I was eight years old when this fire consumed the aging structure. I remember visiting the hotel site several times shortly thereafter. On one occasion, Pina came along with Bronco, my brother and me, to survey the charred remnants of the building. I can still remember the sad look in her eyes as she pointed to various spots in the burnt-out ashes, and how her voice trembled with emotion as she recounted events that had occurred over the years, at various places within the hotel. I knew, even then, that this was a moment of great sadness for my godmother.

According to Thelma, the only asset left after the fire was a liquor license. But a difficulty arose from the fact that Frank Bragazzi (Carabiniere), who had just recently died, still had his name on the license. Therefore, because his estate was still in probate, Pina had to go to court to buy out his interest in the license. This done, and using her license as an inducement, she became a partner with Gilbert and Mary Caiocca. The Caiocca's, along with their sons William and Leo, owned and managed the Davenport Bakery across the road, just to the east of the Hotel D'Italia. At about the time that the hotel had burned down, the Shell Oil Company had built a gas station and store on the southwest corner of Highway 1 and Ocean Avenue. It was here that the Caiocca's—with their new partner—settled in to manage the Miramar. Thanks to Pina's license, the new partnership was able to serve alcoholic beverages, and just as she'd done at the Hotel D'Italia, Pina did the cooking.

Unfortunately, Gilbert Ciaocca died in 1947. William Caiocca, with a partner (Joe Costella), wanted to establish a business in Santa Cruz (The Bubble Bakery). Consequently, the Caiocca's sold their interest in the business to Dominico Della Santina and his wife Nora (Fistolera). Dominico, who was better know by the coastal Italians as "Lambari," and Nora had two sons, Louis and Ricco. Lambari soon found that he did not like the bartending business. I once overheard him complaining to my mother, that it was not at all that conducive to the proper up bringing of two young men. In 1949 the Della Santinas sold their interest to Evelyn and Mac Morelli. This new partnership ended in 1951, when Pina decided to sell in order to move to San Jose, where she could live with Thelma.

I did not know until recently that the fire at the Hotel D'Italia, along with the death of her husband, Frank, and also of Carabiniere, all occurred within the relatively short period of nineteen months. This would have been devastating to a lesser woman, but not to Pina. She did not allow these calamitous events to get the best of her, but continued on, making a living for herself and Thelma. This, of course, was not at all surprising to those of us who knew my godmother. Like most coastal Italians, she would not and did not give up.

On the other hand, the Hotel D'Italia, which originally had been owned by the Coast Dairies and Land Company, was never rebuilt after the fire. Today, the site of the hotel is overgrown with trees and bushes. All that shrubbery now covers the memories of a Davenport past. When visiting the site now, I always wonder what artifacts might be still found in that wistful patch of imperfect green? Perhaps parts from those old slot machines or a broken *bocce* ball. Maybe Carabiniere's oversized coffee cup. Certainly not a torn piece of red curtain. Hmm?

For some reason we rarely went to the Ocean View Hotel. It fronted the Coast Road and was situated just beside where the New Cash Store stands today. (This hotel also burned down *circa* 1962.) It was owned and managed by Charlie Bella and his wife Carmelina, and famous for its "Wild Game Feasts," involving the coastal *Cacciatori* [kah cha **tohrr** ee], as the local hunters were known. Since Bronco was not much of a hunter, my family only attended one or two of these events.

It's funny what sticks in the mind of an eight or nine-year-old boy. As I recall, the Ocean View Hotel had a front porch or veranda. I can remember standing, during one of our infrequent visits, outside on the veranda, looking inside the hotel at where the bar was. I guess all the men sitting at the long bar drinking and talking fascinated me. All of a sudden a man with rather short legs and a protruding belly got off his stool. Walking with a menacing swagger, he came to the open front door where I was standing. Looking at me with a very mean expression on his face, he said in very poor English, "Don't you know that men don't like being looked at when drinking?" In a very soft voice, I told him that I was waiting for my father, who was visiting someone at the hotel. "Well, get away from here," he ordered. "I don't like you looking at me." Crushed, I stepped away from the door and went to the other end of the veranda.

I was so mortified by this incident that I didn't even tell my father about it. I was convinced that I had done something terribly wrong. Afterward, I never felt comfortable when visiting the Ocean View Hotel. Whenever in Davenport, I made it a point to look for that short man with the fat belly. From time to time I would see him hanging around at the local bars. Observing some of his acts of foolishness (such as being drunk and swinging his hips to the music being played on the juke box), I decided that he was nothing but a *ciuco,* and a *poco roba* (lazy, good for nothing). It's no wonder he didn't want anyone looking at him.

Nevertheless, I never forgot that incident. As a young patrolman walking Market Street in San Jose in 1959, I can remember walking into some of those old, notorious bars that still existed at that time. Bars such as the Tico-Tico and Tower Bar were infamous for catering to a rather unsavory clientel. During my "inspectional" tours, I made it a point to take a long look at each and every man drinking at the bar. I guess I looked pretty mean because no matter how hard or long I looked, no one ever came up to me and said, "I don't like you looking at me." Did I just hear the discerning reader ask, "Do you think Carabiniere would have been proud of you?" I certainly hope so. Stern and menacing looks, given at appropriate times and places, plus a police uniform, often helped me avoid physical combat.

Later, after my godmother along with other coastal Italians, moved away from Davenport, our visits to the little town became more and more infrequent. Once my family had relocated to Santa Cruz in 1954, the visits seemed to stop altogether. There was really no reason to go there anymore. Most of our friends now lived in Santa Cruz and the shopping was a lot more convenient there. Still, I will never forget those memorable trips up the green gilded coast every Saturday afternoon—our Old Carrettone squeaking and squawking along; the *chiacchiera* and savory smells that greeted us at the old Cash Store, and the almost mystical ambiance awaiting us, just down the hill, at the Hotel D'Italia.

Endnotes

[36] Most of the historical information on Davenport was garnered from Margaret Koch's book, *Santa Cruz County, 'Parade of the Past'*, published in 1973, by Valley Publishers, Fresno, California. Also used was an essay paper entitled, "A Short History of Davenport," by Alverda Orlando, dated July, 1960, "In Partial Fulfillment of the Requirements of Ed. 183S", found in the Davenport File, at the Santa Cruz City Library.

[37] In 1956, The Santa Cruz Cement Division of Pacific Cement and Aggregates Inc. bought the plant and its operations. Recently, it has been sold to CEMEX, a large Mexican Corporation.

[38] "A Christmas Story," MGM 1983, directed by Bob Clark (III), starring Darren McGavin, Melinda Dillon, Peter Billingsley and Ian Petrella.

[39] Officer Joe Vitto retired from the San Jose Police Department circa 1978. At the time of his retirement, he was assigned to the Traffic Enforcement Unit. Coincidentally, at that time, I was the commander of the unit; thus I was Joe's last "boss."

[40] "The Shining," produced by Warner Brothers, 1980, directed by Stanley Kubrick, starring Jack Nicholson and Shelly Duvall. Novel written by Stephen King.

THE GENTLE GIANT
ROSIE MICOSSI – CARABINIERE – "FAVA"

C. 1930

HOTEL D'ITALIA

C. 1923

THE OCEAN VIEW HOTEL

C. 1950

11. Pino Brovia

As I learned later from my family, I was born in Santa Cruz but actually lived in Davenport for the first six months of my life. Of course I don't remember much of that time, but while they lived there, my mother and father made life-long friends. The Brovias, Pietro (Pete) and Maria (Mary) with their children Joseph (Pino), Virginia, and Lina, lived on First Street in New Town, a block away from our house. (When I see Lina or Virginia, they always remind me that they used to change my diapers. Lina says that I was the cutest baby she had ever seen. Hmmm.) Pete worked for many years at the Cement Plant. Later, *circa* 1950, Mary and Pete moved from Davenport to Santa Cruz and lived at 511 Bellevue Avenue. This is only a few blocks from 729 Seaside Street, where my family eventually moved in 1954. It is somewhat ironical that today my niece Christine and her family live in the Brovias' house while my niece Denise and her family live in the house on Seaside Street. Even more ironical, my parents' burial vault inside Building 7, at the Holy Cross Cemetery, is located just above and to the right of Pete and Mary Brovia's vault. It seems that these two families were destined to be close together both in life and in death.[41]

Pete Brovia, who had a deep baritone voice, often got together with my father, who also sang *basso*. Often, after having a couple of glasses of wine, they began to sing old Italian songs. At times Valentina and Mary joined in, singing soprano. Let me tell you that there was no better singing group *su per la costa*. Between songs, Pete loved to tell jokes. His deep baritone gave him a unique and very infectious laugh. He would look at you over his eyeglasses, tell a joke, and then burst out with a very deep, rolling laugh that seemed to last forever. Before you knew it, you were laughing too, even though the joke might not have been all that funny. To this day I have never heard such an infectious laugh.

Pete and Mary's son, Joseph "Pino" Brovia (known in professional Baseball as Joe Brovia, "The Davenport Destroyer"), stood well over six feet tall and weighed approximately 200 pounds. *Pino* [**pee** no] is also, in Italian, the word for "pine." Pino Brovia's tall, muscular body reflected well those qualities of the tree whose name he bore. In his youth, Pino had played professional ball with the San Francisco Seals, and with the Portland Beavers, the Sacramento Solons, and the Oakland Oaks, of the old Pacific Coast League. Later in his career, Pino was called up briefly to play for the Cincinnati Reds of the National League.

An article appearing in the Santa Cruz Sentinel, dated August 13, 1947, has Pino, then a member of the San Francisco Seals, being the first hitter ever to hit three home runs in one week at Seal Stadium. In addition, Jim Sargent, in his excellent article on Pino, credits him with hitting the longest home run in the history of Seal Stadium. Estimates had the ball traveling some 560 feet, up and over the center field wall.[42] (Unknown to me at the time, Pino's "blast" occurred on my ninth birthday, April 19, 1946.) Because of its significance, a star was place at the top of the wall marking the spot where the ball had left the stadium. After arriving in San Francisco *circa* 1958, Willie Mays, the legendary center fielder for the Giants, was alleged to have said of Pino's homerun, "Hey, that's a five-dollar ride in a taxicab."[43] (Five dollars took you a long way in 1958.)

Although he was a very good baseball player, I mostly remember Pino for when he used to stop by our house on the Coast Road during the War. He was probably home on leave. Like most young soldiers during the war years, Pino liked to drink. On some of his visits, it was obvious that Pino had had too much. He would knock on the door and wait for my mother to come and greet him. As she opened the door, we would see this big, tall curly-haired figure standing in the doorway, slightly swaying and clearly unsteady on his feet. Seeing him in this condition, Valentina would throw up her hands and say, "O Dio buono, Pino! Viene qui subito." ("Good God, Pino! Come here quickly.") She would then make him sit down at the kitchen table and would not allow him out of the house until he was sober enough to drive. She would make him drink black coffee and eat tuna fish sandwiches. This combination seemed to work. Pino always made it back to his home in Davenport safely. Mary would then come to our house and thank my mother for taking care of her boy. Valentina treated the Brovias as though they were part of our family, and *vice versa*. Thus Valentina, unknowingly, made her contribution to baseball—saving Pino for all those home runs he would eventually hit.

In 1953, the Sacramento Solons of the Pacific Coast League held their spring training in Santa Cruz, at Harvey West Stadium. (During this time period, the Santa Cruz Seahawks, a semi-professional team, played both baseball and football there.) Pino was playing for the Solons at the time. This gave my brother and I a rare opportunity to watch Pino play ball.[44] I can actually say that, to this day, I have never seen any ball player using a batting stance similar to that used by Pino. A left-handed hitter, he stood in the batter's box with a straight-up-and-down stance, with feet set close together, and knees slightly bent. Unlike many baseball players waiting for the ball to be pitched, he did not hold his bat high and away from his body in a cocked position. Rather, he held the bat low and straight, with the handle close in at the waist and the barrel tucked in at the shoulder. As the pitcher delivered the pitch, Pino quickly cocked the bat back and then swung it forward, attacking the ball with a vengeance as it crossed the plate.

Pino was a notorious pull hitter. That is to say, as a left-handed hitter he constantly hit the ball to the first-base side of the field. Given the batting stance that he used, Pino must have had incredibly quick hands and tremendous power to accomplish this on a consistent basis. In order to "take away" hits from Pino, some opposing teams employed the "Brovia Shift," positioning three infielders on the first base side of the field. This was not the first time such a shift had been employed against a hitter. In 1948, Lou Boudreau, the manager for the Cleveland Indians, employed this shift for the specific purpose of "taking away" hits from Ted Williams, one of major league baseball's greatest hitters. An exaggerated version of the "shift" is currently being used against Barry Bonds of the San Francisco Giants, the all-time season home run leader (with 73 home runs). A problem with the "shift" is that it isn't high enough to prevent a home run. (My one regret is that I never did see Pino hit a home run.)

Another thing I observed was that Pino was the only player on the field wearing the legs of his pants pulled down low, touching the tops of his shoes. The other players, in order to show more of their colored stockings, wore their pant legs higher up, to just below the knees. Recently, Reno Cantarutti informed me that he had heard a story of Pino having a major dispute over this issue with Birdie Tebbets, the Cincinnati team's manager.

According to Reno's story, Tebbets wanted Pino to pull up his pant legs to allow the team's traditional red stockings to show. Pino, in his customarily stubborn way, refused. Today, many of the top hitters in baseball (Barry Bonds for one) wear their pant legs pulled down to the tops of their shoes. I suspect that Joe "Pino" Brovia, the "Davenport Destroyer," was well ahead of his time in this aspect of the game. On the other hand, his stubbornness in not complying with his manager's wishes, might have contributed to his early exit from major league baseball. (Perhaps Pino should have told Birdie that he didn't want to get dirt in his shoes.)

Recently, while my wife Mildred and I were shopping at a thrift store in Carmel Valley, I found an old 1981 edition of *The Sports Encyclopedia—Baseball*. On a whim I picked up the book and looked up the name Brovia. There it was—listed as: "Brovia, Joe - Joseph - John, with a nickname of 'Ox.'" According to the encyclopedia, Pino was 6'3" tall and weighted 195 pounds. He played for the 1955 Cincinnati Reds, and appeared in 21 games with 18 at-bats, two hits (singles), and four runs batted in. Regrettably, he was not given enough playing time to hit a major league homerun.

Unfortunately, Pino had to wait until he was thirty-three years old (an age considered old for a baseball player) before he could leave his imprint on major league baseball. Pino wasn't the fastest runner in the world and he certainly wasn't the best fielder. This probably kept him from getting to the major leagues at an earlier age. I often wonder what *might* have been, had the designated-hitter rule been in effect during Pino's career. Edgar Martinez, who recently retired from major league baseball, made a very nice living by just going up to the plate and hitting four times a game without taking the field. Pino died in 1994; however, I am sure if he were still alive today, he would say, in his familiar raspy, but confident, voice, "I could have done that, Ivano. I could have 'spiked' a lot more plates in the 'bigs.' Just my luck. I was born too soon."

Perhaps Pino was born too soon to "make it big" at the major league level. But in my eyes he was born at the right time, and in the right place. Davenport, with its insidious wind-blown cement dust was that place—and out of that dust came this tall, lanky action figure who could hit the tar out of a baseball. He didn't have to make it in the "bigs." To my brother and me, and—I'm certain—to many other young boys *su per la costa*, Pino had already made it "big"—as our first real-life hero. So what if San Francisco had Joe DiMaggio? *La Nostra Costa* had Joe "Pino" Brovia. (Pino was inducted into the Pacific Coast League Hall of Fame – Sept. 2005)

Endnotes

[41] Although Building 7, has no inscription, Ed Patrone, Operating Manager for the Diocese, informed me that it is referred to as " St. Charles Chapel". It is here where all caskets bearing the bodies of the faithfully departed are brought for a final blessing before burial.

[42] Mr. Sargent's article dated 9/1/2001, appears on the website, www.baseball-almanac.com/hero.

[43] Article in *Santa Cruz Sentinel*, dated 5/15/77, by sportswriter Bob Putney, entitled, "Brovia's Power Amazed even Mays." (After moving from New York, the New York Giants baseball team, of which Willie Mays was a member, was renamed the San Francisco Giants, and initially played their home games at Seal Stadium.)

[44] Pino made a visit to our house after one of these games. Sitting in our living room, drinking coffee and eating sweet rolls, he revealed to us that he was making $6,000 a season. To me, this was an incredible amount of money. Of course it wasn't. Most of the old ball players had to have second jobs during the off-season to make ends meet.

JOE "PINO" BROVIA AND HIS UNIQUE STANCE

C. 1953

IN THE "BIGS"

C. 1955

PETE BROVIA AND HIS FAMOUS SON

C. 1953

12. La Strada Per Pescadero
(The Road To Pescadereo)

About 22 miles north of Davenport lies the little town of Pescadero. In olden days Pescadero was a favorite fishing spot of the Ohlone Indians who were the early inhabitants of *la costa*. Later, Portuguese and Spanish explorers, who apparently had a penchant for making some "fishy" trades with these Indians, decided on the name Pescadero for their newly founded town. Pescadero means "fishmonger" in Spanish.

In the 1800s, the town of Pescadero was situated on the main road along the coast. Horse-drawn stage coaches brought tourists down from San Francisco to stay at its hotels, and to visit the beach which was, and still is, only a couple of miles away. Later the South Coast Railroad ran through the town, making it more accessible to the earnest traveler. When my family used to visit there in the late 1940s, the Coast Road bypassed the town, but the railroad, which had failed in the early 1920s, was no more. Pescadero was no longer a tourist town. Rather, it was considered to be an agricultural hamlet, mainly growing brussel sprouts and artichokes. During this period, my baptismal godfather, Antonio (Tony) Micossi and his wife Rosie managed the Elkhorn Bar and Restaurant, which was located in the center of town. They, along with their son Frank and daughter Rina, lived at the restaurant.[45] Since Pescadero was in the outermost region to which my parents dared travel in the Old Carrettone, it became quite an adventure for my brother and me. We got to see the best part of the rocky north coast, where the highway almost touches the Pacific Ocean. This was especially true when we approached the Slide Area, near the San Mateo/Santa Cruz county line. Located about seven miles north of Davenport, *La Slida* [**sly** dah], as the coastal Italians called it, was and still is a one-mile stretch on the Coast Road. It was beautiful, but also a little intimidating. As we drove along the road we could see the big waves rolling up and breaking on the rocks below the highway. As a little boy, I would have terrible nightmares about the waves actually breaking over the highway and sweeping the Old Carrettone, with us inside, down into the ocean below.

Driving very carefully, my father kept an eye on the steep and very high cliffs (i.e. Waddell Bluffs) lurking ominously, directly above the highway. This was in the time before the road had been improved, and extensive slide prevention measures had not as of yet been taken.[46] It was quite common for large boulders and rocks to come down from above and land on the road—or worse, on someone's car. Though from time to time we had to drive around some fallen rocks, a boulder never did crush our car. As we crossed the county line, we would all breathe a sigh of relief. We had made it safely, yet we knew that we had to travel back on that same stretch of highway on our way home.

La Slida was always in the back of our minds as we proceeded north on the Coast Road.

Just north of where the Ano Nuevo State Preserve is today, there was a ranch which had a windmill on it. We often stopped here to visit Tita and Rosie Cricco, two Friulani that were very close friends of our family. (The house where the Criccos lived is still there, at number 1703, just off Highway 1.) On our visits, my brother and I would run to the windmill to see it pump water. At times we were disappointed because the wind was not blowing. During these windless spells, the big machine lay dormant as we waited impatiently for *il vento* to pick up. I always wondered how the people got their water when the wind didn't blow. Fortunately, *il vento* was seldom quiet for very long. On cue, the big fins would start spinning and the pump would start pumping. I could tell that it was working because some of the water leaked from the pump as it was being primed. (The windmill can still be seen from the highway today; however, it is now pretty dilapidated and is no longer operational. Its broken tail fin bears painted letters that seem to spell AERMOTOR.)

One of the saddest episodes of my boyhood took place on this ranch. The owners of the ranch owned horses and cows. A large barn was seen at the end of a long driveway as you entered the ranch. On one of our visits, Tita Cricco informed us that a cow was very sick inside that barn. Apparently it had eaten too many oats or perhaps wet alfalfa. Whatever it was, it caused the poor cow's stomach to swell up with gas. Of course, being curious, my brother and I wandered over to the barn. There we saw this beautiful, brown cow lying on its side, its belly grossly swollen. We could see that the cow was suffering greatly. The owners were trying everything they could to save the cow. I do not remember exactly whether the cow's stomach actually ruptured, or if the owners had it put to sleep before that could occurred. Regardless, I was devastated, and I have never been able to forget the sufferings and the eventual death of that beautiful bovine creature in that barn.[47]

Proceeding north on the Coast Road, we passed the Pigeon Point Lighthouse, located about 16 miles north of Davenport. While in operation, this lighthouse guided many a ship safely around the point. (It is no longer operational, but there is now a hostel on the grounds for those who wish to stay overnight.) Onward we would go, another six miles to Pescadero Creek Road. Bronco would make a right-hand turn onto this road, and the Old Carrettone chugged along for another two miles, passing green fields of artichokes and brussel sprouts and finally arriving at the little town of Pescadero.

My godfather's restaurant was located on the southeast corner of the Pescadero and Stage Coach roads. (A U.S. Post Office is now on the site.) We would enter the restaurant through its front entrance on Stage Coach Road, and then proceed past the bar section to the kitchen at the rear, where Rosie Micossi did the cooking. There, surrounded by the savory aroma of Rosie's Italian cooking, my father and mother would sit for long periods of time conversing with Rosie and my godfather. Judging by the multitude of spicy fragrances coming from the kitchen area, I was quite sure that many of my mother's "quando si mangia" cooking skills had been learned from Rosie.[48]

If we were lucky, Frank and Rina would be at the restaurant during our visit. They were very friendly and would not hesitate to talk to my brother and me, which helped to pass the time. (Frank was in his late twenties or early thirties at the time, and Rina was probably in her early twenties.) This was especially true if Frank was there. Frank was of medium height and weighed approximately 170 pounds. I would stand back and take long admiring looks at him and his magnificently sculptured physique. He had developed his body by working out with weights and it was quite obvious by looking at his big bulging biceps that he had done a very good job. At times, he would take time out to demonstrate some of his exercises for us. He would also give us advice on how to begin to develop our bodies using weights. When I made the bold-faced assertion that Charles Atlas didn't need weights to build his body, Frank informed me that he very much believed that Charles Atlas had, in fact, used some weight training to develop his body. This very much confused me because Charles Atlas, in advertisements appearing in popular comics and magazines of the time, claimed that he only used "Dynamic Tension," to transform himself from a 98-pound weakling into a "he-man." In the advertisements, Dynamic Tension was the name given to a natural way of developing the body, by using resistant forces created by the body itself. Later, as a young teenager, I would use a combination of Dynamic Tension and weight training to develop my body. But I was never able to achieve the same results that Frank did.

One of our most memorable visits to Pescadero occurred just after the war. Frank, a captain in the Army, had recently returned home from overseas duty. Immediately after the war, he had spent some time in Nimis, Italy—my parents' and his father's hometown.

While there he bought surplus U.S. Army supplies and food, and distributed the items among the war-lorn citizens. His help was so much appreciated that on my first trip to Italy in 1969, the people in Nimis were still talking about "Il Capitano Micossi"—who had done so much to help them in their time of need.

My parents listened attentively as Frank brought them up to date on what had occurred, and gave them assurance that our surviving relatives were all right. My father had already been notified of it, but Frank confirmed that my paternal grandmother, Carolina Comelli, had been killed when she inadvertently picked up a live electrical wire that had been knocked down during the fighting. Bronco, who was deeply saddened by his mother's death, tried to garner some solace in the fact that no other members of his family had been injured or killed.

Frank then showed us several photographs of what the war had done to Nimis. The German army of occupation, in an act of retribution against the citizens of Nimis, had set the village afire.[49] The pictures depicted many burnt out and bombed out buildings. Every picture attested to the fact that the people of Nimis had suffered greatly during the struggle. Frank had also brought back pictures showing the bodies of Benito Mussolini, "Il Duce," along with those of his mistress Clara Petacci, and of a few of his Fascist supporters, strung up by their heels in the plaza at Milan, Italy. This was the first time we had seen these pictures. My father grew angry when he saw what the Italian people had done. In a very sardonic tone of voice he said, "Che bella figura fan questi Italiani!" To loosely translate: he meant to mock the Italians by saying, "These Italians sure know how to put on a good show (for the rest of the world)."

The suspicious reader might now be urging further comment by asking, "Why in the world would Bronco say something like that? Was he a Fascist supporter?" As far as I know, he wasn't. However, he believed that the Italians had behaved badly, first by desecrating the bodies and then by placing them on public display in such a heinous fashion. Even though Mussolini had committed many grievous crimes (grand stupidity probably being one of them),

Bronco believed that the Italians should have treated the bodies of their former leaders in a more dignified manner. After all, they, the Italian people, were the ones who had originally put them in power. My father was of the opinion that this was not the proper way for civilized people to behave. Bronco found it to be a cowardly act. I think this was the first time I heard my father speak ill of his former countrymen.[50]

Growing tired of listening to the old folks' conversation, my brother and I often wandered outside to take a look at the little town of Pescadero. I must say that there wasn't much there, and not much for kids to do. As it does today, the town consisted then of two streets: Pescadero Road, and Stage Coach Road. The cemetery (Mount Hope) was on the north end of town, and the Portuguese (I.E.S.) Hall was situated, then as now, on the opposite side of town. I think that at the time, there was one other restaurant other than my godfather's in town (probably Duarte's), but not much else. Today, Pescadero is visited mostly by people from the San Francisco Bay Area, who are attracted to the beach at Pescadero State Park, the seals at Ano Nuevo State Preserve, the lighthouse at Pigeon Point, and the Redwood Forest at Butano State Park. Although it now has a few more stores and antique shops than before, it is still small as far as tourist stops go. Duarte's Restaurant, now over 100 years old, seems to be the favorite gathering place. Except for my godfather's missing restaurant, Pescadero looks very much the same today as it did then.

Not wanting to drive through *La Slida* area after nightfall, our parents would soon call us back, and we prepared to say our goodbyes to Pescadero. If we were lucky, we would pass through *La Slida* before the low hanging fog had a chance to creep in from the ocean, engulfing the area in a thick gray, mystical mist. *Il respiro della strega* ("the breath of the witch"), as my mother called it, would make it hard for my father to see other cars or those falling rocks that might come crashing down on us. On the other hand, my brother and I always found driving through the fog, with the sound of the ocean waves crashing below, quite exciting and "spoooky."

Good weather or bad, the Old Carrettone always got us home safe and sound. Bronco would say that the old car knew the Coast Road so well that it could get back home by itself. It seemed that he was right, at least as far as the Comelli family was concerned. As we shall see later, the return trip from Pescadero would prove to be tragic for at least one other family.

Endnotes

[45] The reader may recall that in the 1920s, Tony and Rosie managed the Swiss Hotel in Santa Cruz. Later, in the 1950s, the Micossi Family built Micossi's, a restaurant and bar which was located just inside the northern city limits of Santa Cruz (2830 W. Cliff Drive at Mission Street). Lou Facilli, a long-time Santa Cruz resident, later bought the restaurant. Renamed "Facilli's," the restaurant became extremely popular during the 1960s and 1970s.

[46] An article appearing in the *Santa Cruz Sentinel*, dated 10/02/47, stated that a contract to improve the Slide Area had been approved on June 23. The cost of improvements was set at $505,000, and the job was to be completed by March 18, 1948. It described the Bluffs as being of Monterey shale, and standing 300 feet high.

[47] The barn is still standing at the end of that long driveway. In the front there is an old sign with the words "Ano Nuevo Rancho" and underneath, "Geo. H. Steele Estate." In her book, Margaret Koch states that the Rancho Punto del Ano Nuevo was purchased by Issac Graham, at a sheriff's sale in 1851; later the Steele Family acquired it.

[48] After my mother's death in 1977, Rosie and Rina, who by then were living in Santa Cruz, would invite my father to dinner every Sunday evening. "Vasin," as Rosie and Rina continued to call him, appreciated these evenings no end. Rosie's exquisite cuisine always reminded him of Valentina's cooking.

[49] In 1944, Italian Partisans succeeded in "liberating" Nimis from Nazi control. The German Army, subsequently recaptured the village and, in act of retribution, burned down many of the buildings.

[50] Apparently Bronco wasn't the only one that felt that way. In his final volume on World War II, Winston Churchill, by no means a friend of Fascism, stated that he was "profoundly shocked" after viewing the photographs. He further described the methods of the man who shot Mussolini and his mistress as being "treacherous and cowardly." *Triumph and Tragedy*, Winston S. Churchill, Houghton Mifflin Company, Boston, 1953, page 528.

IL CAPITANO MICOSSI

NIMIS – 1945

13. Tre Famiglie Friulani
(Three Friulian Families)

At times, prejudices and biases based on "old country" regionalism did play a part in the coastal Italians' lives.[51] It was natural for some to favor people from the part of Italy in which they themselves were born. This was more pronounced among the men, who had to compete in the labor force. Bronco often told the story, with some rancor, of being "let go" from a *rancio* during the Depression. According to my father, the Toscano *bosso* of the ranch chose to keep a Toscano worker. This was despite my father's pleas that he had a family with a sick child (my brother, John) to support. The Toscano *bosso*, according to Bronco, turned a deaf ear and kept the Toscano worker, even though he (the Toscano worker) was not married and had no family to support. Understandably, this did not sit well with my father.

On the other hand, most of the women got along just fine together and these biases were seldom if ever imposed on their American-born children. It was as if there was an unwritten law among the Italians *su per la costa*, that declared that these "old country" regional prejudices and biases had to end, once and for all, with their own generation. As for the children, we recognized only one region—**America**.

My father and mother were still living in Davenport when they first met the Cantarutti (kahn tah **rrew**- tee) and Taurian (**tarr** yahn) families. These two families became very close to our family. Guido and Evelina Cantarutti and Mario and Giga Taurian were born in the Friuli region of Italy. They spoke the same dialect, Friulano. This dialect, and being of the same age and region, seemed to bind our three families close together.

I have very dim memories of when I first met the Cantarutti family. As I remember it, they lived just off the Coast Road, a few miles north of Davenport. Their house (more like a shack) was located near a bluff or cliff that overlooked the Pacific Ocean. (Lido Cantarutti recently informed me that their rent had been $5 per month.) I know that the ocean was not too far from their house, because I remember being scared that I would fall off the cliff and that the ocean, waiting patiently for me below, would swallow me up for ever and ever. Actually, I think my mother was probably the one who instilled this fear in me. I'm sure Valentina was just as afraid of me falling into that ocean as I was. To this day, I don't know how Evelina ever managed to keep her two boys from being blown over that cliff.

The Cantaruttis had two children, Carino (kah **ree** no), the oldest, and Lido, the baby. (Norma, a daughter, was born later in 1947, and thus did not get the thrill of experiencing life in the wind-blown shack that hung on a cliff—or pretty close to it). The name Carino, which means pretty or nice in Italian, was soon shortened to "Rino." Somewhere along the line (probably in public schools), the spelling of the name changed to "Reno." One thing that amazed me about Reno—born in Italy—was that he spoke the Friulano dialect. Valentina discouraged my brother and me from speaking Friulano (she believed that Italian was the proper language and that the dialect would only confuse us), but since my father and mother frequently conversed with each other in that dialect, we came to understand it quite well. Reno throughout his younger years, loved to "chew the fat." I still can visualize this kid sitting at the dinner table with his parents and/or my parents, conversing with them in Friulano.

Truthfully, listening to a conversation in Friulano is quite enjoyable. Words spoken in the dialect have a more melodious tone than when articulated in proper Italian. It can also be quite humorous when spoken words are combined with the gestures and expressions of the speaker. It is not uncommon for Friulanos to flail their arms about and to grimace with wild expressions, as they drive home a point in a heated conversation. It was also humorous to hear our parents swear in Friulano when they became angry. It was not humorous when one of the parents lost patience with one of the kids. They would let you know in no uncertain terms that you had done something wrong. "Ti do un pataff" seemed to be a favorite expression. When directed at the kids it usually meant, loosely translated, "I'm going to cuff you one (or worse), if you don't behave." We knew it was time to get our act together.

Another thing I remember about Reno was that he had tuberculosis when he was a kid, in 1943. In order to be cured, he had to spend some time (about 18 months) at a sanitarium near Auburn, California. It must have been pretty scary for a ten or eleven-year-old kid to be taken from his parents and isolated along with other TB patients. I remember some photographs of Reno sent by Evelina to my mother. In the photos Reno was standing around in his shorts. He looked pretty healthy to me, so I asked my mother why it took so long for Reno to get out. I guess that was the first time I heard of TB and how serious it could be.

Reno says he could not have made it back to health without his mother's help. He is eternally grateful to Evelina, for all she did for him during this time. Living in Richmond, his mother had to take a three-and-a-half hour bus ride (she did not drive) all the way to Auburn, to visit her son at the sanitarium. Reno said that when she got there, she was restricted to visits of only an hour or so. Although short, her anticipated visits were all that kept Reno going.[52]

As with the Cantarutti family, I have dim memories of when I first met the Taurian family. They also lived on a ranch just north of Davenport. I remember that their house was near a chicken coop; I have lasting memories of going in and out chasing a bunch of chickens around. Mario Taurian, who had red hair, was known *su per la costa* as Mario "Rosso" (i.e. "red"). His wife Luiga was known as Giga [**gee** jah]. They had two sons, Felicino (Phil), the oldest, and Elso, the baby. Again, Phil was close to my brother's age; Elso was close to Lido's age. They also had a dog named Terri. Terri was a black and white spotted terrier mix. To me, he was the smartest dog in the world. He obeyed our commands and did other amazing things. He was also extremely loyal and a great fighter. Terri, although of medium stature, was afraid of no dog. He took them all on and usually won. However, with the kids he was kind and gentle. I know this for a fact because he was soon to become the Comelli kids' first real dog, as I will explain below. (We would eventually have three dogs *su per la costa*, Terri, Prince and Capi.)

In my memories, it seems that these wonderful people were gone only a short time after I had first met them. From Reno and Lido, I learned that the Venturini Ranch—where Guido was working *su per la costa*—had gone broke. This caused the Cantarutti family to move to Richmond, California, where Guido found work with the Richmond Sanitary Services Company. In 1942 the Cantarutti family had to relocate from Richmond to Asti, due to the wartime restrictions against enemy aliens. There Guido found temporary work with a winery. After the restrictions were lifted, he returned to his old job with the Richmond Sanitary Services Company. Later he bought a share in the company and did quite well for his family. However, I think that he worked too hard, and eventually suffered severe physical problems as a consequence.

According to Phil Taurian, his family's move from *la costa* to San Francisco was strictly economic in nature. Mario, with some foresight, had become a naturalized U.S. citizen prior to the outbreak of the war; thus he and his family were able to avoid many of the restrictions that befell non-citizens of Italian descent. However, Phil does remember that the police authorities searched their home in San Francisco. Apparently they believed the Taurian family was in possession of a short-wave radio. As far as Phil remembers, nothing ever came of the incident.

Mario first found work tearing down the remnants of the World Fair, held on Treasure Island in 1939. He then worked for a butcher business, and later for a malt house. He also did quite well for his family. He stayed in San Francisco until he retired and then moved to Italy. His wife, Giga, worked many years in San Francisco for the Levi-Strauss Company. When she retired, she also moved to Italy. (For many years, Giga was our main supplier of Levi jeans. Later both my mother and my Aunt Lina worked at the Levi Straus Factory on Front Street in Santa Cruz. Thus my brother and I, as well as my father, had a never-ending supply of new Levi pants and jackets. No hand-me-downs here.)

I do remember one important thing about the Taurian family's leaving the area: Terri the dog. For some reason, I remember my family going to the ranch where the Taurians had lived. This must have been just after they'd gone. Of course, no one was there. No one except Terri. He was hanging around the house next to where all those chickens used to be. We thought that the Taurians, out of necessity, had abandoned the dog. My brother and I pleaded with my father and mother to take the dog home with us. After some hesitation they agreed. We loaded the dog into the backseat of our Lafayette and brought him to our home on the Coast Road.

Later, we found out that the Taurians had not abandoned the dog at all. Prior to their leaving, they had given him to Silvio and Elena Moro, a Friulian couple who lived in Davenport along with their sons Fernando and Freddie and daughters Mary and Yoli. The Moros had agreed to take care of the dog. Apparently, Terri, trying to find the Taurians, had run away and returned to his previous home. When we found out about this, my parents, much to my consternation, made contact with the Moros and offered to give the dog back to them. I think that Silvio and Elena were more than happy to let sleeping dogs lie. We were allowed to keep Terri for ourselves. Terri was our first real dog and he lived on for many years, giving us great joy and happiness. At times Terri would disappear for a long period, only to return in a rather haggard-looking condition. I always suspected that on these occasions he was trying to find his way back to Davenport to visit the ranch where the Taurians used to live.

Although these two families—the Cantaruttis and the Taurians—had moved away from *la costa*, they still visited us from time to time. I remember that the Taurians had a Chevrolet coupe with a rumble seat. I don't remember what year it was (probably an early 1930s model), but I do remember that Mario kept it in pristine condition. I'm sure it would be a classic car today. The Taurians, all seated in the front seat, with Elso on his mother's lap, would drive all the way down from San Francisco to our house. I think it must have been a very grueling journey, given the roads of that day and the very small car in which they traveled. I remember how happy we would be to see Mario driving that Chevrolet up into our back yard. And Terri remembered. As soon as he saw them, he jumped for joy and they had a real family reunion. He had not forgotten them.

The Cantaruttis also came to visit from time to time. My brother and I waited with great anticipation for their visits. We knew we were going to have a great time for a day or two. I think that they had a fairly old brown or tan sedan at the time. I remember they had more room in that car than the Taurians had in theirs. (According to Reno, this car actually belonged to a friend of theirs.)

I also remember that, of all the cars among these three families, our 1934 Lafayette was the worst. The Old Carrettone was not too reliable. As a consequence, our visits to the San Francisco Bay Area were infrequent. However, I do remember going to visit the Cantarutti family while they lived in Asti (a small town in the wine country just northeast of San Francisco). For it had been determined by the U.S. government that their home in Richmond was too close to the naval shipyards.

Circa 1943, my mother, brother and I once took a Greyhound bus from Santa Cruz to visit them. I remember the bus driver finally stopping the big, lumbering vehicle in front of an old winery, letting us out, and then just driving away. There we were—on this strange road with no one in sight. My mother must have asked someone at

La Nostra Costa (Our Coast)

the winery if they knew where the Cantarutti family lived, because I remember walking down the road to this house that had a big, empty swimming pool in front of it. Sure enough, it was the Cantaruttis' house. I don't remember how long we stayed, but I do remember that the weather was very hot and that we played Cowboys and Indians in that big empty pool. For that matter, Lido was not much of a cowboy or an Indian. He was still walking around in diapers, "babbling" his way through life.

I would be remiss at this time if I didn't mention the old "club house" *su per la costa*. Immediately after the war, my father, using the Coast Guard's "lookout houses" as a model, built a small, one-room playhouse. It was located in our backyard next to our garage and chicken coop. Inside, my brother and I stored our comic books and other boyhood treasures. One summer, Reno came down and made us a bunch of play rifles and pistols out of broomsticks and other scrap wood. (Reno was good at doing things like that.) We stored the "weapons" in the clubhouse and formed the Artillery Club.

Also stored in the clubhouse was an old stand-up Victrola. It even had that famous picture of that black and white dog, gazing longingly into the megaphone. To set the machine in motion, you simply had to tightly wind the phonograph with the hand crank on the side, and then click on a switch. (This was indeed fortunate because the clubhouse was not wired for electricity.) With an old 78-rpm record already in place on the turntable, you ever so gently set down the needle holder, so that the needle came to rest on the spinning record. Whoa-la! Let there be music! This was our hi-fi system in those days.

Whenever the Cantaruttis or the Taurians came for a visit, we would spend a lot of time listening to records on that phonograph. Guess what? Those records were in Italian and a lot of them contained Fascist songs and propaganda. I remember one record in particular which had "Facciata Nera" (Little Black Face) on one side and "Cara Virginia" (Dear Virginia) on the flip side. I later found out that these two songs were sung by Italian troops as they marched on Abyssinia, in North Africa, *circa* 1935. "Facciata Nera," as I understood it at the time, depicted the invading Italians as liberators, promising that once with them, they would give the Abyssinians a different set of laws and a different king. "Cara Virginia," on the other hand, was a love song, telling the story of an Italian soldier, about to leave for the African campaign, who promises his *amorosa* that once there he would faithfully write to her. He would also send her a beautiful flower that he would (no doubt) find growing under the equatorial sky. Fascist songs or not, we had a great time playing them.

Bronco told us that the Victrola, along with the records, had been abandoned and left in the barn at the Gulch Ranch during the war. Fortunately, our record playing occurred after the end of the war. Can you imagine what the U.S. government would have thought of our Italian parents letting our "Artillery Club" listen to Fascist songs during the time we were at war with Italy? Ouch! They probably would have sent them packing to North Africa to help that poor love sick soldier find his precious equatorial flower.

On this same note: Reno, who was about four years old at the time, still remembers attending a meeting in Davenport *circa* 1935. The meeting was held for the purpose of raising funds for Mussolini and the Fascist Party. Most all of the attendees were Italian immigrants who lived in the Davenport-Coast Road area. Reno even recalls a man trying to entice him to give the Fascist salute by offering to buy him an ice cream cone. (Reno can't remember whether the man succeeded or not.) Our Victrola records had probably originated in that time period.

Perhaps the reader is somewhat shocked and amazed to learn that such Fascist propaganda records and meetings were allowed *su per la costa*. However, having these records or attending the meetings was not at all illegal prior to Italy's involvement with the Axis Powers in World War II. Richard Ben Cramer, in his book *Joe DiMaggio: The Hero's Life,* writes that during this time it was common practice for Italian women living in the North Beach area of San Francisco to send their gold wedding rings to Italy for the glory of a new Italy. In return they would receive copies of their rings crafted from genuine Italian steel. The Italian immigrants were in need of heroes. Up until about 1935, Mussolini, the Italian Prime Minister, was considered a hero—not only among Italians, but also among Americans. To illustrate this, Cramer points out that in 1934, Cole Porter, the famous American song writer, included the lyrics, "You're the tops: you're Mussolini." in one of his hit songs.[53]

Even after Mussolini initiated his wars of aggression in North Africa, some Italians hung in there for the cause, hoping that Italy would establish her empire for the common good. All this turned sour, of course, when *Il Duce* threw in his lot with Adolph Hitler in 1940. Although initially successful, many of the same soldiers who marched into battle singing "Facciata Nera" and "Cara Virginia" were later killed or made prisoners, as the Allies drove the German and Italian armies out of North Africa, forcing Italy to surrender. Mussolini's dream of a new Roman Empire proved to be as elusive as the shifting desert sands he had tried to conquer.[54]

Endnotes

[51] Italy is currently divided into twenty regions. The Friuli Region is located in the northeastern portion of the country, not too far from Venice. Toscana (Tuscany) is located in the west-central section, much closer to Rome.

[52] Reno recently related to me, that one of his most scary experiences at the sanitarium was having to watch two plain-clothes officers handcuff and drag off a ten-year-old Japanese patient. Reno presumed that they took him to an internment camp. Apparently that wartime paranoia had found another victim.

[53] Richard Ben Cramer, *Joe DiMaggio. The Hero's Life*, published by Simon and Schuster, in 2000.

[54] A very poignant film, directed by Enzio Monteleone, entitled "El Alamein - The Line of Fire," depicts, both with courage and pathos, the Italian soldiers' hopeless plight in North Africa. Distributed by Palace Films, it was shown at the 2004, Italian Film Festival, in Marin.

14. Famiglie Insieme (Families Together)

The greatest of times were when the Cantarutti and Taurian families both came to our house on the Coast Road, and we were all together at the same time. My mother would then say, "Let's go have a picnic." One of our favorite spots was Bonny Doon, which is located in the Santa Cruz Mountains just southeast of Davenport. Situated above the fog, the area is noted for its warm weather and forestial beauty. In this area, our parents knew an Italian couple named Luigi and Mary Iacopetti (I believe they were Friulani), who owned a small grocery store and bar. Later this store became known as the "Lost Weekend."[55] (Presently it houses the Bonny Doon Vineyard Tasting Room at 10 Pine Flat Road.) Behind the store, under a grove of redwood trees, was a very special place where the Iacopettis allowed us to set up our picnics. The grove of redwood trees is still there today, standing majestically behind the building.

As our parents sat around the picnic table eating food, drinking wine, and conversing in Friulano or singing Italian songs, the other kids and I would set off exploring through the trees, playing games or just talking. Sometimes, we even thought up practical jokes to play on our parents. One incident in particular, which will be forever remembered as the "Big Mosca Caper," was planned and carried out just adjacent to the above-described redwood grove. Guido, Reno and Lido's father, decided after eating and drinking to take a nap in the back seat of his parked car. The shade provided by the redwood trees kept him cool and comfortable. Soon Guido fell into a deep sleep. I don't remember if it was Reno or Lido (probably Lido, who liked to do these things) who took a pussy willow, and from outside the car (whose window was open), brushed Guido's face ever so lightly. Guido, still sleeping, soon became annoyed and, thinking it was a big old fly, whiffed at the pussy willow with his hand. He then settled back and snored away again. We thought it was great fun and we would laugh each time Guido took a whiff at that "mosca," but not too loudly, because we wanted Guido to continue sleeping so that the pussy willow could be applied again. This went on for quite some time, the pussy willow "mosca" being applied over and over again, and Guido whiffing at it with his hands like a punch-drunk fighter. All of a sudden we heard Mario Taurian yelling "Ti do un pataff!" Apparently he had spotted our antics and was coming to Guido's defense. We knew it was time to quit. Guess what? Guido kept on sleeping throughout the entire incident. I still think he thought it was just a big old *mosca*. Nothing to be concerned about.

Reno and Phil were the oldest, and so they became our *de facto* leaders. My brother was next in line—then me, and then Elso and Lido—all in order of our birthdays. Since my brother, Reno, and Phil were only about one year apart in age, they became close buddies. I was four years younger than Reno and Phil, and about two years older than Elso and Lido. As we grew older it became natural for Lido, or Elso, and me, to pair up and play practical jokes against the two older boys, and vice versa. On one such occasion, Lido or Elso (my memory fails me as to which) and I were for some reason mad at the two older boys. We decided to get back at them. We noticed that Valentina, preparing the noon day meal, was cutting up some garlic cloves. When she wasn't looking we swiped a few. We then proceeded to put the cut-up garlic into a couple of drinking glasses. As I remember, the older boys were allowed to have a glass of wine with their meal—at least I know that my brother was. This was not unusual in Italian families. I think the theory was, that if you trained the boys to drink wine sensibly with their meals, they would not become *ciucos*. (This seems to have worked in my brother's case: I can only remember him getting drunk once.) Lurking in the background, we waited for our moms to set the table. Then, before the two older boys came in, and when no one else was looking, my co-conspirator and I poured the wine over the garlic and set the filled glasses in front of their usual sitting places. Our plan was for the red wine to hide the garlic. To our astonishment, the white cloves could be clearly seen at the bottoms of their glasses. Too late to do anything about it! The two older boys came in and proceeded to sit in their designated spots. We expected them to see the garlic right away. They didn't. Then it became very difficult for my fellow perpetrator and I to keep from laughing, even though we had to keep a straight face in order to pull off this prank.

The two older boys nearly caught on to the whole gag, because it was not the custom to have their glasses filled prior to sitting at the table. They seemed to sense that something was up. Still, to our amazement, they didn't see the garlic cloves. Soon they became engaged in conversation and forgot about their drinks. The meal was served and I sat in my chair with great anticipation as the two older boys sipped their "garlic cocktail."

Nothing happened. In fact, nothing happened until they took their final sip and actually hit bottom. I don't know if they actually tasted the garlic or if they had just spotted it for the first time, but in any event, all hell broke loose. My fellow accomplice and I burst out laughing. The two older boys got really mad and started to come after us, but then, to our delight, our parents began laughing with us and we knew that everything was going to be all right. The two older boys had to swallow their pride and sit back down. I'm sure that the two victims did something later to get back at us, but I can't quite remember what it was. In any event, it was a simple prank, but great fun.[56]

One summer, the Taurian family came to visit us *su per la costa* for a whole month. Better yet, the Gemignanis' house next door was vacant at the time, and they allowed the Taurians to use it. Giga came down and stayed with the boys for the first two weeks; and then Mario came down and stayed for the next two weeks. I remember two important things about that summer. First, Phil and Elso had brought down a big collection of "Joe Palooka" comic books. I loved to read these comic books. Joe Palooka was a boxer, and the comic book was popular during the time in which Joe Louis—a black—and one of the greatest fighters of all times, was Heavyweight Champion of the real world. Conversely, Joe Palooka, a big blond-haired Caucasian with a cowlick covering one of his eyeballs, was Heavyweight Champion of the funny-book world. I didn't think anything about it at the time, but I now believe that the comic book may have reflected the anti-black sentiment that existed during this period. If you can't beat the Black Champion in the real world, crown a White Champion in the fantasy world. As I remember it, Joe Palooka's opponents in the ring always seemed to be white. Joe Palooka never lost a fight and I thought he was a great funny-book Champion. However, there was another, rival "Funny Book Heavyweight Champion" at the time. His name was Curly Kayoe. He, also, was white and he, also, never lost a fight. My greatest wish was that the two champions would one day slug it out in the same ring, and resolve once and for all the disputed "Funny Book Heavyweight Championship." Then we would know for certain who the best fighter really was. Much to my disappointment, they never did.

Notwithstanding my passion for the two White "Funny Book Champions," the comic books never changed my mind about Joe Louis, who was my boyhood hero. I was pulling for Joe even when he was fighting Rocky Marciano, a white Italian-American, on October 22, 1951. I was saddened when Marciano knocked out Louis in the eighth round. Louis, who had been trying to make a comeback, called it quits after that fight.

The Louis-Marciano fight marked the end on an era—but what an era! "The Brown Bomber," as Louis was known, held the title from 1937 to 1949. What a thrill it was to hear the ring announcer, over so many years, bellow out over the radio: "The winner and still Heavyweight Champion of the World—Joe—Louis!" After the Marciano fight, Louis was finished as a fighter. Rocky, on the other hand, went on to win the Heavyweight Championship a year later, knocking out Jersey Joe Walcott in the thirteenth round. The Comelli family had a new hero in their household.

La Nostra Costa (Our Coast)

The second thing I remember about the Taurian family's visit that summer was that Phil introduced us to the rubber gun. Such early-model "weapons" were usually aimed from the shoulder like a rifle. They were clumsy and not very accurate, because of the nature of their trigger mechanism. (Actually, Phil was quite good at hitting his mark.) A long, narrow piece of wood (about half an arm's length or a bit longer) sufficed as the barrel of the weapon. Two or three notches, cut on the top edge of the barrel, locked a stretched rubber band (cut from the inner tubes of tires) in place; a leather thong (or string), strategically placed over the notches and under the rubber, acted as the trigger. When ready to fire, the stick was aimed at an opponent, and the rubber band was launched by means of pulling upward on the leather thong. A clothespin, which we later used, was a much better trigger, allowing for greater accuracy. These early "weapons" served as a prototype for the later rubber guns used in the "duels" yet to come on the Rodoni Ranch.

My family did reciprocate the Taurians' visits on a couple of occasions. On one particular occasion, I remember, we drove up to San Francisco in the Old Carrettone and stayed overnight. The Taurians lived in an old Victorian house on Potrero Hill. There, Phil and Elso showed my brother and me how boys in the big city used their urban environment to entertain themselves. For example, Phil had a homemade go-cart, made out of wood, with roller skates serving as its wheels. The cart could be steered by pulling cords attached to either side of the swiveling front axle. As one boy sat in the cart, another boy, or boys, pushed the cart from behind, getting it to roll along the sidewalk and down the steep Potrero hill. As the cart descended, it picked up speed. At the bottom of the hill there was a major traffic intersection. To stay on the sidewalk and avoid the cross street directly ahead, the driver of the cart had to make a sharp right-hand turn around the corner of a building. I think the cart had some sort of hand brake—or maybe we just dragged our feet to bring it to a stop. Phil and Elso were quite proficient in making this turn safely. My brother and I, being farm boys and unfamiliar with sidewalk games, had trouble making the turn, and crashed the cart several times before getting the hang of it. As we shall see later, my brother and I later used this knowledge to make similar maneuvers on a race track *su per la costa*—but using a modern marvel, the Old Carrettone.

I remember Mario, during one of our visits, driving us to San Francisco's waterfront to see Alcatraz. We listen as Mario told my father this very exciting story about an attempted prison break at the "Rock." I don't remember whether Mario actually witnessed the action; however, he vividly described to Bronco how hundreds of people had lined up near the waterfront to watch the "cops shoot it out with the inmates." Phil then added that you could actually see gun flashes in the darkness and hear explosions. You can imagine how excited my brother and I were listening to this story. In my mind, I could actually see myself there, standing on San Francisco's eastern shore, watching and hearing all the gunfire happening in the middle of the Bay. Gosh! It was just like the movies, only better.

Imagining all that action was fun for us, but there was another side to the story. While the citizens of San Francisco were enjoying themselves, watching the episode develop, the inmates inside the prison were having a terrible time. What San Franciscans were probably seeing was the notorious attack on the "D" block, a cluster of cells adjacent to the west wall of the prison. In his book *Alcatraz From Inside*, Jim Quillen relates that in May 1946, he and several other inmates, including Robert Stroud, the famous "Birdman of Alcatraz," were holed up in the isolation ward—the "D" block. According to Quillen, the entire cellblock was raked with sustained gunfire for long periods of time. Tear gas and concussion grenades were also used in an attempt to dislodge the prisoners. The attacks finally came to an end with the killing of the three principal instigators, Joseph Cretzer, Marvin Hubbard, and Bernard Coy—not in "D" block, but in a service passage near "C" block.[57]

As a nine-year-old boy, I knew nothing of this. Like some San Franciscans, I thought the incident was just great fun. In fact, I was hoping that it would happen again. Maybe next time I could actually see the gun flashes for myself. On the other hand, I really don't think Mr. Quillen and his fellow inmates of "D" block would have appreciated a repeat performance for my benefit.

La Nostra Costa (Our Coast)

On a later visit, I remember, Phil and Elso taking us to 16th and Bryant, to see Seal Stadium, where Pino Brovia had hit his monstrous homerun. This must have been around 1950, because I was just starting to become interested in baseball. The San Francisco Seals played at the stadium and, at the time, were the only professional baseball team in town. I remember listening to the radio and hearing the voice of Don Cline—who later was to broadcast the 49ers games on KCBS radio—announcing the games for the Seals. One of his sponsors was Regal Pale Beer. (At times, I still hear the jingle going through my head, "Take it easy, take it light, with the beer that tastes just right. Regal Pale Beer!")

The Seals had a long history of winning baseball. Joe DiMaggio used to play for them before being sold/traded to the New York Yankees *circa* 1935. According to Richard Ben Cramer, in his book *Joe DiMaggio: The Hero's Life,* Joe went to the Yankees for $25,000 cash and five player-prospects. According to the author, it was rumored that the Yankees were willing to pay as much as $75,000 (a huge sum for that time). However, Joe suffered an off-the-field injury to his knee, which reduced his market value. No wonder that Pino Brovia wanted to play baseball: A player going to the major leagues for that amount of money certainly would get paid a lot more than the workers at the Portland Cement Plant.

Much to my chagrin, after I started listening to the Seals it seemed that they always had a losing season. It was as though I had put a curse on them. I felt relieved when the Giants came to town in 1958. Maybe I wouldn't have to feel so guilty when listening to their games. Even though my "curse" seemed to reappear each time they played the Dodgers, they did assuage my fears by always being in contention for the National League Championship, at least during those first few years.

Our visits with the Cantarutti-Taurian Families were not always filled with fun and games. On a more serious note: In June 1950 the United States got itself involved in a nasty little war with North Korea. President Truman called it a "police action," but I think that when people start shooting and bombing each other, it's a war. I was much too young to be involved (I was 13) but Reno was just at the right age. He was drafted and assigned for basic training to Fort Ord, an Army base located in Monterey County about forty miles south of Santa Cruz. . I remember one Sunday afternoon when the Cantarutti, Taurian, and Comelli families were all getting together to drive down to Fort Ord to visit him. Our plans were to have a picnic right there on the base. Reno came out wearing his fatigues and spit-shined brown boots. (Later, when I was drafted into the Army in 1960, the boots issued to GIs were black.) Reno told us that he could only be with us for a short time. Apparently someone in his Company had gotten into trouble and as a consequence, the Company Commander had placed the whole unit under restriction. This was a great disappointment to us all, but especially to Evelina, who was worried sick that Reno soon would be sent to Korea. As luck would have it, and much to the relief of Evelina, Reno was assigned to an Army unit stationed in Europe. After this, he served in Italy, where he met his future wife, Franca. Reno later said that he indeed had been fortunate in being stationed in Europe. As feared, the majority of his basic training unit was assigned to Korea. Some of the boys never did make it back.

Endnotes

[55] *Memories of the Mountains: Family Life in Bonny Doon*. The Ladies of Bonny Doon Club, published by AuthorHouse, 2004.

[56] Not so much fun some years later, when my daughter Suzanne, then about six years old, turned the tables on me, so to speak. Apparently she had gotten this idea from watching cartoons on television. As I was working at my desk at home, she came in and served me an orange liquid in a tall glass. Not paying much attention and thinking that it was fresh juice, I took a big swallow, only to realize, too late, that it was liquid soap. I didn't blow bubbles as she had anticipated, but I think I did foam a bit at the mouth. Suzanne broke out laughing. On the other hand, I didn't do much laughing as I chased her around the house. Now I knew how the two older boys must have felt. Come to think of it, I would have preferred that "garlic cocktail."

[57] *Alcatraz From Inside* by Jim Quillen, published in 1991 by Golden Gate National Park Association, San Francisco, California.

TRE FAMIGLIE INSIEME

COMELLI – CANTARUTTI – TAURIAN

C. 1947

AMICI DELLA COSTA IN BONNY DOON

C. 1938

BABE IN TRAINING

IVANO FRANCO – C. 1938

15. Il Mare (The Ocean)

During the summer months, Evelina or Giga often sent their kids down to stay with us for two or three weeks. When the sun was shining, my mother would make some sandwiches, and load us all into the Old Carrettone. Then we would head southward for the beach in Santa Cruz. *Spiaggia* [spee **yah** jah] is the Italian for beach, but we seldom used that word when referring to the beach in Santa Cruz. Instead, Valentina usually would announce her intention to go by saying, "Si va al mare" [**mah** rreh]—meaning that we were going to "the ocean." (The word *mare*, which normally is used to mean sea, was also used by coastal Italians to refer to the ocean.) Often, Mario, Elio and Andreina Rodoni, who lived just down the road, came with us in a separate car. Valentina would park the car at the end of Bay Street, near West Cliff Drive, and we would all—one of the boys with a giant umbrella in hand—march down to Cowell's Beach. (Much later the Dream Inn, now the Coast Santa Cruz Hotel, was built on the very spot we used to cross to get to the beach.) There we played in the sand and swam in the ocean. As a very young boy, I remember that one of my favorite pastimes was to mimic the newspaper boys who walked the beach hawking their papers and shouting, "READ ALL ABOUT IT!" I would try my best, but the words always came out a rather shearing, "BEE-ROLL-ABOB-IT!"

After swimming, our mothers called us back to have a snack consisting of a peanut-butter-and-jelly or bologna sandwich, or something similar. After we had eaten our sandwiches my brother and I were given a nickel apiece to buy a single-scoop ice cream cone. A double-scoop ice cream cone cost a dime. Only on rare occasions were we allowed to buy a double-scoop ice cream cone. I remember that we never were allowed to buy a hamburger because it cost 25 cents. I don't remember what the other boys were allowed to buy, but I guess that they had similar restrictions placed on them.

While we ate our sandwiches and ice cream cones, Andreina and my mother would sit in the shade of the umbrella, gossiping about work or events *su per la costa*. At times, a rather perky lady, perhaps in her mid-thirties, displaying a petite, well-trimmed body, succinctly fitted in a tight swim suit of the latest fashion, came by to say hello. I believe that she said her name was Louisa. She spoke very good English and very bad Italian. I remember that she laid her body in the sand near our umbrella and then by adroitly mixing the words of the two languages, she recounted to my mother and Andreina all about her amorous adventures. I soon noticed that, every once in a while, a male sunbather would come near to say hello and to engage her in a few words of conversation. After the man left, she would say, in English and fractured Italian, "See that guy? E caprone!" Literally, *caprone* [kah **pro** neh] is a derivative of the Italian word *capro*, which means he-goat. The reader can readily imagine that used in the manner Louisa did, the word *caprone* figuratively meant that the man was a notorious womanizer, or worse. Hearing this, my mother and Andreina would break out laughing. They really enjoyed her visits. Her conversations tended to add much-needed diversion and amusement to their day. I must admit that I also liked her visits, because much like the *caprones* of the day, I also enjoyed looking at Louisa while she displayed her well-trimmed body in those tight-fitting bathing suits.

I was probably too young to remember, but Reno tells me that Valentina used to bury my brother in the sand (lying on his back) up to his neck. Apparently this was done for therapeutic purposes. My brother, when quite young, suffered from some kind of glandular problem. To this day he bears on his neck the scars where he was operated on. I think my mother believed that a treatment of salt water, sun, and warm sand would help heal the wound. It must have worked. My brother survived and the scar is barely noticeable today.[58]

Speaking of medical concerns, I must mention the big health scare during this time period—*polio*. In the 1940s there was no vaccine or known cure for this disease. It was common for people who contacted the disease to either die or become crippled for life. The newsreels of the time were filled with pictures of children lying in iron lungs or standing with heavy metal braces on their legs, barely able to walk even with the aid of crutches. An Associated Press article, appearing in the Santa Cruz Sentinel, dated July 29, 1949, typifies the heightened attention paid to polio during this time. The article indicated that 1948 was the second worst year ever for reported cases of polio in the United States (27,680 cases). It also stated that reported cases thru July 23, 1949, were running 38.4% higher than 1948. According to the Sentinel article, a pool in Springfield, Illinois had to be closed, and children under the age of sixteen quarantined, after 17 cases of polio, with two deaths, were reported. Even scarier, the Sentinel reported on October 19, 1949 that Dr. Duncan A. Hobert, a well-known and respected Santa Cruz physician, had been stricken with polio. If a doctor was not safe from this dreaded disease, who was?

Since there was no cure, the main focus was on prevention. My mother's preventive measures were: going to the beach, getting plenty of sunshine, and staying away from crowded indoor places. This was not always possible to do because we had to go to school and we couldn't go to the beach all the time. We did go to the movies once a week, but in general we tried to avoid crowds.

Valentina had one serious health concern about going to the beach. At the south end of Cowell's Beach, near the Santa Cruz Municipal Wharf, there was a big drainpipe. The pipe was capped most of the time, but, sporadically, someone would uncap it, and water would gush out and flow like a river onto the beach and then into the ocean. I think the flow of water came from the storm sewers under the streets of Santa Cruz. Because the water flowing out of the drainpipe was warmer than the ocean water, kids and adults alike played and swam in it. Valentina refused to allow us to go into that stream of water. She firmly believed that the water was contaminated and could cause polio. My mother became so concerned that the water could contaminate the portion of the ocean where we swam, that she moved our spot from Cowell's Beach, to the beach on the other side of the Municipal Wharf. (The site is now famous for the professional volleyball tournaments played there today.) I guess she believed that the flow of water could not contaminate the ocean that far away. Valentina might have been right. We survived the Polio epidemic and today the open drainpipe at Cowell's beach is no more.

On special occasions, our parents gave us some loose change to go play the games at the Penny Arcade, which was located at the north entrance of the Santa Cruz Beach Boardwalk. In those days, loose change went a long way at the Arcade because it still had machines that actually accepted pennies. For one cent, I could actually watch the entire Joe Louis v. Max Schmeling fight of 1938, on one of those old-fashioned hand-cranked movie machines. These machines contained sequential still photographs that came into view, one after the other, as a hand crank, located on the outside, was turned. This created the illusion that the fighters were actually moving and boxing. The faster the cranking, the faster the fighters fought. On the other hand, you could also watch the whole fight in slow motion, by cranking very slowly. My eyes must have peered through the viewer on the top of that machine a hundred times. Each time they would see my boyhood idol, Joe Louis, batter Schmeling to the canvass in the very first round.[59] (Let me see—that would be about one dollar's worth of pennies. Such extravagance!)

Also for a penny, Reno and Lido loved to play a particular baseball machine. This machine contained baseball player figurines standing on a miniature baseball field. Each fielder had a hole strategically placed in front of him. On the other hand, the umpire, who was affixed directly behind the pitcher, had a hole implanted in the middle of his stomach. As the machine was set in motion, the pitcher leaned back and a small, round steel ball rolled out of the umpire's belly, and then dropped into the pitcher's mitt. With ball in hand, the pitcher sprang forward, delivering the pitch to the plate. The batter (controlled by the paying customer) attempted to hit the ball as it crossed the plate, by means of depressing a lever at the front of the machine. When the lever was depressed, a spring-loaded metal bat in the batter's box swept across the "plate." The object of the game was to hit the ball, either into the stands or in between the fielders avoiding the holes in front of them. Actually, Reno and Lido got a bigger kick in watching the ball roll out of the umpire's belly than they did in getting a hit. Each time the ball rolled out of the umpire's stomach, they would start to laugh and shriek. Who cared where the ball went. So much fun for so little money. Computer games of today are much more realistic; however, in my mind the "hole-in-his-belly umpire" has proved to be irreplaceable. (Actually, the umpire was quite unforgiving. It seemed to me that every time the batter let a ball go by without swinging the bat, his right arm would go up, signaling a strike.)

Perhaps, on a Sunday or two during the summer, the Comelli, Cantarutti and Taurian families would join together to stroll down the Boardwalk. The Santa Cruz Boardwalk has changed a great deal since then. Most notably, the once-famous indoor Plunge, an enormous swimming pool whose mixture of ocean salt water and chlorinated water tended to sting the eyes and infect the swimmers with telltale red eyeballs, has been replaced by a miniature golf facility. On the other hand, three main attractions—the Merry-go Round, the Bumping Cars, and the Roller Coaster—are still there today. Of the four, the Bumping Car attraction was our favorite. Smashing into one another seemed a great way to work off our excess energy. As we grew older and gained body weight and strength, our "smashes" became more violent. Once in awhile, the operator had to "shut us down," giving fair warning that head-on crashes were not allowed and that further violations were cause for ejection. *Porca la miseria!* Can't kids have fun anymore?

The only Santa Cruz Boardwalk game I ever saw Bronco participate in (he was probably in his mid-forties at the time) was throwing baseballs at dummies—with colorfully painted faces—dressed to represent "tramps." The tramps, rolled in and out of doorways of "Hobo Alley," stiffly turning their heads from side to side as they went by. This concession is no longer there, but for many years customers attempted to win a prize or two by knocking the hinged metal caps off the top of the tramps' heads. I don't remember Bronco ever winning a prize, but he seemed to get a big kick out of hearing the smack of the baseball as it hit a tramp right in the noggin. Bronco had a pretty good fastball, but I think his control was a bit off. Either that, or maybe, he was actually trying to knock the poor tramp's head off.

I can't leave the Boardwalk scene without telling the reader about Tom the Cop.[60] For years this man patrolled the "walk" and in all that time, I seldom saw him with a partner. Tom looked like one of those old-time Irish cops. He was of medium height with a slender, wiry body. Tom seldom smiled, and with a firmly set jaw and piercing eyes to accentuate his stoic, leathery face, he sent an unmistakable message to everyone who looked upon him. "Don't mess up, because I'm very serious about my business."

At that time, the type of cliental on the Boardwalk was probably more law abiding then they are now; however, to patrol alone without the means of portable communication was still courageous. Instead of a handheld radio to alert him, a loud buzzer-sounding alarm, with preset signals (presumably to designate approximately where the trouble was brewing), could be heard from one end of the Boardwalk to the other. After the sounding of the alarm, Tom could be seen quickly walking (never running) to the location of the disturbance. Somehow, when Tom arrived at the scene, things seemed to quiet down in a big hurry. This was even true when an unruly group outnumbered him. In this vein, I always tried to remember Tom when I was faced with similar situations as a policeman. Be resolute and never let them know that you are afraid, no matter what the odds. A policeman in uniform, with the proper demeanor, can do amazing things. Thanks, Tom. I never forgot your example.

One summer, we altered our beach-going routine. It must have been *circa* 1946, because I remember discussing with Reno the second Joe Louis v. Billy Con fight.[61]

Evelina and my mother had rented a house in Felton. The house was big enough to accommodate the two families quite comfortably. (My father and Guido had to work and were not with us.) Felton is located about six miles east of Santa Cruz, on U.S. Highway 9. Felton, because it is inland from the coast, has far less fog and is much warmer than Santa Cruz. The house was situated across from the former Big Trees Park—now Henry Cowell Redwood State Park. (The house is still there at 106 Redwood Drive at Highway 9.) Since the San Lorenzo River ran near the park, we had great fun that summer, swimming and riding the water currents on inflated tire inner tubes.

Phil Taurian had an inner tube that supposedly came from the front tire of an old World War II bomber. He always brought it along when he visited us. When the Cantaruttis came, we made sure that they first went over to the Taurians' house and borrowed it for our use. We were "top dogs," and the envy of all the other kids on the beach, when we rode the river current or the ocean waves, sitting on top of that huge inner tube.

One-day Reno, attempting to get to the river by taking a short cut across Highway 9, severely sprained an ankle while going down the steep embankment near the house. Evelina thought that Reno had broken his leg. To make sure he hadn't, Valentina drove him to Dr. A. E. Allegrini's office in Santa Cruz, where he was checked over.[62]

After determining that Reno's ankle was only sprained, Dr. Allegrini gave him some pain pills and sent him home. Once back home, and not being entirely satisfied with the treatment prescribed, Valentina made one of her famous "medical" concoctions. She beat up a bunch of egg whites and poured the batter onto a white cheesecloth. She then wrapped the "medicated" cloth loosely around the swollen ankle. To prevent the egg whites from seeping through, she wrapped a towel over the cheesecloth. When the egg whites dried they formed a crusty "cast." In the morning, Valentina removed the cast and re-applied fresh egg whites, as needed. Reno said that it indeed made him feel better and that the swelling in the ankle actually went down. (My mother used this concoction many times on my brother and me when we had a sprain. I swear that it did make the injury feel better and the swelling did go down.)

Well, the story does not end there. I remember that I did a very bad thing. While recovering from his injury, Reno, with the aid of a cane, was only able to walk very gingerly. We were still at the house in Felton and I can remember that he was going down the steps of the front porch, ever so slowly. I was behind him and I guess I got tired of waiting. I gave him a push. (Again that "devil guy" made me do it.) Fortunately, Reno was able to hop down the steps on one foot and saved himself from further injury. As you can imagine, he became quite angry and yelled at me. He threw down his cane and started after me, but because of his injury, he was unable to get me. I don't remember the exact punishment I received for that little episode, but I think that Evelina once again interceded, and I got by with only a severe tongue lashing and more *Dio Bouno's* on my behalf from Valentina.

One particular summer, I remember something very special happening. Mario Taurian came down with Phil and Elso and stayed for two weeks. (This was probably the same summer that Phil introduced us to the rubber guns.) Mario, to my amazement, actually went to the beach with us. This in itself was unusual because Bronco, like most all of the *ranceri* I knew, seldom if ever went to the beach. (Bronco had those suntanned arms, but he tended to keep the rest of his body lily-white.) Not only did Mario go to the beach with us, he also wore one of those early 1930s-style bathing suits. This was the type that covered the upper part of the body, leaving only the legs, shoulders and arms exposed. The suit was beautiful. It was mostly bright red (not quite matching Mario's hair), with blue stripes.

Needless to say, Mario, who was not all that tall, but had a muscular, well built body, stood out when he pranced on the beach,

La Nostra Costa (Our Coast)

wearing his antique bathing suit. We laughed and snickered as Mario, clad in his flamboyant costume (the only thing missing was a red cape), rushed past us and dove into the ocean surf. Our snickers turned into shouts of amazement as Mario swam way out into the deep. Mario was an excellent swimmer. Once out there he waved back at us as we stood wide-eyed on the shore. We kids could never go way out there. The rule imposed on us by our mothers was that our feet always had to touch bottom. Since none of us was very tall at the time, this rule limited us to staying very close to the shore. On the other hand, there was Mario way out there. Was his swimming costume making Mario a "super-swimmer"?

The question was soon answered when Mario, noticing that he was the only male on the beach wearing this particular style of swimsuit, asked Valentina to cut off the top. The next time we went to the beach, Mario was wearing only the bottom part of the swimming suit, leaving his muscular upper body exposed to the sun. This, of course, gave him a more contemporary look. We now waited anxiously for Mario to take his plunge into the ocean. Off he went, racing towards the surf and diving headfirst into an oncoming wave. As he swam further and further into the deep, it became quite evident to us that Mario had "super" swimming powers even without being dressed in his full costume.

Mario may not have been a "super hero," but he sure could do some amazing things when it came to swimming.

Several years later (in 1977), my father and I had an opportunity to visit Mario in Zoppola, Italy, where he had gone to live. Unfortunately, Mario had just been released from the hospital. There before us stood this much older man, his once red hair now turning gray, his slightly bent stature making him look shorter than what I had remembered. It was obvious that age and illness had dissipated his once muscular body. This was to be the last time that I would ever see him. Although I was happy to see Mario at that time, now I somehow wish that I hadn't made that visit. It greatly disturbed the image I had in my mind of the strong, young Mario, who could swim way out into the deep. A few years later, Mario, who was born in the same year as my father (1900), died in Italy, at the age of eighty-two.

Endnotes

[58] Four years ago, I had arthroscopy surgery on my knee. Then, instead of going to a physical therapist, my wife and I took a trip to Maui, Hawaii. There for two weeks, I used Valentina's sand and sea treatment. I swam in the ocean and then buried my knee in the hot sand. It worked beautifully. At the end of the two-week vacation, my knee was much stronger and the swelling had noticeably diminished.

[59] In 1936, Max Schmeling, a native born German, and a former Heavyweight Champion of World, had knocked out Joe Louis in one of the biggest upsets in boxing history. At the time of their second fight, Louis was the Heavyweight Champion, having won the title in 1937 by defeating James J. Braddock, known in boxing circles as "The Cinderella Man." In 1938 Schmeling was not well liked by the American public because he was the "darling" of Hitler's Nazi party. Although his sentiments were later proved to be anti-Nazi, the party did use him at the time of the fight to further their claim that the Germans were a "superior" race. After his loss to Louis, Max fell out favor with the party, was drafted into the German Army, and saw combat as a paratrooper. He survived World War II and its aftermath. He subsequently became wealthy as a licensed representative and spokesman for the Coca-Cola Company in Europe.

Schmeling died in February, 2005. At the time of his death he was ninety-nine years old and had outlived the "Brown Bomber" by some 24 years. Although the actors portraying the two fighters seem to be undersized for their roles, the 2002, STARZ presentation "JOE and MAX", now available on DVD, gives a fair account of their story.

[60] My old college roommate, Marvin Del Chiaro, informed me that retired Santa Cruz Police Officer Bert Witte, advised him that Tom's full name was Tom Leonard. However, "da youts" of the time, simply knew him as "Tom the Cop."

[61] On June 19, of that year, "The Brown Bomber," knocked out Billy Con in the eighth round to retain the World's Heavyweight Championship. It was the first fight ever televised, although most of us listened to Hall of Fame announcer, Don Dunphy broadcast the fight over the radio. Like most Americans at the time, we did not have a television set.

[62] Dr. A. E. (Chick) Allegrini, was the son of Ignio Allegrini, an Italian emigrant, born in Lucca, Italy. Because he understood and spoke Italian, he naturally was a favorite among the *ranceri* and their families. When I first was his patient, Dr. Allegrini, who I thought bore a resemblance to Bing Crosby, had an office on Soquel Avenue, near the old Santa Cruz Hospital. Later he moved his practice to an office on Mission Street near Bay.

COWELL'S BEACH

PIA MAZZEI – VALENTINA AND HER BOYS – C. 1945

AL MARE

CANTARUTTI AND COMELLI BOYS – C. 1947

16. Figli Di Ferro (Sons Of Iron)

The Gemignani family house—and our house at the Gulch Ranch—were the only two on the east side of that portion of U.S. Highway 1, which stretched north from what now is Dimeo Lane, to the edge of the gulch. The Gemignani house was very similar to ours, in that it had two bedrooms, one bath, a kitchen, and a living room. Although the living area of the house was on one level, the house itself was raised to allow for a cellar and crawl space beneath. It was in this musty smelling cellar that I have my first memories of Aladino Gemignani.

I must have been about four years old and I remember visiting with Aladino as he was working in the cellar. Apparently my mother didn't know that I was there, because I remember her calling for me in a very loud tone of voice. I told Aladino that I didn't want to go home just then. I found Aladino to be most accommodating in this matter, because he told me to wait until she called again. Valentina called me again. I asked him if I should go now? "No," he replied, "Aspetta che chiama una volta ancora." ("Wait for her to call one more time.") I thought this was a fun game. Valentina called again, this time with a little more authority in her voice. "Ora," Aladino said. "Va casa." ("Now, go home.") I didn't want to end the game; I told Aladino that I didn't want to go home. Aladino, in a calm, reassuring voice, persuaded me to go home by saying that my mother would be really mad if I didn't go now. He was right. Valentina was not too pleased with me when I finally arrived home. But when I told her that I was visiting with Aladino, she didn't seem to mind too much.

Aladino was married to Argentina (Biancalana). They had three sons, Constantino (Augie) the oldest, then Lido, and then Giovanni Giuseppe (Joe), the youngest. They also had an older, married daughter, Marietta, who remained in Italy. All of the Gemignanis were born in the Tuscany region of Italy; thus they were Toscanos. Aladino had immigrated to the United States first, in 1912, then Argentina and the three boys came over in 1932. At the time that I knew Aladino, he was one of the partners in the Gulch Ranch. He was also the cook. I remember that he had a reputation of being a smart businessman and a good cook. I also remember that Bronco liked him very much, and I too get warm feelings when I think about him. Unfortunately, I only knew Aladino for a brief time. Aladino, only in his early fifties, was stricken with cancer and died in 1943. I was six years old at the time.

Aladino's death meant that Argentina and the three boys had to fend for themselves. Of course, the three youths were all much older than my brother and me. Joe, the youngest, was born in 1920, so all three had to be in their twenties when I first started interacting with them. Most of my memories were of Joe, who stayed at the house the longest. I remember Lido being at the house, only briefly. Augie, was already married and living away from the house. However, I do remember Augie and his wife Victoria (Ghio), who was also known as Sista, often coming to visit Argentina with their little girl named Aladina (Aldine). I would always say that Aldine was my very first girl friend because, in truth, she was the first little girl I ever got to play with. Tragically, Aldine died in 1960 at the very young age of twenty-two. According to Sista, Aldine died of Lupine's disease, complicated by kidney failure. (Augie maintains to this day that the doctors were at fault for giving her the wrong medication.) Fortunately, Augie and Sista had another little girl named Donna, who helped them get through this very dark and sad period in their lives.

As I recall, Lido, although not married, was gone from the house most of the time. I remember that he had the reputation of liking the girls and loving to dance. In fact, Lido often told the story about the time, during World War II, when he was arrested for dancing. This tale has now been properly documented in a piece written by Geoffrey Dunn, entitled, "Mala Notte" ("Bad Night"), appearing in the book, *Una Storia Segreta*.

According to Dunn, Lido was arrested in 1942, with his friend Louis Aluffi, while dancing at the Coconut Grove Beach Ballroom, in Santa Cruz. Unfortunately, they were dancing in a restricted area (too close to the Pacific Ocean) after the 9:00 p.m. curfew. Remember those restrictions imposed on Italians during the war? The U.S. government was serious about them. To make sure that Lido and Louis now understood this, they sent them to federal prison and detained them for more than two weeks. (Such a price for "cutting a rug"!) As I recall, Lido never served in the armed forces (due to a medical deferment) during the war. However, Dunn states that Aluffi, who had already enlisted in the Army prior to his arrest, eventually got to participate in the invasion of Germany. I guess the U.S. government had decreed that he was good enough to serve, but not to dance.

My very first memories of Joe, were of him riding his motorcycle around the house. (I think his first motor was an Indian.) He loved that motorcycle. I also liked his motorcycle. I remember that he used to park it in the garage next to his house. As I recall, the garage had been partially converted to a *capannone,* to allow my mother and Argentina to clean sprouts. I was too young to be left alone. Apparently Valentina had convinced the Gulch Partnership to add a couple of those hinged folding tables to one side of the garage. Thus, she could walk directly from our house to the garage, taking little Ivano with her; while she cleaned sprouts, she could keep an eye on little old me.

While she worked, I often went over to Joe's motorcycle and admired it. Then, when I thought no one was looking, I seated myself on the machine and squeezed the handle bars where the throttle and the brakes were, pretending all the while that I was flying down the road, doing a hundred miles an hour.

Later in the day, Joe got up, usually with a hangover, and attempted to start his motorcycle. Most of the time he had a very hard time "cranking it over." In those days, there was no such thing as an electric starter for motorcycles. You had to kick-start the engine using a foot pedal on the side of the motor. I watched with amazement as Joe, who was six foot tall and skinny as a rail, jumped on that pedal, with the weight of his whole body pushing down on one leg, trying time-after-time to kick-start the motor. While doing this, he began to swear to the high heavens—because it just wouldn't "kick over" for him. During these episodes, I tried to hide, shrinking back in a corner, convinced that I had done something really bad to that motorcycle. Finally, much to my relief, Joe got the engine to "kick over" and the motorcycle started. Then, with a few last endearing swear words, he calmly took his leather fighter pilot's cap, with earflaps and goggles, and put it on over his head. Slipping the goggles over his eyes, he gunned the engine, and with a roar (sometimes with a couple of backfires) took off down the Coast Road towards Santa Cruz. As the reader can imagine, this was all very exciting stuff for a boy of three or four. (The best of these sessions were when the motorcycle engine started and then, inexplicably, quit on him just as he was taking off down the road. The cuss words then reigned supreme.)

Now, my mental vision of Joe getting ready to ride his motorcycle, is glamorized by images of actors who play the part of fighter pilots, such as John Wayne in the World War II movie, "Flying Tigers."[63] As he climbs into the cockpit of his P-40 airplane, John Wayne is wearing a pilot cap with goggles. His "flying helmet," as the military called them, reminds me of the one Joe wore on his motorcycle rides. Regardless of the name these caps were given, they were not safety helmets by any stretch of the imagination.

Joe palled around with Freddie Dimeo, Fernando Moro and Albie Rossi. Known in some quarters (perhaps only in their own minds), as the *Figli* [**feel** yee] *di Ferro* (Sons of Iron), you might say they were *La Nostra Costa's* version of the Rat Pack.[64]

Joe's best friend was Freddie Dimeo, who lived about one half mile east of us, not too far from what was then known as the City Dump, or *Il Dumpo*, as the *ranceri* called it. (The road to his house now bears his family name.) Being young and energetic, Joe and Freddie often got themselves into trouble while carousing *su per la costa* and in Santa Cruz. As the story goes, Joe Scaroni, a landowner and rancher, who had substantial influence with the local draft board, got tired of their antics. He exerted his influence and had them made "1A" for local call-up and induction into the Army. (I heard this story as told to me by Joe Gemignani, and I believe he said that Santa Cruz Municipal Court Judge James J. Scoppettone was the one who had had them drafted. Fred Moro, who heard the story from Fred Dimeo, and who passed away in August 2003, had in turn told him that it was in fact Joe Scaroni who'd done it. Scoppettone or Scaroni, the deal was sealed.) Freddie and Joe were drafted and spent the duration of the war overseas. Although they did not serve together, they both survived the war and later met in Berlin after hostilities had ceased. In civilian life, Freddie and Joe remained lifelong friends. Later, as we shall see, Joe's Army service in Europe was going to become very important to the Comelli family.

The next thing I can remember about Joe was his returning home from the war. One day I just happened to be standing outside his bedroom window (probably waiting for him to appear.) All of a sudden, the window opened and Joe leaned out, and he said in a loud voice, "Hey Ivano! Ti piace il ghiaccio fritto?" [tee pee **yah**'cheh eel **gee**' yacho **free**' toh], which simply means, "Do you like fried ice?" Thinking that it was something delicious he was offering me, I answered, "Si." Joe then laughed with his high pitched, infectious laugh and went back inside.[65]

The Army did not mend Joe's ways. Once home, he picked up right where he left off. That meant getting back to his motorcycle and motorcycle-riding friends. One of his buddies was Fernando Moro. As the reader might recall, Fernando was the son of Silvio and Elena Moro of Davenport. Like Joe and Fred, Fernando was also a World War II veteran. He was not as fortunate as they were. In 1944, He was captured and made a prisoner-of-war by the Germans, and remained in their custody until the war was over.

I thought that Fernando had the best motorcycle of the group, and he always kept it in pristine condition. His motorcycle was also one of the loudest. You could hear Fernando coming from a very long way off. He usually started his journey from his home in Davenport and came south on the Coast Road. I can still remember the vibrating sound of his motorcycle approaching the gulch, then quickly descending into *il buco* before roaring up the steep grade. Rushing to the side of the road, I would see Fernando, perhaps for only a split second—hunched over on the handlebars, dressed in a black leather jacket and black leather pilot's hat with the goggles pulled over his eyes—flashing by with a burst of speed. On his trip back from Santa Cruz, I could hear the roar of his motorcycle as it approached the bend near the Rodoni Ranch. Whoosh! Like *il vento*, Fernando and his motorcycle blew by the house, going down into the gulch and up the grade on the other side. All the while his motorcycle's engine roared like an angry, attacking beast. I continued to listen to its loud growling sound until it faded completely away, *su per la costa*. I swear that, on a quiet evening, I could hear that "angry beast" all the way up to Davenport. (Fernando recently informed me that at different times during his riding days, he had owned a Harley and a Triumph motorcycle. Of the two, he thought that the Triumph was the loudest.)

You might think that with all this motorcycle excitement around me, I would grow up to be an avid motorcycle rider. Well, for two years as a police lieutenant in 1978 and 1979, I did command the elite Motorcycle Traffic Unit in San Jose. But I never did ride a motorcycle. Maybe this was because of something that happened to Joe, *circa* 1946.

He was riding with Albie Rossi, one of his "Rat Pack" friends, on a slippery road (Graham Hill Road) in Santa Cruz. Going down a hill, Joe lost control of his motorcycle, which caused him to fall off and break his leg. He was lucky that he did not sustain head injuries. (Remember, they didn't wear safety helmets in those days.) I can still remember Joe, sitting on a couch in his home, with this great, big cast on his leg, complaining about the pain.

The pain must not have been all that bad, because I also remember Joe driving his brother's Pontiac with one foot. This was no easy task, since the car had a stick shift under the steering wheel, with a foot clutch on the floor. With his one good foot, Joe manipulated the clutch, brake, and gas pedal. It got a bit tricky when he had to stop. By positioning his one good foot sideways, he could step on the brake and clutch at the same time, bringing the car to a stop without killing the engine. Joe always seemed to find a way to get around.

Again *circa* 1946 or 1947, I remember Joe getting my father involved in a really weird episode. One night—it must have been after midnight—we heard Joe outside our house shouting in Italian, "Bronco, Bronco! Get up! They stola my car!" Joe apparently had left his car keys in the ignition of his old 1932 Ford. Someone, perhaps hitchhikers, had spotted the car parked in Joe's yard and decided—Joe being so accommodating by leaving the keys in the ignition—to ride instead of walk. Joe had been awakened when the perpetrators started the car, and actually saw them drive away, headed north towards Davenport. Over my mother's objections, my father and Joe both got in the Old Carrettone and with Joe at the wheel started after the culprits. Joe, thinking that he needed a faster car for the chase, drove into *il buco* and enlisted the services of Dante Ramaciotti, one of the Gulch Ranch partners, who owned a newer-model Buick. He also had a 12-gauge shotgun, which he gave to Joe—just in case. Getting into the Buick, the trio, now armed and dangerous, drove out of *il buco* and sped north after the thieves, just like in those old gangster movies.

They were gone for what seemed hours. Valentina was worried to death and was trying to keep my brother and me calm. Finally, Joe and Bronco came back. They never did catch the car stealers. Apparently against Joe's wishes, my father and Ramaciotti had decided to break off the chase when they reached *La Slida*, at the

San Mateo county line. The next day, the Highway Patrol found the vehicle, abandoned and completely wrecked, just north of that area. Afterwards, Joe never would let my father forget—saying, "See, Bronco? I told you, if we would have kept going, we would have caught those sonnabitchas."

After reading the above account of that wild ride *su per la costa*, the reader might now want to ask, What would Joe have done with that shotgun, if they had indeed caught up with the culprits? I don't know and I'm glad we didn't have to find out. Fortunately, soon thereafter, my aunt came to live with us, and Joe's motorcycle riding and shotgun toting days were brought to an abrupt end. Thus, as destiny would have it, this *Figlio di Ferro* was about to be saved by a certain *Figlia del Friuli*.

Endnotes

[63] "Flying Tigers," Republic Pictures, 1942, starring John Wayne, John Carrol and Anna Lee, directed by David Miller.

[64] According to Freddie Dimeo, it was a *rancere* named Maccario who dubbed them *Figli di Ferro*. The name alluded not only to their machines, but also to the riders' abilities to cope with the many bumps and bruises sustained while riding them.

[65] Such a silly phrase, but I never did forget it. In 1998, Joe was lying semi-comatose in a hospital bed, dying from cancer; I gently leaned over him and said, "Hey Joe. Ti piace il ghiaccio fritto?" A big smile came over his face. He had heard me and he remembered. Sadly, these were the last words I ever said to my uncle before he passed away. *Adio, Figlio di Ferro.*

FIGLI DI FERRO IN BERLIN

JOE AND FRED 1945

TWO FIGLI DI FERRO RIDE AGAIN IN SANTA CRUZ

JOE AND FRED – C. 1945

A FIGLIO DI FERRO AND HIS "ANGRY BEAST"
FERNANDO MORO – 1950

17. Lina

Lina Bressani was my mother's youngest sister. She was born and raised in Nimis, Italy. She was sixteen years old when Mussolini, *Il Duce*, brought Italy into World War II on the side of Nazi Germany (1940). Lina's story is one of survival during a very brutal period under German occupation. To give some background on her life during this period, I relied heavily on her unpublished book, *My Yesterdays*.

In July 1943, the Italians, sensing that the war was lost, ousted Mussolini from power. The ever-suspicious Hitler did not trust the Royal Family of Italy, nor Marshal Badoglio, whom they appointed to take over from Mussolini. Withdrawing precious troops from the Russian front, Hitler made preparations to invade Italy. In September 1943, the new Italian government signed an armistice with the Allies, secretly agreeing to join with them in the war against Nazi Germany. As soon as the armistice was signed, Hitler ordered his troops to take control of northern and central Italy. On October 13, 1943, Italy, under Marshal Badoglio's government in the south, declared war on Germany. The Nazis in the occupied zones quickly disarmed the Italian army. Hitler, subsequently, placed the deposed Mussolini in charge of a puppet Fascist government in the north, thus thrusting Italy into a civil war.[66] Attempts were made to coerce Italian men to join the army of the "new" Fascist regime. If they refused to join, they and their families were threatened with being shot or imprisoned as traitors. Many former Italian soldiers who refused were actually interned in Germany.

Despite the severe consequences of being captured, many Italians chose to oppose Mussolini and Hitler's army of occupation. Retreating into the hills to hide, they formed partisan groups called *partigiani* [parr **tee** johnny] and in 1944, using guerilla tactics, they commenced to fight the Nazis and Mussolini's puppet government in earnest. Because a very important railroad, going to and from German occupied territories, passed near Nimis, the little town became a prime focus for the *partigiani* to do their sabotage.

The citizens of Nimis were caught in the middle. The Nazis had decreed that for every German killed by *partigiani*, a certain number of civilians would be killed in retribution and their houses burned to the ground. Lina, in her book, recounts that the *partigiani* came down from the mountains during the night, attacking Nazi headquarters, bridges, and the railroad. In the meantime, Lina and her family hid in the wine cellar in order to avoid the gun exchanges above ground. In the daytime the Nazis took their revenge on the citizens of Nimis. Families were taken from their homes, their houses soaked with gasoline and burned to the ground. Many were shot to death.

To make matters worse, the Germans imported Cossacks from Russia to defend Nimis from the *partigiani*. The Cossacks were nomads searching for a home. The Germans promised them that the Friuli region would become their home after the war. The Cossacks brought their families with them in anticipation of living in the area for a long time. In the meantime, they performed their work as an army of occupation with great zeal and brutality. They plundered, raped and killed. According to Lina's book, her father (my grandfather) almost lost his life when he tried to keep the Cossacks from stealing his two milk cows. He must have been a good talker, because he wasn't killed and he managed to keep one cow for his family.

The Cossacks did their work so well, that for a time the *partigiani* were kept at bay. However, one night in 1944 all hell broke lose. Lina and her family, hiding in the wine cellar, heard explosions and sustained machine gun fire everywhere. The *partigiani* had managed to mount a major attack against the Cossacks and succeeded in driving them out of Nimis. For a few days Nimis was "liberated." This infuriated the German Command. Soon thereafter, the German Army counter-attacked and re-took the town, driving the *partigiani* and many of the civilians back into the hills. After the fighting was over, the Germans coaxed the civilians into returning, promising that nothing would happen to them. Many of the citizens, including Lina, returned, only to be made prisoners by the Germans.

Once captured, the Germans made the citizens of Nimis form two lines. One line consisted of older people and women with babies. Many of the people in this line were sent to concentration camps. Some were never heard from again. The other line consisted of younger persons without children. Lina and her older brother Tita, were placed in the latter line and then taken to the provincial city of Udine, about 30 miles south of Nimis. (During this trek, Tita managed to escape and eventually survived the war.) Once the civilians were out of Nimis, the Germans, in retribution for the uprising, set the little town afire. Lina took note. This was how Hitler's treacherous soldiers dealt with insurrection.

In Udine, Lina, along with several other young Italian women, were taken to a building that was serving as the Nazi's SS headquarters. There these young women were given the tasks of cooking, cleaning, and serving the SS officers, in whatever manner the SS chose. They were told that if they did not comply, or if they tried to escape, they would be killed and, in addition, their families would be found and also killed. Having first-hand knowledge of the brutality that could be inflicted by these hardened Nazi bastards, Lina did not try to escape and spent the duration of the Nazi occupation (seven months) serving the SS in that building. The Friuli region remained under German occupation until near the end of the war, in May 1945.

Once liberated by the Allied Forces, Lina returned to Nimis. There she hoped to start her life anew with her family. Fortunately, the Bressani family had all survived. As I have previously stated, my paternal grandmother, Carolina Comelli, was not as fortunate. It was during this period that she was killed, when she accidentally picked up that live electrical wire that had been knocked down during the fighting.

However, the hard times were not over for Lina. Members of the *partigiani* demanded retribution against those Italians they believed had collaborated with the Nazis. Because Lina had been forced to work for the SS, she became a prime target. One night she was taken without warning from her home by three masked Italians. She was told that she was a collaborator because she had not tried to escape from the SS. Lina tried to state her case. She pleaded that she was afraid that her family would be killed. Her words fell on deaf ears. These supposedly patriotic Italians then cut her hair. This would shame her and alert anyone who saw her that she had been a collaborator. The humiliation was so great that Lina decided to leave Nimis until her hair grew back. (Upon hearing this story, Bronco once again would remark, "Che bella figura fan questi Italiani.")

As unjust as this may seem, Lina probably was lucky. She writes in her book that many in that *other* line of prisoners that consisted of older people and those with babies, were shipped to the Dachau concentration camp in Germany. About 400 of them survived the camp and eventually returned to Nimis. Lina describes them as being "like trembling skeletons, with no resemblance of who they used to be."

Although she eventually decided to return to Nimis, I think Lina still harbored a deep resentment towards those who had marked her as a collaborator. This and the fact that the Friuli region in general, and the Bressani family in particular, was having a hard time recovering from the war, convinced Lina to look elsewhere for a better life. That elsewhere was America. Lina wrote to her sister Valentina, asking for help in coming to the United States. It was under these circumstances that my mother came up with a plan that would eventually bring her youngest sister to *la costa*.

Lina's story of her immigration to America was somewhat different from the stories recounted by other Italian families who had survived the war. For example, members of the Degli Esposti, Donatini, and Orlando families, came over a year or so after my aunt had arrived. They were sponsored by families and friends already here, who promised that the newly arrived immigrants would not become a burden on the United States because they would have jobs here. Chicanery could be kept to a minimum.

On the other hand, because of lingering wartime paranoia against former enemies, and the economic uncertainties (jobs needed to be found for all those returning GIs) in the United States, it was very difficult to immigrate to the United States in the period immediately after the war, from 1945 to 1947. America had strict quotas on how many persons could emigrate from Europe. However, the Americans made an exception for World War II veterans who had served in Europe. If a GI met a girl in Europe and then decided to marry her, he could then apply to have that girl come to the United States. Knowing this, Valentina figured that if she could convince a certain, unsuspecting *Figlio di Ferro* to go along with her plan, she might succeed in bringing her sister to the United States as a "war bride." Normally, this would not be an easy task, even under the best of circumstances. Toscanos did not usually marry Friulanas. However, our relationship with the Gemignani family was such that Valentina believed this to be the least of her obstacles.

The plan was to have Joe Gemignani say that he had met Lina while he was in the Army serving in Europe and that he now planned to marry her. Part of this was true. Joe had served with a military unit in Europe, but he had not met Lina during that time. Valentina, armed with a picture of this beautiful twenty-one-year-old blonde Italian girl, approached Joe and told him of her plan. Seeing the picture, Joe immediately became interested. It didn't take too much to convince him to go along with the rest of the plan. When Lina arrived here, Joe was to marry her. If they did not like each other, or could not otherwise get along, either Joe or Lina could sue for divorce. Of course, they would have to stay married long enough to convince the immigration authorities that the marriage was a legitimate piece of work. According to Lina's book, if the marriage did not work out, my mother had agreed to pay all of Joe's expenses, plus $500 for his troubles. Such a deal for *questo* (this) *Figlio di Ferro!*

As I remember it, there was one small problem. Lina now had a boyfriend in Italy. Immigrating to America meant giving him up. I think Lina had some real concerns about doing this. However, given the situation in Italy at the time, and the prospects of a better life in America, Lina eventually agreed. The stage was set for Lina to meet Joe.

The year was 1947. You must remember that outside of our immediate family, my brother and I did not have any known relatives living in the United States. This would be a first. A real live aunt, right here *su per la costa*. We waited with great anticipation for her arrival.

As the days got closer, it seemed that greater and greater complications set in. I remember Valentina being frantic. Somewhere between Italy and New York, Lina had gotten herself lost. Apparently, the person from the travel agency had failed to make contact with her when she disembarked in New York. A desperate Lina managed to make a telephone call to the Gulch Ranch cookhouse. (Remember that box telephone that hung on the dining room wall: It sure came in handy this time.) Valentina got the word and quickly made contact with Lina, finding out where she was. She then telephoned the travel agency in New York, and had one of their representatives make contact with her forlorn sister. The representative then made arrangements for Lina to stay at a hotel while she waited for her plane. More complications. According to Lina's book, a giant snowstorm hit the New York area. All planes were grounded. Lina had to spend three days in a hotel room, by herself, waiting for the snowstorm to lift. Worse yet, these three days included Christmas Eve and Christmas Day, 1947. One can only imagine the anxiety and loneliness that Lina must have experienced. She was alone in a strange land, unable to speak English.

Meanwhile, back at the ranch, I remember my brother and I playing with our Christmas presents. One game we had received was called "Sorry." We were playing "Sorry" on the couch in the living room when my mother came in and announced, with some sense of excitement in her voice, that Lina had been put on a train and was now en route to "Colliefornia." Apparently, the travel agency had decided not to wait any longer for the storm to clear up. Lina was running out of money and needed to get on the road. The train seemed to be the reasonable alternative. Thus, Lina was to make her trip to *la costa* in the same manner as my mother and father had, several years before.

Finally, the day came when Lina was to arrive in San Francisco. Joe, his mother Argentina, along with Sista, Augie's wife, and Valentina, went to San Francisco to pick her up. I remember that my brother and I spent the day with the Rodoni family, waiting for her arrival. It was in the early evening hours when the car with Lina finally arrived at the Rodoni Ranch. I greeted Lina with a kiss on the cheek, just like my mother told me to do. I remember Lina saying, "Chi e questo?" ("Who is this?") Then for the first time, my mother introduced my brother and me to our aunt. There was much celebration. However, Lina looked very tired, so we took her to our house for a bath and much needed rest. Lina had finally arrived, safely, at the little house *su per la costa*.

At first, all did not go smoothly. We were all strangers to one another. The last time Valentina had seen her sister, Lina had been seven or eight years old. She was now twenty-three years old, a grown woman. But Valentina was a take-charge woman and quickly started telling Lina what to do and what not to do. Lina went along with it, but I'm sure she had a mind of her own, and could not help resenting some of my mother's advice. Also, it must have been hard for Lina. She had left her family in Italy and now she had to live in this very small house with a strange family. My brother and I didn't make it any easier for her. A young lady does need her privacy.

There was not much privacy with my brother and I lurking about. As I recall, Lina slept on the couch in the living room. To get to the bathroom, she would have to go through our bedroom. Valentina, knowing that Lina needed some time to herself, did her best to keep us out of her way. However, we kept bumping into each other.

After awhile, it became difficult for my brother and me to find things to say to her. Yes, we were thrilled to death to have her with us—but what boys aged eleven and fourteen had in common with a twenty-three-year-old woman, we hardly knew. She was also taking up space, our space. We could no longer romp and stomp through the house freely. Worse, when she first arrived, she gave us a good case of the *Pidocchi* ([pee **doh** kee], head lice, or so my mother thought.

Valentina prided herself in being clean and keeping us clean. This was very hard to do since we lived on a farm. We were always getting dirty and she was constantly after us to clean up. Well, soon after Lina arrived from Italy our whole family came down with a bad case of head lice. *Pidocchi,* as Valentina called them, sent her into a tizzy. She was afraid that she would be tainted as an ignorant, low-class Italian mother, unable to keep her family clean. She quickly blamed Lina for bringing over the pests on the boat. In reality that's probably where she got them, mingling with all those strange immigrants. On the other hand, my brother or I might have brought them back from school. Nobody will ever know for sure, but Lina got the blame.

Valentina got in the Old Carrettone and rushed to Mission Drugs, on the corner of Mission and Bay streets in Santa Cruz. There she bought some anti-*Pidocchi* shampoo and medicine. Twice a day, thereafter, she shampooed and medicated our hair. Not being satisfied with a simple medicated shampoo, she submitted us to further torture by combing our hair with a very fine-toothed comb, making sure that any *Pidocchi* egg left behind got the boot. This must have gone on for weeks on end, our scalps being grated with that infernal comb. Finally, our heads stopped itching and the *Pidocchi* were gone, never to return. Valentina saw to that by continuing to inspect our heads on a daily basis for a long time, even after the head lice had ceased to exist. She made darn sure that her good housekeeping reputation *su per la costa* remained safe.

Meanwhile, Lina and Joe's courtship commenced. This was very interesting for my brother and I to observe. Joe usually came over and sat with Lina in our living room. He often stayed late into the night. My brother and I, sleeping in the room next to the living room, would all of a sudden be awakened by Lina's laughter. Joe had a muffled laugh that could hardly be heard; Lina had a loud, hearty laugh that woke up the whole house. Once awakened, we put our ears to the wall and listened in to their conversation, trying to figure out what was going on. I guess something was going on because the courtship progressed. Well, not all that smoothly.

I think Lina was still keeping in contact with her old flame in Italy. Also, after going out with Joe a few times and observing his wild ways, I think that she may have formed some doubts in her mind about this *Figlio di Ferro*. Joe, on the other hand, had no doubts about her. This was the girl he wanted to marry. I remember one particular argument between Joe and Lina that probably had to do with Joe's unruly behavior after he'd had a few drinks. Lina was ready to give it all up. She'd had enough.

Argentina, Joe's mother, sensing that Lina was serious, quickly arranged to have a talk with my mother. She told Valentina that Joe was "oh so sorry" for what he had done and that he would never do it again. Argentina said that Joe was crying his eyes out and that he would do anything to get her back meaning that he would stop drinking, change his wild behavior, etc. She pleaded with my mother to help her out. Valentina must have agreed because I remember my mother and Lina sitting in the kitchen of our house having this very serious conversation. Lina was not sure she wanted to go on with her relationship with Joe. (In her book, Lina writes that she tried to take off her engagement ring, but couldn't get it off her finger.) After a very long discussion, Valentina finally asked Lina for a final decision. Lina responded that she still wasn't sure what to do. That was the wrong response. Valentina hit the roof. In a very stern manner, my mother told Lina to make up her mind, one way or another. Valentina believed that it was unfair to have Lina lead Joe on, if she had no intention of marrying him.

I guess that got Lina's attention, because I remember, one evening shortly thereafter, Lina and Joe driving off to Las Vegas to get married (March 19, 1948). After they had departed, I saw my mother break down and cry. When I asked her, "Ma, perche piangi? [**pee** yan gee]" she answered me in Italian, saying that she was crying because Lina was her youngest sister and, in marriage no one knows what might happen. She was obviously worried that something bad might happen to Lina. Being the instigator of this whole relationship, Valentina would never have forgiven herself if something really bad did happen. At the time, my mother did have good cause to worry. During the previous year, as the reader will find out later, the marriage of a young Italian couple we knew quite well ended tragically, when the husband shot and killed his wife.

Fear not. As in any other marriage, Lina and Joe had their ups and downs. However, the marriage endured 50 years, until Joe's death in 1998. Their marriage produced two wonderful children, my cousin Joanne (Swaney), born in 1951, and my cousin and godson, Aladino (Dino), born 1960. Both of my cousins are married now and have families of their own. I constantly remind my younger cousins that all of this happened because Valentina came up with this crazy idea about her sister and the wild boy who lived next door. Who would have thought that she (or they) could have pulled it off? It's one for the books—at least for this book.

Endnotes

[66] In his biography of Benito Mussolini, author Denis Mack Smith relates that after being deposed by the King of Italy, Mussolini was made a prisoner and held captive by the Badoglio government. Hitler quickly ordered arrangements to be made to free "Il Duce." On September 12, 1943, a commando raid led by Colonel Skorzeny rescued Mussolini from a secluded mountain resort in Italy. He was then flown to meet Hitler in Germany. *MUSSOLINI, A Biography*, by Denis Mack Smith, published by Random House, Inc., New York, 1982.

THE BRESSANI FAMILY IN ITALY

C. 1934

LINA

C. 1942

UN FIGLIO DI FERRO AND HIS BRIDE
JOE AND LINA – 1948

18. Il Rancio Di Rodoni
(The Rodoni Ranch)

The Rodoni Ranch was within walking distance, about two-tenths of a mile south of our house on the Gulch. The Rodoni family house (still there, at 2691 Coast Road) was also very close to the Coast Road, but on the western side. The Rodoni Ranch compound consisted of the family house, a separate cookhouse with living quarters for the Italian ranch hands, a barn with a horse coral, and several garages and work sheds. The Coast Road to the east, the Rodoni house and barn to the north, the garages and sheds to the west, and the cook house, along with an open brussel sprout field, to the south, formed the irregular borders of the "big gravel yard." The "big gravel yard" was where we kids rode our bikes and played our games. Cowboys and Indians, rubber guns, basketball, volleyball, football—you name it; we probably played it in the yard. Although the yard was safe, at times we had to compete with incoming cars and trucks. This was especially true during the sprout-harvesting season. During the non-harvest season, traffic in the yard was sporadic and we were able to play our games without too many interruptions.

To the south, a few paces beyond the yard, stood another house. I don't remember who first lived there, but eventually it became home to the Degli Esposti family, who came to live on the Rodoni Ranch after World War II. To the immediate west of the barn and corral, standing completely separated from the main compound and the "big gravel yard," was another cookhouse, containing living quarters for the Filipino ranch hands. Conditions at Rodoni Ranch being similar to those on the Gulch Ranch, the Italian and Filipino ranch hands worked together in the fields, but did not socialize or eat together after the work was done.

Dante and Andreina Rodoni had two sons, Mario the oldest, and Elio. Jeanne, the daughter, was born a few years later, in 1943. Mario was one year younger than I was, and Elio was two-plus years younger. My first memory of this family was playing in the "big gravel yard" with Mario. Elio was there, but he was still a baby going around pestering Andreina in search for his bottle, and constantly crying, "Tee-tee, Mama! Tee-tee!" As a child, Elio was called "Bebo." Apparently, when Mario was learning to talk, he couldn't pronounce the word baby, so he did the best he could, sounding out the word "Bebo." The name stuck with Elio for quite a few years. I don't think many people call this esteemed *rancere* by that name now, but I will always affectionately remember him as Bebo. (Both Elio and Mario stayed in the ranching business, and along with their families now operate several *rancios* in Santa Cruz County.)

Dante was *il bosso* and manager of the *rancio*. He also had a share in the ranch along with three or four other partners. My family became very close to his during the early 1940s. I remember we visited them quite often at their house, and they visited us at our house. I always loved these visits (usually on a Saturday night), because they meant that I got to play indoor games with Mario and Elio. I also loved them because Dante had an eight-millimeter movie projector. When we visited at the Rodoni's house, we kids would cajole and pester Dante and Andreina into showing us movies. Remember that this was the time before TV and videotapes. Some of these movies were westerns; others were comedies or melodramas. I think Dante even had a movie starring the wonder dog Rin-Tin-Tin. Of course, all were silent films.

I still remember the feeling of great anticipation and excitement as Dante set up the white viewing screen, usually in the kitchen, and

La Nostra Costa (Our Coast)

then brought in the projector. We watched impatiently as he manually threaded in the first reel of film. He then turned off the lights and switched on the projector. A stream of light soon flickered onto the screen and the action began. Throughout the showing, because the movie was silent, you could hear the constant humming and clicking of the projector as the film treaded itself through the machine. As the movie progressed, the adults would make comments about each scene. One thing about silent films: Talking in the audience could not interfere with any movie dialogue. We watched the same films over and over again. The other kids and I never got tired of watching these films. Our parents must have gotten very tired of seeing the same old films. Nevertheless, at times they too seemed to get into a "picture show," even though everyone knew the ending.

Dante also had a movie camera, which he used extensively to document the history of his family, and of others who lived *su per la costa* during the 1930s and 1940s. He even filmed the Comelli boys, in front of their house, sawing a couple of pieces of wood. I must have been about seven or eight at the time. Recently, these films were used in a TV documentary about Davenport.[67] (When I saw the documentary for the first time, all the memories of those nights spent at the Rodoni's came back to me. In fact, viewing those film clips gave me inspiration to write this book.)

Not only was Dante a "movie entrepreneur," but he was also very mechanically inclined. In the late 1940s or early 1950s he constructed one of the first sprout-cleaning machines. This machine made the task of sprout cleaning less arduous. Dante's machine consisted of a large rotating barrel, constructed of long, curved aluminum tubes of about six feet in length and one-half to one inch in diameter. A small open space was left between each tube. An electric motor produced the power that rotated the barrel. The sprout cleaning process was set in motion by dumping sacks of brussel sprouts, one at a time, into an opening (about 36 inches in diameter) located at the front of the barrel. As the sprouts rotated inside the barrel, they began dropping their yellow and loose leaves through the spaces between the tubes, and onto the floor. The rotation and tilt of the machine caused the sprouts to move forward to the end of the barrel. There, they dropped onto a conveyer belt that routed them in a perpendicular direction, away from the barrel itself. On either side of the conveyer belt stood three or four women and/or men, who sorted, discarded, and peeled the sprouts, using their hands and curved knives. A wooden crate was placed at the end of the conveyer belt and, as their journey ended, the cleaned sprouts dropped off the belt and into the crate. When full, the crate would be loaded onto a truck and an empty one would take its place at the end of the line. As one can see, this method of cleaning sprouts was much more efficient than the old cleaning-by-hand method so meticulously performed by Valentina.

As I recall, a very important event happened in 1943: Jeannie was born. I was six years old then and I must have noticed that Andreina was not around. I remember asking my mother if she knew where Andreina had gone. She told me that Andreina had gone to Santa Cruz to buy a baby girl. I asked my mother if we could go to Santa Cruz and buy one, too. My mother answered, "Per dio, no. Costan troppo." ("For God's sake, no. They cost too much.") That's how I learned that Jeannie was born. Jeannie, of course, was a girl, and she was too young to participate in our juvenile antics. Later, when she was about six or seven years old, she became a very valuable member of our football team. At the yard we used Jeannie to center the football. She was so good at this task that she got to play center for both teams. More about Jeannie and our yard football teams later.

In late 1949, the Degli Esposti family arrived from Italy. Vanda Degli Esposti was Andreina's sister. Much like my aunt Lina, the Degli Esposti family, having lived through the horrors of the war years, was having a very rough time in the old country. Andreina made arrangements for the family to immigrate to the United States. Vanda's husband, Luigi Degli Esposti (Moro), was the first to arrive.

One morning, as usual, my brother and I walked to the Rodoni Ranch to wait for the school bus. When we got there Mario told us that his uncle had just arrived from Italy. Andreina then took us inside the cookhouse and led us to a small room in the back. There still in bed, just waking up, was a very thin, dark-skinned man, with a big smile on his face. This was the first time I saw Luigi Degli Esposti. Later his friends gave him the nickname Moro. Italians often use the word *moro* to describe a man with dark skin.

About six months later, Vanda with her sons, Roberto and Fabrizio (Fabby), arrived in California. Roberto was about six months younger than I was; Fabby was about three years younger. Dante hired Moro to work on the farm, and the family occupied the house that was just south of the cookhouse. None of the Degli Espostis spoke a word of English. Fortunately, Mario, Elio, Jeannie, my brother, and myself all spoke Italian. It wasn't long before all the kids became fast friends. Later, of course, the Degli Esposti boys learned to speak English quite well.[68]

Endnotes

[67] The Davenport Oral History Project is a series of videotaped interviews with "old timers" of Davenport and the coast. Francisco Serna, Project Director, P. O. Box 97, Davenport, CA 95017. Website: www.drsc@cabinc.org

[68] In the mid-1950s, the Degli Esposti family moved to Santa Cruz and became our neighbors at 741 Seaside Street. During his early twenties, Fabby did some radio announcing for an Italian-speaking radio station. Later, he also did some screenwriting for movies and television. He is now a teacher of English and Italian, living in Las Vegas. Roberto went on to be a supervisor with the Coca-Cola Company. He is now retired and lives in Rocklin, California.

WELCOME TO "LA AMERICA"; THE DEGLI ESPOSTI FAMILY SHORTLY AFTER ARRIVING FROM ITALY.

FROM LEFT TO RIGHT: FABBY, VANDA, MORO AND ROBERTO.

C. 1949

(Courtesy of the Degli Esposti family collection)

19. Giochi (Games)

The Degli Esposti's arriving from Italy was a very fortunate happening. Now we could really have fun playing *giochi* [**joh** key], i.e., games. In fact, we now had enough kids (just about) to play team games. We started out with the simple Cowboys and Indians and gradually advanced to playing football and basketball. In between we played our favorite game, Rubber Guns!

Unlike the ones introduced to us by Phil Taurian, these rubber guns were cut out of pieces of scrap wood and then shaped into "pistols" with handgrips. The "ammunition" we used was the same: rubber bands approximately 1" in width. These rubber bands were cut out of old inner tubes. The majority of the car tires at the time had inflatable rubber inner tubes. Once discarded, these tubes became an endless resource for producing the "ammunition" needed for our rubber guns. Retrieving these inner tubes was quite easy for us, because *Il Dumpo*, where so many of these tires were deposited to be later burned, was about one mile east of the Rodoni Ranch.[69]

This was just a short bike ride and a strong smell away.

The length of the gun varied in size. The longer the gun, the farther the rubber band could stretch, but also the harder to keep the "weapon" loaded. After serious experimentation, we found that a length of about 18 to 20 inches was best. Behind the handgrip, we placed a wooden clothespin. (The kind that has a metal hinge in the middle.) Wooden clothespins were in abundance during this period of time, because our parents did not have electric or gas clothes dryers. We affixed the clothespin to the gun by tightly wrapping a rubber band (cut out of one of those same inner tubes) around the pin and handgrip, and then nailing or screwing the rubber to the wood. The gun was loaded by inserting one end of the rubber band into the clothespin. The rubber band was stretched out and then secured by slipping its opposite end over the end of the barrel. To ensure that the stretched rubber did not slip out of the clothespin, the back of the pin was re-enforced by wrapping more rubber around it.

The "weapon" was held with one hand, the palm and the inner fingers covering both the grip and the back of the clothespin. When ready to fire, the "gunman" aimed the gun carefully and tightened his grip simultaneously on the handle and clothespin. The pressure from the hand on the back of the clothespin caused it to open, thus releasing the rubber. If the back of the clothespin was too tightly wrapped, the pin became difficult to open and the gun would be slow in "firing"; if it were too loosely wrapped the rubber slipped out and the "gunman" would be left with an unloaded "weapon" in his hand. Many a "gun duel" was lost by a malfunctioning clothespin trigger.

The rubber gun, as constructed by the "gunmen" on the Rodoni Ranch, was a marvelous "weapon." One must remember that this was the time before laser or paint guns. Before the advent of the rubber gun, we played Cowboys and Indians, using cap pistols or inert wooden guns that didn't shoot anything. Sometimes we just used our middle and index fingers—just pointed them. There was no way to know for sure if you "hit and killed" your opponent. Now, this new *pistola* [pee **stoh** lah] changed all that. You could shoot something at a person without hurting him (unless you hit him in the face at close range), and actually see whether you'd hit him. It changed the whole dynamics of the game.

The teams playing this game usually pitted Roberto, myself, and sometimes Elio, against Mario and Fabby. (Jeannie played this game infrequently and my brother, who was older, never played.) In essence, it was my team versus Mario's team. The object was to shoot and hit the opposing players. Once hit by a rubber band (anywhere on the body), the player was "dead" and eliminated from the game. When all the players on one team had been hit and "killed" the game was over. When Elio played, my team usually had three players. Since we did not have anyone else to play, Mario was allowed to carry two guns, to even things up. In order to win the game, my team had to "kill" Mario twice. I can still hear Roberto or Elio calling from inside the barn, "Mario is dead—one gun!" This, of course, meant that Mario had been hit once, and so one player on his team had been eliminated. However, he got to play on until he was hit and "killed" a second time.

We mostly played this game in the barn. Sometimes we played outside in the yard; however, the wind caused havoc with the flight of the rubber bands, making hitting an opponent difficult. In the non-harvest season, the barn was largely empty of people. This made it an ideal arena for playing the game. Not only did the barn shield us from *il vento*, its largeness also provided us with abundant space to hide and play the game. One team was assigned to defend the barn from the inside. Team members found suitable places to hide, such as behind a stack of crates, bails of hay, a parked truck, or other stationary farm machinery. The other team was assigned to attack the barn from the outside. Once inside they attempted to ferret out the defenders and then "shoot" them "dead." The team with the "last man standing" was declared the winner.

One of the rules of the games was that a "gunner" could not shoot an opponent in the face. (We did not wear protective goggles.) If this should happen, the person doing the shooting was immediately disqualified. Well, maybe not so immediately. This rule caused many drawn-out arguments. Sometimes a rubber "bullet" would hit an opponent in the shoulder and bounce into his face. Other times it would bounce off an object, like a crate, and then into the face. Should the player be disqualified? After heated debate, and still being unable to arrive at an equitable resolution, we would usually reload our *pistolas*, and the "duel" was played once again.

A "stinging" problem, not so easily resolved, occurred when a "gunner" accidentally "zinged one in," hitting an opponent directly in the face without benefit of a bounce. This could cause some hard feelings. Shouts of "dirty player," could be heard from the injured player. (Fabby, when hit, was particularly adept at using this as a technique to disqualify an opposing player.) We had some walk-offs and suspended games because of it, but we usually came back the next day and went at it again. On the whole, I think we played the game showing good sportsmanship. But I do feel that Mario's team had an advantage, because he was the best "gunman" and a lot of times he had two guns.

As the reader probably has surmised, I had a lot of fun playing "Rubber Guns." However, I must confess here that the hand-squeezing method of firing the rubber gun caused me a great deal of trouble when learning to fire a real revolver. At the San Jose State Police School, one-hand shooting at a bull's-eye target was used. Instead of squeezing the trigger nice-and-easy, I would squeeze the handle and the trigger at the same time. This caused the revolver to pull off target. It wasn't until I joined the San Jose Police Department—where two-hand combat shooting at human silhouette targets was emphasized—that I became comfortable firing the revolver. My favorite method was to jam the fist that held the revolver into the palm of the free hand. The opposing forces of the two hands (Dynamic Tension?) steady the revolver as a shot is being fired. This method is much more akin to firing a rubber gun.

When I first attended Mission Hill Junior High School in Santa Cruz (in 1949), I was introduced to touch and flag football. We had never played football at Laurel School. (I don't think the all-female faculty teaching there felt comfortable teaching us the game.) I found out that I was pretty good at it and I really enjoyed the game. Naturally, I brought the game to the "big gravel yard." At first we used a round rubber ball. Later, someone, probably me, bought a regular football. Since we had only four players (five if Jeannie played), our game consisted mostly of passing the ball. Sometimes we would run the ball, which usually required a reverse, or a pass behind the line.

Roberto (the slowest) was usually on my team, Fabby (the fastest) on Mario's team. Elio seldom if ever played this game. Sometimes, Leo Bargiacchi, the son of Pietro and Emma Bargiacchi, who along with his sister Flora lived on a neighboring *rancio*, would show up and play with us. That created a problem. He must have been in his early twenties at the time, and of course he was much bigger than any of us. When he was on Mario's team, I would try to even things up by bumping and shoving him before he caught the ball. Even these illegal tactics didn't work: the team that had Leo always won.

To add depth to our teams, we often recruited Jeannie to be our center. (I think this might have made Jeannie the very first female football player.) This allowed one player to line up as a flanker when going out for a pass. Of course, if one team on offense had Jeannie for a center, the other team also had to have her when on offense. So Jeannie got to play center for both teams. Soon she got bored with it all and left the game. Then we had to revert back to doing our own centering, which eliminated the flanker formation. (Sadly, Jeannie left us for good in 1998. She died of cancer at the young age of fifty-five.)

Mario was an exceptional player. I always thought that he would have made a great fullback or halfback for the high school team. He was fast and shifty and had powerful legs. I know that he was better than some of the boys I was later to play with. Mario, however, was more interested in hunting and fishing than in playing football. This probably proved to be a wise decision. Unlike myself, Mario still has sound knees.

Endnotes

[69] At times, *il vento* would send some of these fires out of control. Alerted by their sirens, we often saw fire engines speed up the road towards *Il Dumpo*, to quell the potentially dangerous flames. I remember one such fire in particular, which spread alongside what is now Dimeo Lane, nearly reaching the Coast Road.

20. Sesso E Altri Divertimenti
(Sex & Other Amusements)

Being in our adolescence years, the "big gravel yard" boys naturally became interested in sex. Mario and I were the first to see how the real thing was done. Remember the beach where the Coast Guardsmen used to keep watch during the war years? Well, at times we noticed an unfamiliar car parked on the bluff near where their "lookout house" used to be. We then would get on our bikes and ride down to the beach to investigate. At times, we would discover a young couple on the beach, kissing and fondling each other, but nothing more. I remember one such covert episode, when the man doing the fondling spotted us spying from the bushes above. Before we knew it, he was running up the side of the bluff, causing us to jump to our feet and run to our bikes. Luckily, we were able to high-tail it out of there without being caught. This rather exciting escapade taught us that people "making out" do not appreciate being spied upon. Greater stealth was needed.

Although watching a boy and a girl kissing was stimulating, it was nothing compared to what we were about to see. On one particularly informative day, Mario and I, being ever vigilant, spotted a car parked on the bluff. Naturally, we took our trusty bikes and rode down to the beach to investigate. We found a spot on the bluff where we could see a couple on the beach below. Nothing happened for a long time. Then, the couple started fondling and kissing each other. Nothing new here. All of a sudden they stopped. The man got up and looked to his left, and then his right, but he never did look straight up where Mario and I were lurking. What happened next really blew our minds. Thinking that no one was around, the man removed his bathing suit. At the same time, the woman, to our utter delight, also removed her bathing suit. Laying her gloriously naked body on the sand, with open arms (and thighs) she beckoned the man onto her. After standing his naked and aroused body over her for a second or two, the man proceeded to get on top of her. There before us, bare buttocks and all—we observed and learned, for the first time, how the sex act was performed. Certainly, being raised on a ranch, we had seen dogs and other animals do it, but somehow we had never associated the act with human beings. No book, no sex education class, could have been more informative.

Regrettably, our moment of enlightenment was cut short. Mario, trying to get a better look, inadvertently pushed an empty sprout crate over the bluff. (I believe he was using the crate as camouflage for greater stealth.) Thinking that the crate had fallen directly on the lovers below, we once again got on our bikes and high-tailed it out of there. Nearby, we found a suitable hiding place and got a chance to catch our breaths. There I noticed that Mario's right eye was filled with dirt. Mario, in his continuing attempt to get a better look at the entwined couple below, had dug a hole through the dirt cliff. As he placed his eye to the hole, *il vento* had apparently sent blasts of dirt up and into his eye. Not wanting to miss any of the spontaneous lovemaking going on below him, Mario tolerated this minor inconvenience. Now he was almost completely blind in that eye. I couldn't stop laughing because Mario looked like one of those movie pirates that wore a black patch.

After taking time out to clean Mario's eye, we began a serious discussion on what we had just seen. The man and woman certainly looked like they were having fun. It was Mario who first suggested that this might be how babies were made. He said that he had read this in one of those books his father had. "Naw!" I responded. "This couldn't be. You mean that our parents had to do the same thing to have us?" We eventually came to the conclusion that this was indeed how babies were made. However, we still had a tough time accepting the fact that our parents had so much "fun" in having us. Nothing would ever be the same again.

Naturally, when we got back and told the other "big gravel yard" guys about this adventure, they all became very interested in seeing how the "whole thing" was done. Elio, Roberto, and Fabby became instant voyeurs. From then on, we were all on the lookout for those cars parked on the bluff. It was a matter of who got there first. On one occasion we even saw a bunch of young men prancing around in the buff. I think Elio or Roberto was with me. Not liking what we saw, we made our presence known. One of the men put on his swimming trunks and came up to talk to us. Puffing out our chests we promptly informed him that our parents owned the ranch, and that he and his boy friends were trespassing. Guess what? He bought it and they left. Now, if they had been girls, this would have been a different story.

Having been thoroughly indoctrinated on how the whole sex thing was done, we naturally became real interested in attracting the girls. We figured the best way of doing this was to improve our bodies. As kids growing up, we read about Charles Atlas and how he had supposedly transformed himself from that 98-pound weakling into a strongman. (We didn't know it at the time, but Charles Atlas was an Italian emigrant: his real name was Angelo Siciliano.) The comic books of the time always showed him getting the girl (who usually hung out at the beach) after he had developed his body. This is what we wanted to accomplish — get strong, look good, and get the girls.

Although Mission Hill Junior High School had a very good Physical Education program, the curriculum under the direction of Milo Badger centered on the playing of team intramural sports.[70] It was fun to play the various games, but it did very little to build our bodies. There were too few physical exercise classes or calisthenics. Consequently, when I entered Santa Cruz High School, I found that I was very weak in upper body strength. I could only do one or two pull-ups, and I could not manage the rope climb. I was very embarrassed about this. But I was fortunate to have very good gym teachers at that time. Under the guidance of Franklin "Lindy" Lindenberg, Don Lehmkuhl, and Roger Baer, I gradually built up my upper body strength, until I was able to do the required physical exercises quite easily. However, to actually build up the body to where I thought the girls would like me to be — more work was necessary.

Mario, I'm sure was of a like mind. Somewhere along the line Mario got a set of weights. He stored the weights in back of the old barn (the same barn where we used to play rubber guns.) There, during the summer months of 1955 thru 1959, amidst the dusty smells of hay and left-over *pattume*, I joined Fabby and Mario (grunting and groaning) as we tried to lift heavier and heavier weights.(Roberto seldom lifted weights; and Elio and John never did.) Naturally, Mario was the strongest. He could out-lift and out-bench press all of us. As we lifted and performed other weight lifting exercises, we told jokes, laughed, and listen to rock-and-roll music on the radio. I even remember demonstrating an Elvis Presley dance for the boys, between my lifting routines. I think my gyrations were quite good. (Hmmm.)

Needless to say, after following the above routine for three months in the summer, plus working on the *rancios*, we were in pretty good shape when we returned to school. Talk about hard bodies. At the time I was 6'2" tall and weighted 195 pounds. I can still remember walking on the San Jose State campus wearing a tight t-shirt and imagining that all the girls' eyes were on me. Once in school, I enrolled with Bob Mann's San Jose Health Club at 9th and Santa Clara streets in San Jose. Although I kept up the weight lifting, it was never as effective as when we had worked out in that old barn.[71]

Endnotes

[70] *Circa* 1960, Coach Badger and his wife, Dorothy, bought a home directly across from my parents' house in Santa Cruz. They lived at 734 Seaside Street a good many years, raising their family of two daughters and three sons.

[71] Sadly, while I was writing this story about the Rodoni Family, Andreina passed away, on December 5, 2001. Once again that vicious disease, cancer, had claimed another wonderful lady who lived and worked *su per la costa*. Maybe Mario and Elio, and their families, can take solace in the fact that Andreina, unlike my mother, lived a relatively long life and was given the time to enjoy her extended family. Yet, with this came the pain of having her beloved daughter and husband precede her in death. Undoubtedly, she is now reunited with Jeannie and Dante in a place where we all must go. A place where all are reborn young and strong and free of disease. A place where the memories of the past go on forever and can be recalled with the vividness of the present. Adio, Andreina Rodoni.

21. Serafina's

Battista (Bob) and Serafina Beltrami owned and managed a small bar and gasoline station on the east side of the old Coast Road, about 2.5 miles north of the Gulch Ranch. The actual name of the bar was Beltrami's. But because my mother and Serafina were such close friends, we followed Valentina's lead, and called it Serafina's. The Beltramis had two daughters, Angelina (Angie) and Ebe. Angie must have been in her early twenties and Ebe was in her mid-teens during this time period. Since they were older I do not remember too much about their activities. I do remember one visit that Angie made to our house *circa* 1948 or 1949. She was all dressed up that day, sporting a "California girl" suntan and looking like Rita Hayward. Even at my young age, I could see that she was radiantly beautiful. (Hmmm. This being pre-sandy beach days, it actually might have been my first awareness of my own sexuality.)

During the war years, Serafina's became a very important stop for the Comelli family. In 1942, the United States had imposed gas rationing. On occasion, the Old Carrettone ran short and we didn't have the necessary ration stamps to buy additional gasoline. Battista saw to it that we got the additional gasoline to keep us on the road. This stop was also important to me, because it was here that I first started becoming attracted to police work.

The Beltramis' living quarters and the bar section were housed under the same roof. A wall, with a large opening for a door, separated the bar section from the living room/kitchen area. Through this door one could go from the bar section directly into the living room and vice versa. In this way, Serafina or Battista did not have to stay in the bar section all day waiting for customers. I can remember my family sitting in the living room visiting with the Beltramis. As a customer came in, either Battista or Serafina went into the bar to render service. After the customer left they returned to the living room to resume their visit with us. The bar section was small, but it did have room for a dance floor and jukebox. I remember that my brother and I played the song "Beer Barrel Polka" by the Andrew Sisters over and over again. Another disk we played featured this guy who kept urging this gal to behave, by singing, "Lay that pistol down, Babe. Lay that pistol down. Pistol Packing Mama, lay that pistol down." His words, sung to a catchy western beat, sparked all sorts of imaginary scenarios in my budding police mind. I didn't know it at the time, but I was later to find out that this guy was the one and only Bing Crosby, who in 1946 had the hit record, "Pistol Packing Mama."

The jukebox also contained some Italian songs. My mother used to listen to a couple of songs by Carlo Buti, a famous Italian singer. I don't remember the titles of the songs, but I am sure that they were arias from famous operas. My parents often got into a discussion with the Beltramis, comparing the famous Italian singers. Each had their favorite, so a consensus on who was the best was never reached.

Here in this small bar, I got to see up close my first real uniformed police officers. As they patrolled the Coast Road, county sheriff's deputies and California Highway Patrolmen stopped by to take a break. Battista served them sodas at the bar. (At least I think they were sodas.) These police officers made a real impression on me. I liked their badges and uniforms, and of course their revolvers, smartly holstered on their belts. I also noticed that the people at the bar showed great respect towards them. This was especially true of Battista. He liked the policemen. *Su per la costa*, Battista's favorite was Vic Calhoun, a highway patrolman. Battista talked about him

La Nostra Costa (Our Coast)

as if he were his long lost brother. Officer Calhoun patrolled the Coast Road for many years and had a reputation among the coastal Italians of being a fair and honest policeman. When I was at the Beltramis, I waited with great anticipation for Vic Calhoun to come striding into the bar. The reader can imagine my disappointment when, at times, he failed to show up.[72]

Although Battista liked the police officers, he did not particularly favor the game warden, Forrest McDermott. Battista did not dislike McDermott but—as was not the case with the policemen—he was always glad when McDermott left. Many of the hunters and fishermen up the coast were Battista's patrons; they didn't hide their feelings about McDermott, who would issue them citations if they were over the limit or hunting out of season. The Italian poachers told many great tales regarding how they outwitted the game warden. None were better than the ones told by Pete Pianavilla, a big, fun-loving Italian lad. In a loud booming voice and with great relish, Pete often told tales about his hunts and how he had outfoxed that "S.O.B." McDermott. At the end of a story Pete would burst out with a deep loud laugh which let everyone in the place know that Pete Pianavilla was around. If all these tales were true, then McDermott never did catch anybody. This would not have upset Serafina, who was an avid hunter. She was one of a select few women up the coast that actually went out on hunts with the men. She would always say, "Mi piace la caccia." (I love the hunt.) Naturally she was wary of the Game Warden.

I will always remember one special evening, *circa* 1945 or 1946. Valentina had just passed her examination and had become a naturalized United States citizen. To celebrate we went to Serafina's. There in the living room, while Serafina and Battista served drinks from the bar, my father and mother with a few friends sang songs and told stories about their "school days." Bronco, who had become naturalized a year or so before, told a particularly funny story that I remember to this day. During one of his classes the teacher asked an Italian lady, who lived in Davenport, whether she knew the name of the Capitol of the United States. The lady, who had been seated directly in front of my father, had been dumbfounded and could not answer. Bronco, always the great kidder, had prompted the lady by whispering, "Davenport." The poor women then blurted out, "Davenport!" The whole class burst out laughing. According to my father, Mrs. Sonnebern, the teacher, didn't appreciate the humor and scolded him for misleading the befuddled lady.

The above story always reminds me of the radio program "Life with Luigi," popular during the late 1940s and early 1950s. J. Carroll Naish, a non-Italian actor, played the part of an Italian immigrant named Luigi, who was trying to become an American citizen. Just like the lady from Davenport, he often misunderstood the English language, which got him into various humorous situations. Valentina often said that the program made fun of Italians. However, I noticed that she too, laughed along with us, when she listened to the program.

Another story Bronco told was not so funny. When my father was taking his oral examination before a Superior Court Judge, the United States Attorney asked him if he had any objections to fighting for the United States against Italy. Bronco answered that he had no objections. The Attorney then asked him a rather odious question. According to my father, this question had to do with whether or not he would shoot and kill his brother, if he saw his brother on the battlefield fighting for the enemy. Bronco, who had two younger brothers still living in Italy, knew exactly what the Attorney wanted him to say. However, he responded by saying that he did not understand the question. This infuriated the Attorney, who wanted the Judge to compel my father to answer. Bronco had made up his mind not to answer and resigned himself to the fact that he wasn't going to become a naturalized citizen. As my father told the story, it was Mrs. Sonnebern, his wonderfully gifted teacher, who came to his rescue. She told the Judge that she had not instructed her students in matters concerning politics or war; rather that she had instructed them in matters of government and the Constitution, which pertained to the United States of America. She implored the Judge to direct the U.S. Attorney to question my father on these matters only. Apparently her argument prevailed. Fortunately, Bronco did not have to answer the question regarding his brother. He went on to answer correctly all the other questions regarding the United States government and the Constitution. He passed his examination with flying colors and became a naturalized citizen.

While Bronco was telling his stories Valentina was having a real good time. She was very happy that she had passed her examination. This was the only time that I would ever see Valentina even halfway intoxicated. She had had quite a few drinks and was singing and dancing. This was indeed unusual. The Valentina I knew usually did not drink and was quite the serious lady. I became quite embarrassed over my mother's rather bizarre antics. What if Vic Calhoun or one of those policemen came into the bar and saw her like that? They might take her to jail and my reputation would be ruined. I would never be allowed to become a police officer. I found a corner to hide and waited for the evening to end. Finally it was over. When we were driving home, I remember telling my mother (I was all of eight or nine years old at the time) that I didn't like her being a "ciuca." Valentina answered back that she was not "ciuca," but that she was only play-acting to have a little fun. I don't think any of us believed her and I never did see my mother "play-acting" in that manner again.

Endnotes

[72] Not surprisingly, in 1952, Battista's youngest daughter, Ebe, married Don Silva, who soon became a highway patrolman. Ebe and Don later divorced. However, from time to time while working for the San Jose Police Department, I would see Officer Silva, who was then assigned to the San Jose Area. He later was re-assigned to Santa Cruz County.

SERAFINA'S

C. 1940

A LA CACCIA

SERA FINA AND BATTISTA – C. 1950

FIGLI DELLA COSTA

MARIO AND ELIO WITH NORMA DINELLI AND LAURA NERI – C.1946

22. Laguna

If the reader ever should travel towards Davenport on the new Coast Road, to about one half mile north of Serafina's, there on the eastern side of the road he or she will find a small sunken enclave called Laguna. The reader will no doubt notice that the new Coast Road is straight and level, and bypasses Laguna on its backside. I can assure you that the *old* Coast Road was not straight and level. It hugged the hillside, and sloped steeply downward, at the bottom passing Laguna and what was then the Laguna Inn. (Though the inn is now gone, the building is still there.) The road then continued up and around the hillside in a semi-circular manner. This was known as the infamous Laguna Curve. Along with another horseshoe-bend segment of road known as the Yellowbank Curve (about seven miles north of Santa Cruz near Respini Creek), the Laguna Curve was noted for its many wrecks. It was especially dangerous on a moonless night, when the coastal fog hung low over the road. Drivers, unable to see clearly through the eerie mist, could easily lose their bearings and drive their cars off the road or directly into the path of an oncoming cement truck.

Bronco, to his credit, successfully negotiated this curve on many of those visually obscure nights. Typically chugging along home after a visit to Davenport, the Old Carrettone would start to pick up speed as it began its descent of Laguna Curve. "Per Dio! Va piano!" ("For God's sake! Go slow!") Valentina would yell at my father.

"No vedo niente!" ("I can't see a thing!") Bronco, already aware of the obvious, would apply more pressure to the brakes, slowing the lumbering car to a crawl. Once at the bottom, near the Laguna Inn, he abruptly shifted into second gear. The Old Carrettone shuddered and groaned as it jerked forward, beginning its slow, laborious climb up the steep incline. We would all hold our breaths, expecting one of those big cement trucks to suddenly appear in front of us, and heaved a collective sigh of relief when we reached the top safely. As the Coast Road straightened before us, Bronco would shift the Old Carrettone into high gear, and with ever less effort the family car would pick up speed, as we headed south past Serafina's and towards home. Once we'd arrived home we would chalk one up for the Old Carrettone and the Comelli family. Safe again, though each time, Valentina swore she would never do it again. Of course, we always did.

Attilio Tomada (Massimo) once managed the Laguna Inn. This was the same Attilio Tomada whose name my father had put down on his ship records, on first arriving at Ellis Island—as the person he knew in Davenport, California. In the 1930s and early 1940s, many parties were held at the Laguna Inn. My brother has a photograph of his baptismal party (*circa* 1935) showing a gathering of many of our friends from *la costa*, on the front steps of the inn. Massimo was the Godfather that day, and he is seen in the photograph playing his accordion.

The Laguna Inn was also the scene of many famous—or infamous—poker matches. Roy Castiglioni (Lina Brovia's husband), once informed me that he had witnessed many *ranceri* lose their entire annual earnings at some of these matches. Since dividends earned by partners on the *rancios* were usually paid out at the end of the year, it meant the losers had to go a whole year with very little money in their pockets. No wonder they spent so much time in the "cookahousa" drinking wine.

Circa 1940, the Viviani Family took over management of the inn. Lina and Cuneo Viviani, along with their daughter Dolores and son Eddie lived at the Laguna Inn. At the front of the inn, along the highway, were two gasoline pumps. Dolores recently mentioned to me that her family had sold Polly Gas—which for me brought back memories of that familiar parrot symbol which was always on the tanks. The pumps were manually operated. Gasoline was hand-pumped into a glass cylinder at the top of tank. Through the glass you could see a vertical gauge, which indicated the different gallon amounts. A customer, desiring to gas up his car, pulled up to the pumps and requested a certain number of gallons. The attendant then hand-pumped the desired number of gallons into the glass cylinder. The customer, as well as the attendant, could verify the number of gallons, because he could actually see the gauge, and the gasoline as it reached the proper level in the glass cylinder. Gravity did the rest. Just like nowadays, a rubber hose with a nozzle was placed into the automobile tank and the gasoline flowed from the pump into the car. (Some of these antique pumps still exist and replicas abound. They are often displayed in front of restaurants or other establishments, for nostalgic purposes. One such display is in front of the Baja Cantina Restaurant in Carmel Valley. Seeing it always brings back memories of the Laguna Inn.)

Today, most of the flat terrain behind the building that was the Laguna Inn, has been cleared, and is being used for growing brussels sprouts. During the time of my childhood, this same flat area was covered with trees. Italian families from Davenport and the Coast Road gathered here to have many of their picnics and barbeques. Under the canopy of all those trees were numerous picnic tables and a great, big old brick barbeque pit. The Italians brought their picnic baskets, tableware, and utensils, setting up at the tables for a day of enjoyment and festivities. While several Italian "cooks" working in the barbeque area prepared and then served up steaks and chicken, beans and salad, my boyhood friends and I commenced hopping from picnic table to picnic table, making a visual inspection of all the desserts and savoring the ever-so-spicy smells of the hot *pastaciutta* (pasta) dishes. A scene in the movie "Picnic," depicting the gathering around the picnic tables covered with food, with boys and girls running and jumping about, is to me very reminiscent of my boyhood antics at the Laguna picnics. Of course, Laguna did not have a lake, and William Holden and Kim Novak were nowhere to be seen.[73]

These festive events were usually well attended, as attested by an article appearing in the *Santa Cruz Sentinel*, dated September 6, 1949. Beneath the caption, "ITALO-AMERICAN BARBECUE SLATED UP COAST SUNDAY," it went on to quote publicity chairman John Battistini (according to the article, Mario Lazzerini was general chairman) as saying that the event, first held in 1934, usually attracted more than 1,000 people from Santa Cruz, San Francisco, Sacramento, and Monterey Bay cities. I guess it was just to be understood that people living in Davenport or along the Coast Road would be there, since the article made no mention of their expected attendance.

After eating a great quantity of food and drinking many glasses of wine, the crowd broke up into groups. The singers gathered together and started to belt out different Italian songs. A favorite song of the *cantatori* [khan **tah** torie] was "Quel Mazzolin Di Fiori" ("That Little Bouquet of Flowers"). The alto singers opened the refrain, singing in their very high pitch *Quel mazzolin di fiori…* Then the bassos would respond in a very low pitch *…che vien dalla montagna* ("…that comes from the mountain"). After each verse of the song, the refrain was repeated, with the alto notes even higher, and the basso notes even lower. The more wine the singers drank, the higher the alto voices rose, and the lower the basso voices fell. After a few more drinks of wine, it became a contest of who could sing the loudest, and/or hit the highest or lowest notes. Reno Rinaldi, at the time a young American Italian lad in his early twenties, often reigned as champion for hitting the high notes. Reno had a high-pitched voice and, being a little hard of hearing, he was used to speaking in a loud tone. This carried over to his singing. Pete Pianavilla or Pete Brovia, reigned supreme at the low end of the scale. Of course, the louder they sang, the more off-key they sounded. This made for much laughter and amusement. The singing continued throughout the afternoon until the singers' vocal cords finally gave out with one last drunken-sounding rendition:

Quel maht'zoh-lean dee fee-yioree   (high pitch)

khe vien dah la montonya   (low pitch)

*eh quarrda ben khe no'l see **bah-nya***

khe low volyo rreh-gahlareh

low volyo rrehhh—gah-la-reh   (high pitch)

pearr keh leh un bel maht-zetto

low volyo dahreh al mee-oh more-etto

qwestah serrah qwando veeyen.[74]

That bouquet of flowers

that comes from the mountain

make very sure it doesn't get wet

because I want to give it as a gift

I want to give it as a gift

because it is a beautiful bouquet

I want to give it to my sweetheart

When arriving tonight.

Near the picnic area was a big, old barn-like building that had a large dance floor. After eating and singing, a good number of the gathering went inside to dance. Usually a local trio or combo provided the music. The accordion was an essential (maybe even required) instrument for the musical group: a drummer and a saxophonist, or clarinetist, usually accompanied the accordionist. Jimmy Dal Porto, who passed away recently (August 2003), frequently played his accordion at these picnics. Jimmy was well known *su per la costa*, and for years brought enjoyment to coastal Italians, by playing his instrument at their weddings and other ceremonial events.

As the afternoon wore on, the wine and spirits took their effect on both the players and the dancers. The atmosphere became livelier and livelier. It was not uncommon for a dancing couple, performing whirls and twirls to the tune of a lively "Tarantella," to lose their footing and end up on the floor. The next day *la costa* would be abuzz with the news of who had hit the floor. I never hit the floor, but I remember one incident, during the playing of the "Tarantella," when the drummer got mad at me and hit me over the head with his drumstick. Apparently he thought I was seated too close to his drums, thus inhibiting his musical genius. I guess that's one way to get someone to move.

At one end of the building was a long bar. I never knew this bar to be used during these dances. Taking advantage of this fact, my childhood friends Elio, Mario, Jim Ceragioli, Jerry Mungai, and Marvin Del Chiaro, and myself, set up operations behind it, pretending to be bartenders. Not having the essential alcoholic beverages to sell we attempted to sell glasses of water drawn from the faucet behind the bar. I believe we tried to sell glasses of water for two cents each. Would you believe it—we didn't sell one glass of water. Those Italian tightwads didn't know a good deal when they saw one. Personally, I think we were far ahead of our time. If only we would have thought of bottling it, labeling it "Laguna Springs Water," and selling it. Then we could have made a fortunate—don't you think?

The Laguna picnics presented and opportunity for the Italian families living on the Coast Road, and those living in Davenport, to get together and socialize. As young boys, my brother and I seldom interacted with the Davenport youths. One reason was that we went to different schools. Kids living in Davenport, or just north of Laguna, went to the Davenport School. Those of us living south of Laguna went to Laurel School in Santa Cruz.[75] Later, in their high school years, the youths living in the Davenport area were bused to Santa Cruz to attend the local high school. At that time, they became better known to us.

La Nostra Costa (Our Coast)

It seemed to me (I was two or three years younger than they were), that those Davenport kids were nothing but a bunch of ruffians. I always thought they went around with a chip on their shoulder, always wanting to quarrel or pick a fight. I can remember quarreling and almost getting into a fight with one of them during a Laguna picnic. To make matters worse, there was even an ugly rumor going around, during this time, that a Davenport boy had been arrested and sent to jail because of a "hazing" incident at Santa Cruz High School.

Not surprisingly (to me), as they grew older some of these boys started to drink and smoke. I remember one Laguna Picnic, when I saw a carload of Davenport boys parked in back of the dance hall, drinking wine and smoking. (Their names are withheld here to protect the living.) A couple of them got real sick and vomited all over the car. This didn't seem much fun to me. I couldn't understand why these boys wanted to become *ciucos*. It only re-enforced my image of the Davenport boys as ruffians. Fortunately, most of these ruffians, grew out of their stage of rowdiness, and did not become serious wrongdoers, or *ciucos*.

One incident in particular, which took place at a Laguna picnic *circa* 1948, will forever be embedded in my mind as the "Fagioli [fah **jo** lee] Incident." The usual Italian people, including my family, had gathered and began their day of enjoyment. We ate the food we had brought, and also the steak and *fagioli* (beans), prepared by the Italian cooks. Everything seemed normal, with the usual singing and dancing. Day passed into night and we went home feeling good about the event. That evening, after going to bed, my brother and I were awakened by noises coming from our bathroom. Bronco had become violently ill and was vomiting and experiencing bouts of diarrhea. After vomiting he got the "dry heaves." He was sick all night long. This was very unusual because Bronco seldom became sick. It was later determined that he had been suffering from a bad case of food poisoning. Apparently one of the Italian cooks had allowed a batch of cooked beans to sit overnight in a pot without being refrigerated. Bronco had eaten some of these contaminated beans. He managed to survive the incident, but, because of the strain on his body caused by the "dry heaves," he developed a hernia.

Bronco attempted to live with the hernia for several weeks thereafter. It eventually became too painful, and he decided to have it operated on. The operation proved successful, yet during this incident it was discovered that my father had an irregular heart beat. For a time it was thought that he would have to give up his job. Fortunately, a doctor was found in San Francisco, who prescribed medication to control the irregular heart beats. Bronco did not have to quit his job, but he did have to take this medication for the rest of his life.

Bronco always remembered the "fagioli incident" as one of the most painful and discomforting experiences of his life. However, the event might have saved his life. My father did not go routinely to a doctor for physical examinations. His heart condition might have gone on undetected for quite some time, causing him to have a serious heart attack later. Although this malady caused some disruption and anxiety in the family routine, all returned to normal when tests indicated that Bronco's heart medication worked.

Recently, Reno Cantarutti and I paid a visit to Laguna. As I have previously stated, the flat area where all the picnic tables and the old dance hall once stood, is now under cultivation. The tables are gone, the barbeque pit is gone, and the barn-like building is gone. The building that once housed the Laguna Inn is still there, looking rather weather-beaten. Of course the gasoline pumps at the front have long been gone.

Stopping in front of the Laguna Inn building, Reno and I paused and then, as if the walls of the old building were beckoning to us, we broke out singing, first in a very high voice, "Quel mazzolin di fiori..." and then in a loud basso, "...che vien dalla montagna." Of course, our singing could never do justice to those Italian singers of the past. Yet, perhaps wishing just for a moment that someone *did* hear us, we listened for their voices, in the hope that they would join us for one final refrain. Alas! Only the wistful sound of the wind blowing over the flats of Laguna could be heard. Sadly, we resigned ourselves to the reality of the present: *I cantatori di Laguna, no cantan mai piu.* The singers of Laguna will never sing again.

Endnotes

[73] "Picnic," Columbia Pictures, 1955, produced by Fred Kohlar, directed by Joshua Logan, starring William Holden, Rosalind Russell, and Kim Novak.

[74] This song, and many others, are known as the songs of the Alpini, Italy's famous Military Mountaineers. So that the reader could get a sense on how the *cantatori* sounded, I have spelled the words phoneticly. The words can be found, in their original form, on the website at www.alpini. torino.it/coro

[75] Lea (Grossi) Lambert, reminded me that Alice and Betty Santos, the daughters of Don Santos (our milkman), lived north of Laguna, near Yellow Bank Curve. They did indeed attend Santa Cruz schools. It would seem that the demarcation line was somewhat flexible.

THE LAGUNA INN

C. 1934

ONCE THEY WERE YOUNG

LAGUNA – C. 1929

ITALO-AMERICAN PICNIC AT LAGUNA

C. 1952

AT THE OLD BARN

BRONCO, LINA, VALENTINA, JOE, ANDREINA – C. 1948

23. Il Rancio Di Lorenzi
(The Lorenzi Ranch)

Located across the road from Serafina's was the Lorenzi Ranch. In addition to the Beltramis, my family visited four families who lived and worked on that ranch. These families no longer live there, but their houses remain standing today. The new Coast Road bypasses those houses now, but you still can get to them by turning west off the new Coast Road, and onto the frontage road. (For the reader who might be curious as to what the old Coast Road looked like, this frontage road, which hasn't change much in appearance over the years, was part of the old Coast Road.)

As my father drove the family car north on the old Coast Road, we would pass the Scaroni Ranch, later to become the site of the "Red, White and Blue Beach," and soon come to an old rock quarry that had a steam shovel always present on the site. Spotting the quarry, I, being three or four years old at the time, would immediately begin to jump up and down in the back seat. "TEEM SHABOL! TEEM SHABOL!" I would shout, as if to alert everybody that we were almost to the first of the four houses which belonged to Antonio (Tony) and Albina Cerri.

Tony was a working partner at the Lorenzi Ranch. The Cerris had a daughter named Gloria. Gloria was my brother's age. Since

I was three years younger than Gloria, I always thought of her as being an older sister. As a very young boy, I renamed her "Glo-Glo." I loved to visit the Cerris because Albina made the best peanut butter cookies and Gloria was always willing to play with my brother and me. The Cerris were a happy family, always smiling and laughing. They made us feel very welcome when we visited them. As Tony and Albina conversed with our parents in the kitchen, Gloria took my brother and me, back into the living room; there she allowed us to play with her toys.

In the living room, there was this giant grandfather's clock. I loved to stare at that clock, watching the pendulum swing back and forth, back and forth. I waited with great anticipation for the clock to go "bong, bong, bong," as it hit the top of the hour. To a little kid, watching and listening to this mechanical marvel as it designated the time of day, was just plain fun. (Again, I must remind the reader, that this was before the advent of video games and computers. Any mechanical device that moved and made noises, seemed to keep us entertained—at least for a while.)

As we grew older, Gloria became our Coast Road information center. This was especially true after we all got our telephones, *circa* 1950. She loved to tell us all that she had heard about the happenings *su per la costa*. What she didn't know was that I also kept abreast on what was happening by eavesdropping on her when she talked to her girl friends on our mutual party line. This was particularly interesting when they talked about their boyfriends. Although she suspected that someone was listening in on the telephone, "Glo-Glo" never found out that it was me. The reader probably remembers that I was particularly adept at this form of chicanery.

Because Gloria was about the same age as my brother, it was naturally hoped by both sets of parents, that she and my brother would eventually get together and possibly even marry. This never did materialize. Eventually, my brother married Donna Moro, and Gloria married Sam Torrisi. Ironically, their two spouses were both from San Jose.

La Nostra Costa (Our Coast)

After marrying Sam, Gloria moved to San Jose. Later, when I joined the San Jose Police Department, I often stopped by, dressed in my uniform, first at the house on Eugene Avenue and later at their new house on Graystone Lane. I often noticed that their two boys Mark and Michael, would look at my uniform and gawk at my sidearm, just as I did, when Vic Calhoun and those other officers used to stop by at Serafina's. I guess I didn't impress them that much, because neither one became police officers when they grew up.

When Tony died in 1962, Albina moved into the house on Eugene Avenue. At times, I stopped by to see how she was doing. After inviting me in and offering me a cup of coffee, we then reminisced about the good old days *su per la costa*. When my mother died in 1977, Albina took the loss of her friend quite hard. Every time she mentioned Valentina's name, she started to cry. She always reminded me that it was my mother who had persuaded her to see a doctor Valentina knew, which resulted in a successful hip replacement. Crying as she spoke the words, Albina would say, "If it wasn't for your mother, I probably wouldn't be walking today."

Albina came back home to Santa Cruz in 1992. She passed away at the age of eighty-six, and was buried at the Holy Cross Cemetery. Sadly, Gloria also came home to Santa Cruz. She was buried at Holy Cross Cemetery in 1996. "Glo-Glo" died much too young at age sixty-two. Cancer had claimed another friend from *La Nostra Costa*.

The house next door to the Cerri family home belonged to Battista and Angelina Lorenzi, who owned the Lorenzi Ranch. To this day, the ranch remains in the Lorenzi family's name. The Lorenzis were a few years older than my parents and had two grown children, Gino and Lina. When we visited them, Gino was there infrequently, but Lina was usually there.

Battista must have been a World War I veteran because I remember sitting in the Lorenzi's living room, eating cookies, supplied by Angelina, and staring at a full-length photographic portrait of a young Battista. He had a stern look on his face and was dressed in his brown World War I soldier's uniform with wide-brim Campaign Hat. The picture hung on the wall and it seemed as if Battista's eyes were always focused on me, even when I moved around the room.

My father and mother had great respect for Battista Lorenzi, who was a founding father of the Santa Cruz Artichoke and Sprout Growers' Association. They leaned on him quite heavily for advice. I know that whenever my mother and father had a problem concerning business or finance, they went to visit the Lorenzis to seek Battista's advice. During the war, he even gave them advice on how to display their loyalty to the United States. He told my father and mother to buy war bonds to show their support for their adopted Country. Although money was hard to come by, my mother and father did exactly that. Going through the contents of my mothers safety deposit box after her death, I came across a $25.00 War Bond issued during World War II. It doesn't seem like much now, but I know my mother could have used that money elsewhere at the time.

Angelina Lorenzi, who was somewhat overweight, was a pleasant woman who had rosy cheeks and wore glasses. She usually braided her long hair, affixing the strands over her head. I can still remember Valentina and Angelina sitting in the Lorenzi's kitchen, having coffee and cookies. As they talked, they concentrated on crocheting with their hooked needles. Angelina would give my mother frequent advice on how to "loop the loop" or "knit one pearl two," etc. In those days, visits and conversations with one's neighbors were a favorite pass time *su per la costa*. I know that Valentina enjoyed these visits with Angelina very much.

I also enjoyed these visits because it gave me a chance to play with the Ceragioli kids who lived next door to the Lorenzis. James (Jim) Ceragioli [chair ah **gee** ollee] was my age and we were in the same grade at Laurel School. In the sixth grade we both served as Traffic Boys at that school. We remained good friends throughout our school years. Rudy was about two years older than we were. Barbara, the sister, was about three years younger than Jim and me. Their parents Raymond (Ray) and Zelda (Fistolera) worked on the Lorenzi Ranch.[76] In the early 1950s, Ray sold his share in the Lorenzi Ranch and moved his family to Santa Cruz. When I was going through my high school and college years, Ray and Zelda kind of became my foster parents. I often stopped by at their new house on Escalona Drive in Santa Cruz, seeking advice and direction.

I must mention one last family that lived across from the Lorenzi Ranch and right next door to Serafina's. We visited the Dinelli family infrequently. Dante and Diana [**dee** ah-nah] Dinelli had a daughter named Norma, who was a couple of years younger than I was. Mostly, we saw this family when they visited the Rodonis. I remember that the Dinellis had a green 1950 Chevrolet. The car was similar in style to ours, but it was a "Deluxe" model. My father often said, with a touch of envy in his voice, "If I had waited a little longer, I could have gotten the 'Di Lusso' model, just like Dinelli." (Personally, I really didn't think that there was that much difference between the two models.)

I also remember being inside the Dinellis' home, once or twice. Their linoleum floor was always highly waxed and polished. Unlike our linoleum floor, it did not have any scuff marks made by rubber-soled shoes. Valentina would always lament, "Diana does not have to contend with two boys running around the house. Things are easier when you have a girl."

Could it be possible that my mother wanted me to be a girl? I don't know for sure, but every Saturday morning, Valentina had my brother and me help her clean the house. I don't know about my brother, but I hated Saturday mornings because it meant dusting, sweeping and moping. This was girl's work! During these times, I kind of wished that Norma were my sister. Maybe then I could get off the hook.[77]

I can not leave this area without recounting to the reader the following woeful tale of deception and deceit, which I have entitled, "Sleep on Auntie Dear, Your Nephew is in the Rear."

Previously, I have alluded to the fact that the above families lived just north of a coastal beach that later became known as the "Red, White and Blue Beach." This beach became famous, or perhaps infamous, for its clothes-optional policies. In the times before the "Red, White and Blue Beach" craze, the California Coastal Commission did not exist, and access to many of these coastal beaches was denied by the ranchers who did not want people trespassing on their land. The only way to get to the future "Red, White and Blue Beach," which was one of the best beaches on the coast because it was sheltered from the wind, was by driving through the Scaroni Ranch. Public access was normally denied, but the Scaronis allowed access to certain people they knew. Thanks to Katie Scaroni, my school mates and I (then aged eighteen to twenty-two years old), were able to visit this beach several times during our youth (clothes on, I think) and have some outstanding beach parties. These parties were so popular that students from the University of California, Stanford, San Jose State College, Monterey Peninsula College, and Hartnell College in Salinas would often attend. Youths would shirk their duties and responsibilities, even throw caution to the wind, in order to attend these parties.

During the spring semesters, 1956 through 1958, we would regularly organize such a beach party, usually on a Friday or Saturday night. Actually, Jim Ceragioli, who used to live on the Lorenzi Ranch, knew the Scaronis the best, and so it was he who made all the arrangements with Katie. This is important to remember, because all that follows was undoubtedly Jim's fault.

One of our friends who was attending Hartnell College (name withheld here to protect the living, at least for now), had to baby-sit his elderly aunt on weekend nights. His assignment, if he chose to perform his duties honorably, would have prohibited him from attending these parties. The temptation was too great. The word had gotten around that the best-looking girls were attending these parties. He was not going to pass that up. He made arrangements with a buddy to pick him up at his aunt's house, on Peyton Avenue in Santa Cruz. (Later, the appropriately named location caused some of us to remember these as our "Peyton Place" adventures.) The pickup occurred after the aunt had fallen asleep, usually around 8:30 p.m. Then "our hero" would sneak out a window and jump into his buddy's car, conveniently parked at the curb. Seated behind the wheel, his buddy (accomplice) would gun the engine and post-haste drive him to the Scaroni Ranch to attend the party. Later when the party was over (usually around 2:00 a.m.), this friend's buddy would, dutifully, drive him back to his aunt's house, whereupon, using the greatest of stealth, he would nimbly crawl back into the house by the same window through which he had exited. The next morning his aunt would wake up to find, in a rear bedroom, her nephew (probably with a hangover) fast asleep. Fortunately for my friend and his accomplice, nothing ever happened to the aunt who just kept on sleeping through it all; no one ever found out about it, even though this risky business was repeated on more than one occasion.

The dubious reader, noting the various risks involved and the difficulty of keeping such an affair a complete secret from my friend's parents, might now ask, "How do you know for sure that this so-called story of the sleeping aunt is true?" Fair question. I probably would have had some doubts indeed about its veracity, given the improbability of it all—that is to say, if I hadn't been there, and if I hadn't played the aforementioned role of accomplice in this misadventure. Beach party, anyone?

Endnotes

[76] Lea (Grossi) Lambert, the daughter of Settimo and Inez (Fistolera) Grossi, has reminded me that there were six Fistolera sisters: Inez, Winnie (Giraudo), Nora (Della Santina), Zelda, Vivian (Rodoni) and Lena (Shaw). Her grandparents, Paul and Barbara Fistolera had a *rancio* in Swanton. Later, Lea lived on a ranch with her father and mother, just north of Laguna.

[77] Like Andreina Rodoni, Diana Dinelli passed away during the writing of this book (November 18, 2004). She lived to be eighty-eight years old. *Adio*, Diana.

24. Il Carrettone Vecchio
(The Old Carriage)

I'm sure it is not often that one devotes a whole chapter to a car. However, in this instance it must be done. My family, especially my brother and I, had many adventures in this miserable car. I guess I'm being too hard on *Il Carrettone Vecchio* [**veh** kee-yoh]. To be fair, it was the Old Carrettone that took us up and down the Coast Road to visit our friends; it was the Old Carrettone that took us to the beach in Santa Cruz and to the Saturday night movies at the old Santa Cruz Theatre. Finally, it was with the Old Carrettone that my brother and I learned to drive. It was our family car from 1937 to 1949, and I must give the car its due. But it did give us some miserable times.

The reader might recall that the Old Carrettone was, in fact, a 1934 Lafayette. In the 1920s, the Lafayette road car was manufactured by the Lafayette Motor Company, based in Indianapolis. *Circa* 1924, the Company was taken over by the Nash Automobile Corporation. In the 1950s, the Lafayette Motor Car faded out of existence, as the Nash Company merged with Hudson Motors to form American Motors. (American Motors later merged with Chrysler.) Thus, the Old Carrettone did indeed play a part in American automotive history. I even heard Paul Harvey, the famous radio commentator, mention during a paid advertisement that he still owned his 1938

Lafayette car. According to Mr. Harvey, he used this car on his honeymoon and it was still in running condition. Yes, Mr. Harvey, but did you ever do "wheelies" in it?

I guess that in the 1930s, it was considered a nice-looking car. On the other hand, I always thought that it looked like one of those "getaway" cars seen in those old gangster movies. It was a two-door, dark green sedan, with black fenders over the wheels and iron running boards on either side of the car. The headlights were set on top of the front fenders. The front end had one of those old-fashioned oblong-shaped radiator grills. At the top of the grill was an inset with an engraved profile of the Marquis de Lafayette, the French military leader who commanded American troops in the Revolutionary War. I believe the engraving was copper-plated and about the size of a fifty-cent piece. On the floorboard, the Old Carrettone had a foot clutch, to go along with the brake and gas pedals. To the right of the steering column, a long metal gear shift (three forward gears) with a black-rubber hand-knob affixed on the top end, protruded upward from the floor. It had no radio, no heater and of course, no power steering.

Because the car was a two-door sedan, the front seats had to be folded down in order to get into the back of the car. Guess what? My brother and I sat in the back seat. Sometimes we folded down the seats and at other times we just crawled or jumped over them. This often exasperated my mother because we dragged our dirty shoes over the front seat. Of course, once in the back seat, my brother and I would jump up and down and think of other things to do that caused further wear and tear to the car. When not in use, we made believe that the car was an airplane. Whoever was behind the wheel was the pilot and whoever jumped in the back seat was the tail gunner. From our positions, my brother (or some other kid) and I would shoot down imaginary enemy airplanes. Coupled with the fact that my mother was constantly driving a carload of kids back and forth from the beach in Santa Cruz, the inside of the Old Carrettone suffered a considerable amount of wear and tear. Eventually, my mother had to cover the seats with some new car upholstery—an expense—and extra work—that she was not too thrilled about. She swore that her new car would be a four-door sedan and that the car would be treated more mercifully. She finally got her wish in 1949, when we got the new Chevrolet. My brother and I were so thrilled to have a new four-door car with radio and heater, that we treated the Chevrolet with greater kindness. At least for a while.

Valentina was one of the first women on the coast to have a driver's license. I am sure she felt it necessary because she was a working woman and at times had to have a car to get to work. Also, because my brother was sick during his early childhood, she needed transportation to get to a doctor when my father was not available. Because she drove, friends and neighbors often called upon her to drive them to various places. Valentina seldom refused; she was a familiar sight on the Coast Road driving up and down in the Old Carrettone. Given the fact that the car had a manual gearshift, she did quite well. I can not remember her being involved in any accidents while she drove. On the other hand, I can remember Bronco being involved in a couple of fender benders.

The Old Carrettone faithfully took us to the movies in Santa Cruz. Prior to 1947, Santa Cruz had two movie theaters: the older Santa Cruz Theater, on Walnut near Pacific Avenue, and the newer Del Mar, on Pacific near Lincoln. The Santa Cruz Theater first opened its doors in 1920, and kept them open until 1955, when damage caused by floodwaters forced it to close. The Del Mar Theater first opened in 1937, and is still showing movies today at the same location. Old-timers seem to think that the old Santa Cruz Theater had a long run (35 years), but its record is nowhere near as long, as the one being established by the neophyte Del Mar Theater—67 years and still going.[78]

Almost every Saturday night, my mother and my father, driving the Old Carrettone, took my brother and me to one of these two movie theaters. Usually we went to the older Santa Cruz Theater, because for seventy-five cents for adults and fifty cents for children, it offered a double-feature movie. Usually this consisted of a western and a drama or comedy film. A newsreel, a cartoon, and a serial also accompanied the featured films. (I can remember actually being a bit disappointed after World War II had ended. The newsreels got a bit boring without all those planes and ships shooting at each other.)

After parking the Old Carrettone in the Purity Foods' parking lot at Cedar and Lincoln Streets, we walked down Pearl Alley to the theater. Then my brother or I would walk up to the ticket booth to get our ticket. There we would be attended to by Miss Edith Young, who was moonlighting from her job as a math teacher at Mission Hill Junior High School. (Because of an incident that occurred in the fourth grade, I had been constantly afraid of taking math courses. In junior high school, Miss Young and Mr. John Evans became my math teachers. They were such good teachers, that I found out that math could be fun.) After buying our tickets, the Comelli family entered the theater, walked past the concession stand with its enticing smell of popping popcorn, and climbed the winding stairs that led up to the balcony. (Smoking was allowed only in the balcony section.) At the top of the stairs we were met by an usher, usually a boy in his late teens, wearing a brown and tan "Johnny" uniform. The curious reader now asks, "What the heck is a 'Johnny' uniform?" I am sure my brother and I weren't the only ones who did, but we called it a "Johnny" uniform because in the 1940s, Phillip Morris Cigarettes had advertisements on the radio and in magazines which featured a rather short young man wearing a brown-and-tan bellman's uniform, with brass buttons on his chest, and a round page hat on his head. He was called "Johnny" and he went around yelling at the top of his lungs, "Call—for—Phillip—Morrr-eeesc!" (According to the Santa Cruz Sentinel, "Johnny" even made at least two appearances at the old Vans Food Market on Front Street in Santa Cruz, on August 20, 1948 and June 20, 1949.)

The "Johnny clad" usher carried a flashlight, which he used to guide us to our seats in the front row of the upper balcony. The lower balcony was called the Lodges and was reserved for folks that were willing to pay a whole dollar for their tickets. There, they got to sit in cushy, more comfortable chairs. (I always wonder whether sitting in the Lodges made the movies any better than they actually were.) During the intermission, Valentina would give John and I a couple of nickels. We then went downstairs to the concession stand, where we usually bought two Baby Ruth candy bars. A nickel in those days could buy a big Baby Ruth, with all that chocolate, caramel, and nuts. This gave us plenty of energy to watch the second feature.

After the movie was over, we walked back to the Purity parking lot where the Old Carrettone was waiting for us in cold, ominous silence. We all held our breaths, as Bronco pulled on the hand-starter with his left hand and manipulated the manual choke with his right hand. (Both the starter and choke were located on the dashboard. As I recall, we had to change the starter several times, finally ending up with a push-button starter. This made it easier for the driver to initiate the action, but it didn't improve the starting capabilities of the engine.) The cold engine coughed and sputtered. After a couple of tries, Bronco usually got the engine to turn over without flooding. When it did flood, we just had to sit and wait in the dark until the flooding eased. Our biggest fear was running down the battery after too many start attempts. Then we were really in trouble. Most of the time, the Old Carrettone would finally start up, but there were no guarantees.

Circa 1949, I learned that Mario was driving a truck on the Rodoni Ranch. It was common for farm kids to learn to drive at an early age. It was not unlawful because all of the driving was done on the ranch and not on public highways. Mario was younger than I was. I couldn't let him get away with it, without an appropriate challenge. I don't know how I did it, but I convinced my parents to teach me to drive. My brother, three years older, was not yet interested.

I can remember Bronco driving us across the Coast Road to the Southern Pacific Railroad tracks, which ran north and south, between the Coast Road and the Pacific Ocean. Adjacent to and running parallel to the railroad tracks, was a dirt road that extended about a quarter of a mile. On this dusty road, at age eleven or twelve, with my brother observing from the back seat, I took my first driving lessons. Up and down this road I went, slowly at first, grinding the gears and frequently popping the clutch. Like all drivers learning to drive a stick-shift car, it took time for me to learn to coordinate my movements between the gearshift, the gas pedal, and the clutch. As

I recall, low gear was down and to the left, second gear was up and to the right, and third gear was down to the right. Stepping on the clutch, and shoving the gearshift up and to left, put the car in reverse. Of course to accomplish the latter, the car had to be at a complete standstill. Sometimes I forgot, and much to Bronco's consternation, my forgetfulness caused the gears to clash, causing bone-vibrating, grinding sounds.

I don't know how many times the car lurched forward and stopped because I had let up on the clutch too fast, or because I had shifted into high gear instead of low gear. After a few times of this happening in a sequence, the Old Carrettone's engine "flooded over" and would not start. We would have to wait until the flooding had receded before the engine would re-start. My father showed great patience with me. He was actually a better teacher than a driver. Bronco was known to grind the gears, and to flood the engine, a few times himself.

Shortly after I learned to drive, my brother became interested. Now the roles became reversed. While my father sat in the passenger seat next to John, I sat in the back seat and observed. I was not a quiet observer. Being an "experienced" driver I had much to say about how my brother was conducting himself behind the wheel. I would laugh as he popped the clutch and killed the engine. I couldn't understand why it took him so long to master the art of shifting. After a while, it all became too much. They left me at home, as my father tried to teach my brother without me. It took a while, but he finally learned. Of course, being older he got to drive on the highway sooner than I did, but I never made him forget that I was the first brother to learn to drive the Old Carrettone.

Years later, I still attribute my relatively safe driving record to some of my father's early teachings. I never did get involved in an accident driving the Old Carrettone. In fact it wasn't until I was a senior in high school (1954 to 1955), that I got into my first automobile accident. By that time I had my own driver's license. I was driving up Laurel Hill, near Santa Cruz High School, in my parents' Chevrolet. (My high school friends and I called it the Old

La Nostra Costa (Our Coast)

Torpedo.) As I approached the top of the hill, a car pulled out from the stop sign on California Street. I applied the brakes, but I was unable to stop in time. I hit the other car broadside. Fortunately, only my pride was hurt: I got the ticket. I was framed! Later as a police officer, I learned that the primary fault in these types of accidents belongs to the driver pulling out from a stop sign. It's his responsibility to enter the intersection only when it is safe to do so. The perceptive reader might argue that I was probably going too fast. Well yes, but still, you don't pull out in front of a runaway freight train! Just my luck. There was some loose gravel on the roadway, and so the Police Officer decided to cite me for going too fast for the existing conditions. *Porca la miseria!*

I was ordered to appear before Judge Scoppettone—the same judge who might have sent Joe Gemignani into the Army. Since this was my first time as a defendant in any court, my parents contacted John Battistini, who owned John Battistini Insurance, Inc. in Santa Cruz. (I'm quite sure that the Old Torpedo was insured through his Company.) He was also an Italian emigrant, but he had educated himself and, most importantly, he knew how to read, write, and speak English. My father and mother, as well as many other coastal Italians depended on John and also his wife Angelina, to help them whenever they had to fillout papers in English or needed an explanation of what they were actually signing. This was most important when applying for American Citizenship. The Battistinis were an immense help to many Italians living *su per la costa* during this time.[79]

Well, I spoke English, but my parents felt that I needed help in this matter. John took me under his wing, and told me to plead guilty, and to say that I was very sorry about the accident. John told me that it was very important to be very respectful when before Judge Scoppettone. Although I didn't feel that I was completely at fault in the matter, I listened to John, and pleaded guilty. John got up before the judge; and told him that this had been my first accident, and that otherwise I was a good boy. After questioning me and giving me a stern lecture on safe driving, the judge ordered me to write an essay on why I was going to drive safely from then on. That was it. After I wrote the essay I was a free man—but I still believe I was "framed".

On the other hand, Judge Scoppettone's sentence must have done some good. Since that time, I have driven a million-plus miles, mostly commuting to work and patrolling the streets of San Jose. Notwithstanding even emergency driving (with red lights and siren) in my police car, the most dangerous driving I had to do was the daily thirty-mile commute to San Jose from Scotts Valley, where I lived for twenty years. There, on Highway 17, I came close to being involved in several major accidents, but I was able to avoid all of them, except for one. My car hit a deer. I survived, though unfortunately the deer didn't.

The reader, being mindful of the dangers of high-speed chases in police work, might ask, "How did you do on the job?" Through the grace of God, I came through all those chases without being involved in a serious accident. I believe that because of those good driving skills instilled in me at a very early age, and the special practice I had with the Old Carrettone (which I will describe below) I suffered only a limited number of on-duty traffic accidents. I was involved in a few fender-benders—but only one major accident.

While I was driving in downtown San Jose, a car ran a red light and plowed into my patrol car. Fortunately, the impact hit on the passenger side of the vehicle. The offending vehicle struck the police car with such force that it (the police car) was sent careening out of control across the intersection. The wheels on the driver side of the vehicle hit the curb at the corner of the sidewalk. I could feel the right side of the car rising up beneath me. Although I was wearing a lap seat belt, the jarring impact with the sidewalk caused my body to fly up off the seat just enough so that the top of my head hit the roof of the interior. Blood started flowing down my face. I could see the windshield shattering before my eyes and I could feel the car start to roll over on its left side. Suddenly, I felt an impact on the driver side. Fortunately for me, my car hit the tall metal pole of a street sign on the corner. This prevented the car from rolling over. Instead, the police car bounced off the pole, and settled upright on its wheels. I did not lose consciousness, so I knew that I was hurt. As I'd been trained to do, I immediately tried to call for help on the radio, but the impact of the accident had caused the controls on the radio to jam. I could not communicate my predicament to headquarters. At that moment, I could feel a little bit of panic setting in. A police car without a radio is like a lighthouse without a beacon. People know that it's out there, but they do not know quite where. As luck would have it, a nurse who had witnessed the accident called for help. An ambulance soon arrived and I was transported to San Jose Hospital. The blow to my head had caused a deep laceration in my scalp that required suturing. Fortunately, I survived without any major damage to my hard head. This time, the car that didn't stop at the light got the ticket.

I can't say for sure that all that driving in the Old Carrettone helped me keep my accident count relatively low, but one last adventure with that old car did provide me with excellent training for future police pursuit driving. This adventure, or misadventure, occurred *circa* 1949. By then the end was in sight for the Old Carrettone—because the brand new Chevrolet (the Old Torpedo) had arrived at our house *su per la costa*. For a time, then, we used the Old Carrettone as a second car. We usually took the old car when we went to the beach or drove to Davenport. (My mother didn't want any of that loose beach sand inside her new car, and when going to Davenport, my father didn't want any of that damp cement dust to ruin the exterior paint.) When not in use, we parked the Old Carrettone behind or alongside the house. The new Chevy, of course, was parked in the garage.

The Old Carrettone soon became an attractive nuisance for my brother and me. Remember, we now knew how to "drive." At certain times when my mother and father were not at home, we would practice our driving. This was usually done on a dirt road that ran in an easterly direction away from the Coast Road, and passed near our house on its north side. This road proceeded up a slope to the easternmost boundary of the Gulch Ranch, where it intersected a second dirt road which ran in a southerly direction, and it ended near the paved road that led to *Il Dumpo* (Dimeo Lane). This "road course" of ours was about a half-mile or so in distance. Up the slope we would drive, making a right turn at the top, driving to the end of the second dirt road, and finally turning around and driving home.

After a while, driving the "road course" got boring. To make it more exciting we naturally began to drive the course at a higher rate of speed. The most exciting part of this was coming down the slope back toward our house. To avoid going straight and entering the Coast Road itself (shades of Potrero Hill in San Francisco), we had to make a sharp right turn on a third dirt road running parallel to the Coast Road, and heading in a northerly direction. (This was the path Bronco took when walking to work in *il buco*.) This was fine if you were going at a safe speed; however, the faster we went down the hill, the harder we had to apply the brakes, and the sharper the turns became. As the steering wheel was turned and the brakes applied, the Old Carrettone leaned on its left side causing the wheels on the right side to rise off the ground. Simultaneously, the tires on the left side dug into the soft earth causing the rear end of the car to swing sharply from right to left. As the old car came to a sliding stop, the wheels on the right side would settle back to earth.

The alarmed reader might now blurt out, "My gosh! Weren't you two idiots afraid that the old car would flip over?" Oh, yeah! Not being completely stupid, however, my brother and I did begin to worry that the car might roll over some time, unless we slowed down. However, we didn't want to slow down: we had to devise a plan whereby we could maintain maximum speed without tipping over the car on a turn. We came up with the ingenious "designated weight" method of stabilization. We figured that if we weighted down the right-hand side of the car, the added weight would keep the right-hand wheels on the ground. In fact, if we did this right we probably would be able to go even faster. We determined that the best (and, by the way, the most fun) method by which to weigh down that side of the car, was for one of us to ride on the outside of the vehicle. First, we experimented by standing on the running board, hanging on with our hands to the inside of the window frame. After a few tries employing this method, we found it to be too precarious. It was too damn hard to hang on. Later we found that it was much easier to hang on to our runaway contraption by simply lying on the front fender, and holding on to one of the headlights.

I will always remember the first time I came down that hill, riding on the right front fender as the "designated weight." My brother drove down the hill, picking up speed to maybe 40 miles per hour. I can remember that exhilarating feeling as the car approached the Coast Road. Now I knew what Joe must have been experiencing on his motorcycle rides. As we hit the appropriate spot in the road, my brother hit the brakes hard and turned the steering wheel sharply to the right. The wheels locked and the car's rear end spun from right to left. The car lurched up onto its left wheels; the right wheels came off the ground just for a split second, and then settled back down as the car slid to a stop. The "designated weight" theory worked.

After this, the notion that the car could have rolled over or that we could have been thrown from the car never entered our minds. We believed that our "designated weight" would hold the car in place; there was no way the car could roll over. My brother and I continued to drive the "road course," alternating as driver and "designated weight," for many a glorious ride, until one day when a meddling *rancere* saw our daredevil maneuvers. He quickly "snitched us off" to our mother. Needless to say my brother and I caught holy hell for our escapades. Our extra-curricular driving was quickly put to an end. *Porca la miseria!*

Why didn't the Old Carrettone roll over? We certainly were going fast enough, and the turns we made were sharp enough to induce a rollover. Did the "designated weight" actually work, or was the Old Carrettone watching out for us one last time? Perhaps a combination of both—or maybe just plain luck.

As time went on, we used the Old Carrettone less and less. A Mexican laborer named Salvadore wanted to buy the car. After haggling over the price, Valentina agreed to sell the car to him for $200, to be paid in installments. I think that Salvadore made one payment of $50 and then "flew the coop." The last time I saw the Old Carrettone, it was parked on the side of Dimeo Lane. Apparently

Salvadore had returned to Mexico, abandoning the vehicle. A few days later the car was gone, never to be seen again.

I guess I never realized how lucky we were to have the Old Carrettone, and with it, my mother's ability to drive. Norma (Dinelli) has told me that her mother did not know how to drive. They, along with other coastal Italians who either didn't have a car or didn't know how to drive, had to take the Greyhound Bus in order to get to Santa Cruz. So, why do I have such disdain for a car that was so much a part of our family? I have already written that the car was unreliable. I can remember one evening when my mother, brother, and I went to the old Sisters' Hospital, by the beach at Bay Street and West Cliff Drive in Santa Cruz. I believe we went there to visit my father, who had just had his hernia operation. When we finished our visit and got into the car to go home, the headlights would not come on. My mother must have fiddled with the light switch for at least 15 minutes until finally, after many of Valentina's *accidenti* and *Dio Buonos*, the lights came on. As we drove home on the Coast Road, the lights kept fading on and off. We finally made it home safely, but it was one miserable, scary experience. The Old Carrettone liked to do things in that way throughout its career. It was as though it were getting back at us, for something we had done to it—probably all that jumping around my brother and I did, or perhaps it didn't like taking us to the beach all that much.

Above all, I think the car made me feel poor. My family did not have all that much money, but we always had plenty to eat and never suffered from a lack of clothing. I really never felt poor (although Valentina kept reminding my brother and me that we *were*), except when I was in the Old Carrettone. It seemed to me that all the other people living on the coast then had newer-model cars. At school, the parents of my schoolmates all drove newer-model cars (or it seemed so at the time.) I remember one time when Valentina picked us up at Laurel School to take us to the circus. A couple of my friends rode with us. I was mortified. Now the whole school would know that we were poor.

When my family bought the new Chevrolet, it was like announcing to the world that we were no longer poor. I will always remember the Old Carrettone, but I will never regret the time we got rid of it. It was like a "right of passage" to a better life. At least for the moment.

Endnotes

[79] John Battistini died on September 6, 2003. His obituary, appearing in the *Santa Cruz Sentinel*, noted that, among other things, "Mr. Battistini was known for his compassion and willingness to help others. He assisted many Italian immigrant families in their quest for a better life after coming to America." On behalf of my family, I can certainly attest to that fact. John lived to be eighty-nine years old.

IL CARRETTONE VECCHIO

C. 1948

JOHN BATTISTINI

25. La Scuola (The School)

Our yellow school buses employed the Coast Road to take coastal kids to and from *la scuola* [**skwoa** lah]. Laurel School of Santa Cruz was at the intersection of Laurel and Center streets. The Louden Nelson Community Center is now housed in that same sprawling one-story stucco-and-tile building, which was originally built *circa* 1930.

Some of my very first memories from this time are of waiting for the bus to return from the school with my brother. John, being three years older than me, must have been six or seven at the time. Initially, going to school must have been quite an experience for my brother, since he didn't speak a word of English. Italian was spoken in the Comelli home, and it was my first language, although as my brother learned the language at school, I soon picked up a few words of English from him. Because I was three or four years old at the time, I didn't go to school. So everyday, I waited patiently for my brother to come back from school.

While waiting, I devised a very interesting way of keeping my eye out for the bus, without having to leave for "potty time." My mother and Argentina would be cleaning sprouts in the garage, where Joe kept his motorcycle. Apparently my mother had instructed me to use the bathroom in our house whenever I felt the urge to go "poop." Being too busy with her work, she often did not have the time to go with me. I have to tell you that I was scared to death, going into that old empty house. I imagined that every monster in the world lived there and that I was their primary target. Being such a little guy, I wanted my mother to be with me. I had to come up with something to alleviate my fears. Besides, I couldn't see the returning school bus while sitting on the pottie.

I must have been a very observant child. Gazing out across the planted sprout and artichoke fields, I must have seen *ranceri,* every once in a while, squat down among the plants and disappear from view. My young, fertile mind probably deduced that they were doing "caca" (this was before the common use of porta-potties), right there in the field. This apparently struck me as being the answer to my problem. Behind the garage and next to the Gemignanis' chicken coop was a zucchini squash patch. I figured that I could go poop right there and, in doing so, I could keep an eye out for the school bus. Plus, those invisible monsters wouldn't dare get me with my mother being so close by. Besides, the only ones that knew I was doing it were the clucking chickens, and they didn't seem to mind.

Thus, whenever I felt the urge, I simply squatted down among the zucchini plants, and did my thing, *rancere* style. However, I kept forgetting one thing: toilet paper. The better-prepared *ranceri* always kept a folded piece of newspaper in their rear pocket. When the need occurred, they used it as toilet paper. Apparently being unaware of this aspect of the game, I improvised by using the zucchini plant leaves for toilet paper. I must have been really enterprising for my age, because I even recycled the toilet paper, by feeding the used zucchini leaves to the chicken. No need to flush.

Everything went well, at least for a while. Then one day Argentina, an excitable woman even under the most normal of circumstances, came into the garage, wildly waving her hands in the air and screaming to the high heavens. Using my mother's nickname, Argentina screeched, "O Dio! O Dio! Vale! Merda! Merda in il giardino! O Dio! E vero Vale! Merda insieme i zucchini! O Dio!" ("Oh God! Oh God! Vale! Shit! Shit in the garden! Oh God! It's true, Vale! Shit in there with the zucchini! Oh God!")

La Nostra Costa (Our Coast)

It soon became obvious to me what had happened. While searching for zucchini, Argentina had accidentally stepped on some of my deposits. Right away, Argentina believed that a *rancere* working on the ranch must have done the dirty deed. Subsequently, her suspicions fell on a worker nicknamed Mazza [**maht** zah]. Mazza means sledgehammer in Italian, and for reasons known only to himself, Mazza went around constantly saying, "Quel uovo [**o**-voh] infernale!" ("That infernal egg!"), probably referring to some nocuous egg out of the depths of Hell. Infernal egg or not, Argentina was convinced that Sledgehammer was the culprit, and accused Mazza of lying when he denied the charges.

The astonished and perhaps somewhat embarrassed reader may now ask, "Did Argentina ever find out that it was little Ivano, who was messing up her plants?" Oh, yes. Seeing the distress that I had caused, I finally garnered enough courage to tell my mother. Using my very best Italian and in a very apologetic tone of voice I told her, "La caca era mia." After learning that "it was my shit" in the zucchini patch, Vale started to laugh uncontrollably. Calming herself down, my mother tried to be very serious, when she explained to me that I wasn't a *rancere* yet, and that little kids were only permitted to make "caca" in the toilet. Much to my consternation, she then informed me that she had to tell Argentina about my confession.

I know that my subsequent statement of contrition, did in fact cause Argentina to forgive me for my fecal misbehavior, however, I do not know if she ever apologized to Mazza for falsely accusing him. I think that she may have because after that incident, Sledgehammer kept giving me dirty looks every time he saw me. Mazza probably thought that I had been hatched from that *uovo infernale,* or perhaps that I had been fertilizing it.

One thing about this inglorious event about which I am sure, is that I had learned an invaluable lesson which stayed with me for the rest of my life. That is, if you want to stay out of trouble, don't ever make "caca" in your neighbor's garden.

When I was old enough and had learned my lesson about correct fecal behavior, I joined my brother in waiting for the school bus at the Rodoni Ranch. After dressing, we ate our morning meal, which included an after-breakfast spoonful of cod-liver oil. My mother was a firm believer that strong doses of vitamin D went a long way to prevent illnesses such as colds, influenza, tuberculosis and perhaps even polio. She may have been right. Unlike my brother (the daily "spoonful" must have started after my brother's illness), I was pretty healthy growing up. After this morning ritual, John and I grabbed our lunch pails, and walked along the right-hand side of the Coast Road, to the Rodoni Ranch. Knowing that the ever-present traffic on the road caused a danger to us, my mother attempted to get the school district to have the bus stop in front of our house. Her request was denied because they thought that stopping the bus at the top of the Gulch would pose a danger to the kids riding inside. Obviously, it was safer for the bus to pull off the road and onto the "big gravel yard" at the Rodoni Ranch.

During these early years, Pete and Rina Rinaldi lived on the Rodoni Ranch with their two daughters, Sally and Alma. (This was the same Pete Rinaldi that eventually had trouble with my father). I remember that when I was in kindergarten, Alma, who was in the fifth or sixth grade at the time, used to watch over me for a half a day. Kindergarten was only a half day, but the problem was that the bus taking us back to our homes didn't come to pick us up until school was over at around 3:30 p.m. My mother was working at the time and probably was not able to pick me up. She made an arrangement with the Rinaldi family and the school to have Alma look after me. Thus, Alma, willingly or unwillingly, became my babysitter.

The arrangement was that after kindergarten let out, I was to report to Alma. After lunch she took me to her classroom. The teacher seated me in the back row somewhere, and gave me paper to draw on. I spent my entire afternoon with these older kids as they attended to their studies. Fortunately, one other boy my age was in the same predicament. His name was Jerry Mungai. Jerry was the son of Dino and Edith Mungai. Along with his older brother Donald, Jerry lived on the Mungai Brothers Ranch, which was located about one and half miles south of the Gulch Ranch. If it wasn't for Jerry, it is quite conceivable that I would have gone bonkers in that classroom.[80]

After I moved on to the first grade, I met Jim Ceragioli and Marvin Del Chiaro. The four of us—Jerry, Jim, Marvin and I—became close buddies. We were all from Italian families and we all lived *su per la costa*. Actually, Marvin, with his sister Dolores, lived closer to Santa Cruz. Their parents Lisandro and Effie Del Chiaro had a small ranch near where the Wrigley plant used to be. (For years, the Wrigley Company employed Santa Cruzans to make their famous chewing gum at this location.) It was unknown to us at the time; however, all four of us would go on to get our college degrees.

There was also a girl named Jeanette Benedetti (Shaw). The daughter of Eraldo and Emma Benedetti, Jeanette was our age and also lived on the Coast Road, not too far from the Gulch Ranch. We all had a lot in common and we especially liked talking in Italian so that the teachers and other classmates could not understand us.

Jeanette hung around with us; however, Laurel School made it difficult for the boys to play with the girls, since the teachers separated the boys from the girls during recess. The playground was surrounded by a tall wire fence and divided into two halves. The boys played on the half closest to Laurel Street, and girls played on the half closest to Maple Street. Thus, our time interacting with Jeanette and other girls was limited to class time, and when we rode the bus together.

Circa 1949, we were shocked to hear that Jeanette had been accidentally shot. According to Jeanette, she was visiting relatives in Dinuba (near Fresno, California) at the time. A shotgun was left lying, fully loaded, behind the front seat of a parked truck. Her three-year-old cousin apparently found the weapon and accidentally pulled the trigger. Jeanette, who was standing outside the truck about four feet away, received a portion of the shotgun blast, directly in the face. Fortunately she survived. However, the surgeons were unable to save one of her eyes. This disturbed us greatly, because she was our age and we knew her so very well.[81]

Laurel School's faculty consisted entirely of women. When I was first enrolled in the school, Miss Viola Meints was the principal. Because I was only three or four feet tall at the time, I naturally had to look up at Miss Meints. She sure looked very tall from where I was standing. I always suspected that it was she (not President Roosevelt) who was responsible for the "Mi chiamo Ivano" incident. I like to think that she suggested the name change, to protect me from undue prejudices during that time of war against Italy. (Come to think of it, I was the only one in my group with an Italian-sounding first name.) Although the restrictions against "enemy aliens" usually applied to our parents, it was not uncommon, during these years of wartime paranoia, for some children of Italian emigrants to suffer from undue prejudices from the American community. I, for one, never experienced any overt prejudices either from my schoolmates or the teachers.

Under Miss Meint's leadership, the faculty ran a tight ship. Assisting them in this endeavor was a group of older children (sixth graders) known as Traffic Boys and Traffic Girls. Each day, I watched the Traffic Boys as they put on their white-cloth, Sam Browne-type belts, and then, with stop signs in their hands, walk to one of the four intersections around the school.[82] The red and white stop signs were attach to short poles easily gripped in one hand. At intersections, the Traffic Boys stopped traffic by bravely walking out into the middle of the street, with their stop signs held high over their heads. Once the traffic was stopped, they signaled for the younger kids to cross the street.

While the Traffic Boys monitored the intersections, the Traffic Girls monitored the "traffic" in the school hallway. As we entered the hallway, these Traffic Girls used to shout out, in very authoritarian-sounding voices, "No talking in the hallway!" or "Single file down the hall!" Also, prior to entering the hallway, Traffic Boys and Traffic Girls would inspect the children's hands to see that they were clean. If your hands weren't clean, they pulled you out of line and made you go to the lavatory to wash them. If the children broke the rules, they were sent to the principal's office for punishment. No one wanted to go to the principal's office. "Paddling" was still legal in those days.

I must have liked what I saw, because I decided at a very early age that I wanted to become a Traffic Boy. This was no easy task, because the Traffic Boys were selected by the principal, who, I am sure, listened to recommendations from the other teachers. A certain amount of "brown nosing" with the teachers was necessary as you progressed through the grades. Excessive brown-nosers were called "kissees." I always believed that Jerry and Marvin were the two biggest kissees in the group, although Jimmy ran a close third. (I think that I kept my brown nosing to an absolute minimum.) Of course, you still had to keep your grades up, and show a certain amount of leadership ability.

Our efforts must have been successful, because upon entering the sixth grade (in 1948), the principal, Miss Edith King, selected all four of us to be Traffic Boys.[83]

As luck would have it, the Traffic Boy system was changed when we were assigned to the "Force." The loose-knit group of boys that had been supervised mainly by the principal, was now to be formalized into the Santa Cruz Junior Safety Patrol. We were to be trained and supervised by a regular member of the Santa Cruz Police Department, Officer Charles Derby. This dramatic change was even announced in the *Santa Cruz Sentinel*, in an article appearing on August 6, 1948, which featured a warning from Officer Derby "...that traffic safety near schools would be rigidly enforced beginning this Fall, with the junior patrol in full charge, and the public obligated to comply with directives given by the young safety cops." Wow! Just what I was looking for—power and authority.

Officer Derby probably had the greatest influence on my becoming a police officer. At the time we were first introduced to him, Santa Cruz was celebrating "Old Timers Days." To honor the celebration, the police department allowed Officer Derby to grow a closely trimmed beard. (During this time period, Santa

Cruz celebrated its birthday by holding an annual event called "the Fiesta." *The Santa Cruz Sentinel*, dated October 2, 1949, has a picture of Officer Derby with his beard, along with other "Fiesta"-bearded officers.)I had never seen a police officer with a beard. During this time, police departments were influence by the rules and regulations of the military. Many members were veterans of World War II. They wanted their officers to be clean-shaven, with short haircuts. Later, in the late 1960s and early 1970s, the new Vietnam generation of officers, showing disdain for the military look, wanted to wear their hair long and grow mustaches. Police departments spent a great deal of time trying to regulate beards and mustaches, all in a losing cause. It is not uncommon today to see police officers wearing beards and mustaches. However, I now see many younger policemen clean-shaven and sporting short military haircuts. What goes around, comes around. That is, if you live long enough.

Beard or no beard, I thought that Officer Derby, in his blue policeman's uniform, looked like a knight in shiny armor. He was of medium build and not all that tall, maybe 5'10". The Traffic Girls thought him quite handsome. He spoke softly, except when giving military commands. Of course, the boys' main interest was with Officer Derby's revolver, which he wore on his right side, encased in a black leather clamshell holster.

We all drew close to Officer Derby as he demonstrated how this piece of equipment worked. First, gripping his swivel holster at the bottom and turning it upside down, he gave it several hard up-and-down shakes. Amazingly, the revolver did not fall out of the holster. Then, swiveling the holster back to its upright position, and gripping the brown walnut handle of the revolver with his right hand, he gave the gun several hard upward pulls. No matter how hard he pulled, the gun would not come out of his holster. Then with the revolver still encased in the holster, he once again gripped the handle of the revolver and using his index (trigger) finger, he pressed a hidden button built into the holster, just inside the trigger guard. The spring-loaded encasement sprang open to the front, and in a split-second, the revolver, with finger on the trigger, cleared the holster, ready for use. Wow! All the kids thought that this was a marvelous piece of equipment. Those crooks would never stand a chance against officers like Charles Derby, with their lightning-quick draw.

I never did get a chance to prove this theory. By the time I became a police officer in 1959, the San Jose Police Department did not recommend the clamshell-style holster for use. Apparently some holsters failed to open when needed, and on occasion the button inside the trigger guard, being accidentally hit, caused the revolver to fall out of the holster. Yet, during my last year as a Police Captain, I was given cause to remember Officer Derby's demonstration with his clamshell-style holster.

Tragically, on January 20, 1989, Officer Gene Simpson, while attempting to make the arrest of a mentally disturbed person, had his holstered handgun taken from him. He was subsequently shot and killed with his own weapon. A fellow policeman, Officer Gordon Silva, who responded to the scene, was also killed. In turn, other officers fatally shot the mentally disturbed gunman. The scene of two uniformed police officers lying dead on Santa Clara Street haunts me to this day. An "easy draw" holster was not helpful in this situation, and I often wondered if a more secure type holster could have prevented this tragedy.

Besides showing us the workings of his "state of the art" holster, Officer Derby also taught us the rudiments of parade ground drill. The commands—*Platoon, Attention, Dress Right Dress, Left Face, Right Face, About Face,* And *Forward March*—were indelibly implanted in our minds. With continued practice, we all became quite good at executing them. In fact, our platoon became so good at it that we won first place at the 1949 year-end Junior Traffic Patrol Picnic (sponsored by the Optimist Club) held at De Laveaga Park in Santa Cruz. We beat out all the other elementary schools in our district. (Marvin Del Chiaro recently presented me with a photo of our Junior Traffic Safety Squad seated on the steps in front of Laurel School. Proudly, displayed at the front, are two shiny trophies. Wow! We really must have been good.)

Our winning efforts gave us bragging rights over all the other schools. This was important, because the following year most of us attended Mission Hill Junior High School, located on Mission Street. There we joined other students from the very same schools we had competed against. I still remember arguing with some of my new classmates, who thought their school should have won the competition. One classmate even went so far as to insinuate that one of the judges was a graduate of Laurel School, and that, of course, was why we had won those trophies. The fix was in.

I'm certain that we won legitimately, but I do recall that one of my most embarrassing "want to get away" moments occurred at this event. After we had performed flawlessly on the parade ground, the platoon was called to present itself at the front of the grandstand. There we were awarded our winning trophies. We were then called to attention and given the order, "Left face!" Everyone executed a perfect left face. Everyone, that is, except me. I was so excited about winning, that, just as in an old "Three Stooges" movie, I executed a perfect *right face*. Since I was always at the front of the platoon (probably because I was the tallest), I had to endure the glares of each and every one of my fellow cadets as I faced them. Recovering quite quickly, this "stooge" made an about-face to point his conspicuous carcass in the proper direction, "juu-hust" in time to execute the "Forward march!" command. For a time after this incident, I was afraid that the school district might take our trophies away. This didn't happen; however, my buddies kept reminding me of my gaffe for who-knows-how long. (During my time in the military and later as a member of San Jose Police Tactical Unit, it seemed that I was always placed at the head of my squad or platoon. I must record it here in this book, for the benefit of my fellow Traffic Boys, that I never made that mistake again!)

In addition to the training, we got new uniforms and new stop signs. The white-cloth Sam Browne belt was discarded. Instead, we got red knit, button-down sweaters, and yellow, military-style cloth field caps. The field cap was the type that folded and when not worn looked like an empty pocket sandwich. (Later, my army buddies and I used a somewhat derogatory term for the female genitalia to describe this style cap.) Affixed on the left side of the cap was a white safety-first cross with the letters SCJTP embroidered in red. The short, stubby stop signs were replaced by ones on long poles (approximately five feet long). Prior to going on duty, we proceeded to the boys' lavatory. At one end of the lavatory, someone had built us a dressing room, in which we stored our uniforms and stop signs. (To the best of my recollection, the husband of our school custodian built this room.)

After putting on our red sweaters and yellow field caps, we broke up into squads of five, and with our long stop signs at the shoulder-arms position, we marched to one of the four intersections. The squad consisted of a sergeant, a corporal, and three cadets. The corporal and the three cadets positioned themselves on the sidewalk, 50 to 100 feet from one of the four corners at the intersection. The sergeant, who did not carry a stop sign, positioned himself at the corner of the intersection closest to the school. He had a hand-held whistle by which he controlled the crossing of the younger kids. One whistle blast called the squad to attention. Two whistle blasts, and the squad put out their stop signs, holding them up with two hands. Once the traffic was stopped, the sergeant motioned for the children to cross the street. A final blast from the whistle and the squad pulled back their stop signs and returned to their original positions.

Originally, my squad had a sergeant named Damon Knight, whose whistle *blasts* were more like *tweets*. The squad felt that his *tweets* were not manly enough, which negatively effected our moral. Eventually, our classmate Dennis Soo Hoo replaced him. Dennis had joined us at school during the fourth or fifth grade, after his family had emigrated from China. Known to us at the time as Newy, he had a very strong whistle *blast that* made the squad feel real good.[84]

At times, standing at the intersection with our stop signs got rather boring. We looked for things to break up the monotony. One fun thing was to look for a driver who was "asleep at the wheel," or had simply chosen to ignore the stop sign. Once it was determined that a driver was not going to stop, one of us quickly reached across with our long pole and hit the car's windshield with our metal stop sign. This got drivers' attention all right, but it made them very angry. After a few complaints from these recalcitrant drivers, Officer Derby ordered us to not "bang the windshields anymore." We were only allowed to take down the license plate number and give it to Officer Derby for follow-up. *Porca la meseria!* We never believed that was as effective as the old "stop sign across the windshield" method. "Instant justice" was our motto.

I must say that I enjoyed my stay at *La Scuala*. I had a lot of fun playing with my classmates on that old fenced in school ground. Although we didn't play football, we did play most of the other sports, such as baseball, basketball, and kickball. My one regret is that none of the teachers ever taught me how to grip a baseball bat correctly. Not knowing anything about the game of baseball at the time, I just picked up the bat and hit the ball. I hit it pretty hard, too. The problem was that I was gripping the bat cross-handed, i.e., strong hand on the bottom, weak hand on top. Not only is this incorrect, it can cause serious injury to the wrists. No one ever corrected me until I got to Mission Hill Junior High School. By then it was too late. I never felt comfortable swinging the bat using the correct grip. Alas! A promising baseball career, down the tubes, because of inferior coaching.

Although playing inside the school fence was generally very safe, I did witness one of the bloodiest fights ever in that yard. I must have been in the second grade at the time. Two older boys, probably fourth or fifth graders, went at it. The bigger of the two boys was named Howard (Hodgie) Wetsel. The other was none other than my boyhood friend from the Gulch Ranch, Ray Fambrini. This was no "pussy footing around" shoving match. This was a full-fledged fistfight. Hodgie, having the longer arms, kept hitting Ray in the face with his closed fist. Ray, because of his shorter arms, couldn't quite land an effective blow to the face. Pretty soon, the blood started to run from Ray's nose. This did not deter him; he kept coming, trying to get at Hodgie. In the meantime, Hodgie kept hitting Ray in the face, causing more blood to flow. To his credit, Hodgie did try to back off, but Ray would have none of it. He kept coming and coming, trying to land that one punch that would equalize the match. Mercifully, one of the teachers spotted the fight and put an end to it before anyone got seriously hurt. Ray, with blood smeared all over his face, still wanted to fight. He was one hell of a tough kid. He stood his ground and never did give up. In our eyes he was the hero. Poor Hodgie got tagged as the villain.[85]

The teachers at the school for the most part were quite good and I did very well in most of the grades, except for the fourth grade. There, I received my one-and-only F. I guess I just could not get the hang of that "multiplication thing." My mother really got depressed when she saw the F on my report card. I think she was really sorry for not having helped me more. Having only a fifth-grade education, she believed that the schoolteachers were more qualified than she to teach arithmetic. Seeing that I was having a serious problem, she quickly set out to help me.

Valentina did know how to multiply numbers. On a piece of paper she illustrated how she had learned multiplication at her school in Italy. Horizontally across the top of a sheet of paper, she put down the numbers 1 through 12, and vertically down the left edge of the paper she wrote the same numbers. She then divided the paper with a pencil and ruler, giving each horizontal number its own column and each vertical number its own row. The intersecting lines formed 12 squares for each horizontal and each vertical number. Then, working across the paper, she filled in each square, by first adding each vertical number with itself and then with its subsequent sums.

For the computer literate, younger generation, who may have never seen such a graph, I will attempt to explain further. Working across in the *2* row, Valentina wrote the numbers *2, 4, 6, 8, 10, 12,…24*. In the *3* row she wrote *3, 6, 9, 12, 15, 18,… 36*. (Of course, this also can be done by using a number at the top of the page and working down the column in a similar fashion.) Then she invited me to stand closer, as she demonstrated a marvelous trick that opened up a new world for me. By placing her finger on a number at the top of the page and going straight down the column to any square corresponding to a number listed at the vertical edge of the paper, I saw that her finger came to rest on the correct multiple product for the two numbers. She then did the same thing by placing her finger on a number on the vertical edge of the paper and moving directly across the row and stopping at a square corresponding to another number at the top of the column. To my amazement, the square contained the correct product of the two numbers. Marvelous! I didn't know it at the time, but my mother had made me a real "hands-on" computer.

The reader probably wishes to ask, "Why are you making such a big deal about this? Hasn't this matrix been around for many years?" Yes, it has. The point I am trying to make, dear reader, is that after my mother taught me to use this teaching aid, I quickly learned how to multiply (and also to divide). It always amazes me that my mother, with a fifth-grade education, was able to teach me how to multiply, when a college-educated, supposedly trained teacher wasn't. Unfortunately, this incident so negatively effected me that I always had anxiety attacks when taking a math test. On the other hand, the lesson my mother taught me paid dividends. With Valentina's "hands-on" computer, and with a lot of concentration and considerable help from Mr. Evans and Miss Young, those two very special teachers, I was able to do fairly well when taking future math courses. No more F's for me.

Recently I made a visit to the old school. The schoolyard where Hodgie and Raymond had held their main event was now a community park, with trees, lots of green grass, and a basketball court. The only thing that seemed the same was the basketball court. As I remember it, while I had attended school a good portion of school ground had been paved over with asphalt. It certainly would have been nice to have had all that grassy area to play on. Although it has more trees now, I was disappointed to see that a particularly beautiful maple that had stood on the girls' side of the yard (near the corner of Maple and Washington streets) was gone. And what about the classrooms? Were they gone too? I would find to my surprise that the configuration of the classrooms, with only a few exceptions, was basically unchanged.

La Nostra Costa (Our Coast)

I parked the car on the Washington Street (northern) side of the school. I walked across the park and tried to enter through the Laurel Street entrance where the Traffic Boys once had stopped us to inspect our hands. This entrance was now reserved for children attending the Community Children's Center (for day care). I observed there was now a main entrance in the center of the building where the second grade room had been. This, along with the wooden deck abutting the entrance, was new. As a matter of convenience, I used this entrance to enter the school. Once inside I notice that the reception desk was where the principal's office used to be, near the Center Street entrance. Having desired to enter the school through the Laurel Street entrance, I turned to my right and walked to that end of the building.

This entrance, where once the boy students were stopped by the Traffic Boys, is now designated as an emergency exit, but the younger children are still allowed to use it to get to the playground. I looked to my right and saw that the boys' lavatory was still there. This was where the Traffic Boys had sent all those kids to wash their dirty hands. I walked inside and to my surprise found it basically the same. Our old dressing room, where we had changed into our red knit sweaters and picked up our long-poled stop signs, was still there. I tried to open the door, but it was locked. It is apparently being used as a storage closet.

I then returned to the hallway and took a look down the opposite end of the building. I tried to find the spot where the Traffic Girls had stood as they monitored the hall traffic. It seemed to me there was a drinking fountain in the middle of the hallway, just about where they had stood. At about that spot I saw there indeed was a drinking fountain, although I'm sure it wasn't the same one as before. I tried to imagine Jeanette Benedetti, Barbara Silva, Marion Hagler, Ellen Hermann, Barbara Jean Smith, and the other Traffic Girls, standing there and shouting out those ringing commands: "No talking in the hallway!" "Single file down the hall!" Oh yes, girls, I can still hear you now.

I noticed that the old kindergarten room (now designated Room 8) was still there on my right side at the beginning of the hallway. I thought it was only right that this room is now being used as the Children's Community Center room. I hope that these little kids were having as much fun as Jerry Mungai and I had during our day.

I then walked a few paces down the hall and there on the left-hand side was Miss Sampson's old first-grade room (Room 1). I found it basically unchanged. But the second-grade room had drastically changed. (Miss Peck, who got married to Mr. Twowig during my tour of duty here, had been our teacher.) In its place was the exit to the park. Room 2, next to the exit, was designated to be a smaller senior lounge. This may have been part of the second-grade room or the old nurses' room where we had gotten all those vaccinations. (Our parents and the school district had really believed in giving us all those shots. Ouch!!) Room 3 was the old cafeteria. It is now being used as a classroom, but part of the old kitchen is still there.

I walked to the end of the hallway, to where the auditorium had been. It too is still there. On this particular day of my visit, a group of senior citizens were practicing their line dancing steps. I went inside and saw that the stage where many of us had performed our first plays was still there, curtains and all.

Suddenly, looking at the stage, I was reminded of one particular night when the fifth grade put on a marionette show called "Mr. Wiggs' Birthday Party." I was the voice of a marionette called Mr. Wiggs. (Part of the project was to have the class make their own marionettes. The best marionettes were chosen for the play. Mine wasn't among the cast.) According to the story line, the more Mr. Wiggs laughed, the more he filled up with air, causing him to become airborne. It was my job to keep Mr. Wiggs afloat by doing a lot of laughing. The more I laughed, the higher the boy holding the strings raised Mr. Wiggs. By the end of the play I had everyone in the auditorium laughing with me, or so I thought. I later found out that the kids were actually laughing at a "girl" marionette who was attending the party. As she laughed, she too rose in the air, alongside

La Nostra Costa (Our Coast)

Mr. Wiggs. But apparently, the student manipulating her strings brought the marionette's legs up too high, causing her to show her white underpants. She was the hit of the show. Nevertheless, Mrs. Edythe Grayson my fifth grade teacher, would compliment me on a job well done. (Thanks, Mrs. Grayson. I needed that to bolster my confidence after flunking arithmetic in the fourth grade.)

Now, looking back from the auditorium towards the Laurel Street entrance, I saw that all the other rooms were still there, on the Center Street (southern) side of the building. As I *silently* walked back *single file down the hall*, I stopped and paused at Miss Andersen's third-grade room (Room 4), then Miss Giffin's infamous fourth-grade room (Room 5), where I got that "F," then Mrs. Grayson's fifth-grade room (Room 6), and finally Miss King and Mrs. Carruthers' sixth-grade room (Room 7). (Mrs. Carruthers had taught us in the morning; Miss King, the principal, in the afternoon.) All seemed to be in place and virtually unchanged, except that there is no longer a principal's office. As I best remember, the principal's office was adjacent to the sixth-grade room and next to the Center Street entrance. As I have previously noted, this section is now being used as a reception center.

At the reception center, I almost stopped to talk to the receptionist. I wanted to ask her whether she knew that she was probably standing on the very spot where the decision had been made to *change my name*, forever and ever. I thought better of it, since this historical fact was probably of interest only to me, myself, and I. Whether as *Ivano Franco* or as *Ivan Frank*, I had, I knew, benefited a great deal by attending this particular *scuola*. So, just before leaving, I hesitated. As if drawn by a magnet, I turned and walked back to my old kindergarten room. There, standing before the door, I felt compelled to once again speak those words of so long ago. In a low, but very firm tone of voice, I said aloud: "Mi chiamo Ivano." Now I was ready to leave. (For the life of me, I can not remember my kindergarten teacher's name. How apropos.)

Endnotes

[80] The Mungai Ranch is now part of the Wilder State Park. Jerry's father, Dino Mungai, was only 48 years old when he died of cancer in 1955. I still have memories of him riding a big horse along the rocky coast line *su per la costa*. Jerry has recently informed me that the horse was a Palomino named "Blaze."

[81] Jeanette was staying with her cousin, Rita Giannandrea (Franceschini). According to Rita, who grew up *su per la costa*, it was her youngest son who accidentally pulled the trigger. The accident occurred during the summer months. Jeanette had to endure a month long stay in a hot Fresno hospital with no air conditioning in her room while doctors attempted unsuccessfully to save her eye. In a letter to the author dated June 15, 2005, Rita writes that, "Some families in such crisis sever their ties —in our case it cemented our relationship even stronger than ever. To this day, Jeanette and her family are precious to us."

[82] In 1961, as a Military Policeman, I actually got to wear a real Sam Browne belt. The Army version was a wide leather belt, which went around the waist, and a thinner leather strap, worn diagonally over one shoulder and attached to the front and back of the belt at the waist.

[83] By this time, Miss Meints had transferred from Laurel School. A picture appearing in the *Santa Cruz Sentinel*, dated September 10, 1950, shows the "very tall" principal standing in her office at the new Bay View School, located at Bay and Mission streets.

[84] Later, as a young police officer, working traffic control at the intersection of First and Santa Clara streets in San Jose, I emulated Dennis' whistle *blasts* when controlling pedestrian traffic. Mine were so loud that they eventually drew complaints from the office workers who worked in the buildings near the intersection. My sergeant ordered me to tone them down. Maybe Damon was right: a *tweet* sometimes is better than a *blast*.

[85] It appears that Ray went on to make good use of his toughness. According to an article appearing in the *Santa Cruz Sentinel*, dated 5/25/52, Ray won the Top Athletic Award in his Senior Year at Holy Cross High School.

LA SCUOLA

SANTA CRUZ'S FINEST – 1949

26. La Costa Spaventousa
(The Scary Coast)

While I was writing this book, a very disturbing incident occurred, *su per la costa*. According to articles in the *Santa Cruz Sentinel* in the week of March 24, 2002, three bodies, two female and one male, were found on the bluffs overlooking Bonny Doon Beach, just south of Davenport. The two young girls were shot in the back of the head with a 12-gauge shotgun. The male apparently had died from a self-inflicted shotgun blast to the head. This incident reminded me that at times *La Nostra Costa* was and probably still is *spaventousa* [spah ven **toes** ah]—scary.

I have already written about the electricity blackouts and Bronco's near arrest as a spy during the War, and of the midnight ride involving Joe, Bronco, and Dante Ramaciotti, chasing unknown desperados up the Coast Road, and of Jeanette Benedetti accidentally being shot in the face. These were pretty scary incidents for a little kid. There were other scary and sometimes tragic incidents that have stuck in my mind after all these years. Just thinking about them sends shivers up and down my spine. Two of the most upsetting incidents occurred in the same year, 1947. As I later found out, both incidents were interrelated in a strange and scary way.

Ivano Franco Comelli

On Sunday, January 19, 1947, the marriage of a young Italian couple who we knew very well and who we visited quite frequently, ended tragically. According to the *Santa Cruz Sentinel* (January 21, 1947), Frederico Raffin [Rah **feen**], then forty-two years old, shot and killed his estranged wife, Norma (Rocchi), age thirty-two. This violent act occurred in the kitchen of their home on Market Street in Santa Cruz. (This was near to where Adolph's Restaurant was later built.) Raffin, also known *su per la costa* as "Boccetta" (a nickname most probably derived from the game of bocce ball), escaped the death penalty, but was sentenced to life in prison.

I quite vividly remember Frederico Raffin, a short and very thin Friulano with piercing dark eyes, coming to our house on the Gulch Ranch. On occasion, he would go into the fields with my father to pick artichokes for his family. On one particular occasion he brought along a friend. Ironically, he was also an off-duty Santa Cruz police officer. On our visits to the Raffin home on Market Street, I remember playing in the back yard with their two sons, Peter, the oldest, and Richard, the baby. The double tragedy here was that Frederico Raffin's violent and senseless act left these two boys, then ten and three years old, without a mother or a father.

In the late 1950s, Raffin was freed on parole and actually came to visit my father and mother. As fate would have it, one of Norma Raffin's sisters (Jackie) was living in the house next to ours (at 725 Seaside Street). From time to time, Peter and Richard would come over to visit their aunt. During Raffin's visit, Valentina mentioned this fact to Frederico and suggested that he stay awhile to see if he could get a glimpse of his sons. Raffin became very agitated and flatly refused, saying he had no right to see the boys after what he had done to their mother. Seeing them, he said, would upset him greatly. After a short visit he left, and we never did hear from him again. (Norma [Dinelli] Wilson also remembers Frederico Raffin visiting the Lorenzi Ranch during this period of time, apparently looking for work.)

A few years ago, John Battistini, who was used by the court in the Raffin trial as an interpreter for Italian-speaking witnesses, informed me that several years after the trial he received a call from an official of the Italian government, who wanted to know whether he knew a Frederico Raffin. Apparently Raffin, who had returned to Italy, wished to get remarried, and had told the official he was a widower. The official needed to have someone verify that fact. John informed the Italian official that Raffin was indeed a widower, and had become one under the most unusual of circumstances. Presumably, this information did not prevent Raffin from getting permission to marry again.

The other distressing incident that happened in 1947, was an automobile accident involving a fire truck and a passenger car, carrying members of the DeLucca family, which was well known *su per la costa*. The accident saddened the entire coast for months if not years to follow. The accident was reported in the *Santa Cruz Sentinel*, in articles dated August 2 and August 3, 1947.

According to the Sentinel articles, the accident occurred on Friday evening, August 1, at approximately 6:30 p.m., and involved a car with eight passengers, and a California Department of Forestry (CDF) fire truck, carrying a crew of six men. The passenger car was apparently traveling north on the Coast Road, and the CDF truck was traveling in a southwesterly direction on Swanton Road. The CDF truck, driven by William Wellhausen, age twenty, was responding from the Big Creek station enroute to a brush fire, with red lights and siren activated. Apparently the driver of the car, Amerigo DeLucca, did not see the fire truck, which entered the Coast Road at the Swanton Road intersection, soon enough to avoid the collision. DeLucca's car hit the truck broadside. Five people in the DeLucca car, including two children, were killed.

The Sentinel identified the dead victims as Amerigo DeLucca, age thirty-six, Donna DeLucca, age four, Anthony DeLucca, age nine, Mr. Manual Quandros, age sixty, and Mrs. Manual Quandros, age fifty-five. (The Quandros were neighbors of the DeLucca family. The Sentinel reported that the DeLuccas were taking the Quandros to San Gregorio.) Passengers in the car seriously injured were identified as Dolores DeLucca, age ten, Marie DeLucca, age twelve, and Matilda DeLucca, age thirty. None of the Forestry crew was killed. The most serious injured was the driver of the truck, William Wellhausen. Other members of the fire crew were identified as George Alphine, Allen W. Day, Vincent Buta, Allen Rupperechi and Peter Merrill.

The August 3, 1947 edition of the *Santa Cruz Sentinel* gives some evidence on just how violent the collision was. It describes the front end of the DeLucca car being, "smashed back into the front seat, completely demolishing the sedan; the fire truck was a total wreck, with its strong, reinforced steel frame bent and the cab knocked right off the frame, smashing wheels and axle." The year-end edition of the Sentinel, dated 10/31/47, re-published a picture of the accident, and stated that it "was probably the worst traffic accident in the history of Santa Cruz County." So badly damaged was the DeLucca automobile that the only identifying item clearly distinguishable was the California licenses plate, number 35 H 170. The Sentinel articles do not identify the make of the automobile. Some coastal Italians remember it as a black Buick, others as a black Cadillac.

Norma (Dinelli) Wilson told me that the DeLucca family had been at Serafina's earlier that evening, and that she, then about seven years old, had been talking to the DeLucca children as they sat in the car. They had waved goodbye to her as they left on their ill-fated trip.

Norma's friend, Patty Morelli, who at the time lived in Davenport, remembers the DeLucca's car stopping in New Town shortly before the accident, apparently to visit Julia Stefani, the sister of DeLucca's wife, Mathilda. According to Patty, everyone in New Town came out to see the beautiful new car. Patty remembers that it was only a short time after the car had left, that Julia Stefani burst into the Morelli's home screaming hysterically about the accident that had just occurred just up the road. Suddenly, the nighttime air *su per la costa* was filled with the piercing wails of sirens and screeching of ambulances and other emergency vehicles coming to the accident scene.

Norma now recalls hearing these sirens as the emergency vehicles raced past her house on the Coast Road, enroute to the accident, and then as they returned with the victims. It took Norma several years before she could hear the sound of sirens or see ambulances again without becoming frightened. Norma says there were so many people injured, that Abbie Novelli's bread truck was commandeered to help transport the victims. (During this period of time Abbie Novelli was a familiar sight up and down the Coast Road, making daily bread deliveries in his paneled truck for the Davenport Bakery.)

Some time after the accident, I remember Dolores DeLucca (later Dolores deJoiner), who was my age, being in one of my classes at Laurel School. She was a pretty girl, but her face was still greatly disfigured by ugly gray scars. Norma later told me that the doctors had informed Dolores she probably would develop cancer later in life because of the injuries she had incurred in the accident. Dolores died in the 1970s. According to Norma, the cause of death was cancer.

How tragic. It was even more so, and somewhat ironic, when I discovered that Amerigo DeLucca had been the half-brother of Norma Raffin. What really caught my attention was that at the time of the Raffin killing, Frederico Raffin gave his address as 45 Dufour Avenue in Santa Cruz. This is the same address cited by the *Santa Cruz Sentinel* articles as being the address of Amerigo DeLucca. We know that the DeLucca Family probably started their very regrettable journey *su per la costa* from that address. Did Raffin, in fact, leave from the same address to go murder his wife, Norma? Just thinking about it makes the hairs on the back of my neck stand on end. The ghosts of the coast have a strange way of speaking to you. Brrrr![86]

Articles in the Santa Cruz Sentinel have cited many other deaths in traffic accidents on the Coast Road, especially between Santa Cruz and the *Slida* area. In scanning some of these articles, one in particular caught my attention. On November 11, 1948, the *Santa Cruz Sentinel* reported that a nine-year-old boy, Carrol E. Wallace, was killed on Highway 1 after falling off the flat bed truck his father was driving. The boy, who was riding in the back of the truck with his younger brother, struck his head on the pavement, causing intracranial hemorrhaging. The Wallace family lived at 6006 Coast Road. This accident hit close to home, for one of Carrol's older brothers (I believe his name was Vernon) was in my sixth grade class at Laurel School. This accident naturally devastated the brother and saddened us all. It also dramatized for those of us who lived on the Coast Road, how deadly it could be.

Even closer to home, I can remember when this same Coast Road handed a personal reminder to the Comelli family of how hazardous it could be. One evening *circa* 1948, we got in the Old Carrettone and proceeded to the movies, traveling south on the old road. Bronco was driving, Valentina was in the front passenger seat, my brother was in the back seat behind my mother, and I sat directly behind my father. It must have been in the wintertime, because it was already dark and cars had their headlights on. I remember staring out the window looking at the oncoming headlights. Near the Wilder Ranch (now a State Park) the road curved slightly from west to east as it descended a small hill. (The old road, which is still used by park officials, passes in front of the Wilder Ranch compound; the new Coast Road passes behind the compound.)

As Bronco began his descent at the apex of the curve, I noticed, only for an instant, oncoming headlights directly before us. With a loud crash, bang, and blur of lights, the oncoming car struck the Old Carrettone just in front of where I was sitting. Bronco wasn't driving very fast, so he was able to keep control of the car and bring it to a safe stop a short distance down the road. Fortunately, no one was hurt, but as you might imagine I was all shook up. All I could remember was that crashing sound, the jarring impact, and those blinding headlights.

The driver and passengers from the other car were not Coast Road residents. They were apparently driving on the road to get to Half Moon Bay. At first they were mad at Bronco. They accused him of crossing over the white line and causing the accident. (I always believed that they tried to intimidate him because he spoke broken English and drove an old jalopy-looking car.) The California

La Nostra Costa (Our Coast)

Highway Patrol soon arrived and investigated the accident. Much to their chagrin, the CHP Officer found the driver of their car to be at fault. Not being familiar with the road, he apparently was going too fast to negotiate the curve safely. His car veered into our lane, causing the accident.

Needless to say we didn't get to the movies that night, although I seem to remember that my brother got to go with the Rodoni family. They were going to the movies also, and happened to come upon the accident shortly afterwards. I guess my brother wasn't as shook up as I was. The damage to the Old Carrettone was repairable, and it was on the road again after a couple of weeks, sporting a new paint job. Apparently, I quickly got over the accident with little ill effect, because I retained my usual seating in the car — behind my father. Either that, or my brother wouldn't trade with me.

Unfortunately, although many improvements have been made to the Coast Road, it is still dangerous—*spaventousa*. During the writing of this book, the *Santa Cruz Sentinel* reported that on Wednesday, June 26, 2002, a woman and a two-year-old girl were killed in an automobile accident on Highway 1, near Four Mile Beach, only about a half-mile north of the Gulch Ranch. The victims were later identified as Sonia Avila, age twenty, and Silvia Areli Ortega Mena, age two. Sonia Avila's daughter Monica, age four, was seriously injured; fortunately she survived. The three victims were on their way home from, of all places, Pescadero.[87] Obviously, the road from Pescadero, over which the Old Carrettone had on numerous occasions returned the Comelli family safely home, proved not to be safe, on this particular day, for this unfortunate family.

The Gulch Ranch became really scary when a single-engine plane crashed, plowing into a sprout field just west of the railroad tracks and near the Pacific Ocean. Ironically, this also occurred in 1947. Not only did we have to worry about the traffic on the Coast Road, we now had to worry about airplanes falling from the sky. My brother and I probably were at school at the time, but my mother was working in the old barn cleaning sprouts. She told us that she heard a big loud bang that caused her to run out of the barn. Valentina couldn't see anything, but she soon got word that an airplane had crashed and that the pilot and his passenger were both killed. *The Santa Cruz Sentinel* article estimated the time of the crash as between 11:45 a.m. and noon on Friday, October 3, 1947. It described the crash as so bad that "parts of the plane and what was believed to have been two bodies were scattered over more than 200 yards." According to the article, "identification of the bodies was impossible at this time, as limbs and the like were spread over a wide area." Two days later the Sentinel identified the dead as Ensign R. W. Koller, age twenty-three, of Alameda (the pilot), and Army Lieutenant W. J. Cunningham (no age given), of Oakland. Both were Air Reserve pilots on an orientation flight out of the Oakland Naval Air Station. According to the Santa Cruz coroner, Walter Bettencourt, the two were apparently students at San Francisco State College. As an aside, the first article identifies CHP Officer Victor Calhoun (the same Vic Calhoun who used to drop in at Serafina's) as being the first police officer on the scene.

Later, after the wreckage had been cleared, Bronco took my brother and me to the scene of the crash. There in the middle of the brussel sprout plants I saw a gigantic hole. I remember that we had to walk through the sprout plants to get to it. I stood at the edge and gazed in amazement at its size. The plane must have come straight down and hit very hard to cause a hole like that. Just imagining what the two occupants must have been thinking right before the final impact sent shivers up my spine. I guessed the pilot might have been trying to get to the ocean before crashing. My brother didn't think that would have helped, given the force of the impact. It was just lucky that no one was out harvesting at the time of the crash. That certainly would have been a disaster.

Walking away from the hole, I must have been looking at the ground, for under a sprout plant I spotted what looked like a scrap of meat embedded with dirt and debris. I pointed it out to my father. He took a closer look. Sure enough it was a piece of human flesh. Trying to disturb it as little as possible, Bronco dug a small hole in the recently cultivated soil and very carefully nudged the piece of human remains into the hole. He then covered the hole with topsoil.

La Nostra Costa (Our Coast)

When this was completed, he made the sign of the cross over the makeshift grave and prayed: *Dominus vobiscum. In nomine Patris, et Filii, et Spiritus Sancti. Amen.* My father didn't speak Latin, but he knew, from his early Catholic upbringing, those words, which mean, *The Lord be with you. In the name of the Father, Son, and Holy Spirit.* Bronco must have told someone about the incident, because soon after the whole field was disked under. Thus, any uncollected human remains were forever buried in this field on the Gulch Ranch.

In 1952, we were awakened from our sleep by Moro's alarming voice outside of our house calling, "Bronco! Bronco!" My father and mother got up and learned that there had been a fire at the Rodonis' house. As I remember it, the Rodoni family had been painting the interior of their house. Someone spilled a can of gasoline on the floor. The spill flowed underneath the hot water heater with disastrous results. The combustible fluid was ignited by the pilot flame, causing a flash fire. The Rodonis scrambled to get out. Mario dove out a side window, breaking the glass and cutting his arm. Fortunately for Mario, he was not hospitalized, though the cut in his arm did require several stitches.

Andreina and Dante got out suffering only minor burns. As I recall, Jeannie did not sustain any injuries. Elio was not so lucky. Before escaping from the fire, he sustained second and third degree burns over his legs and upper body. An article appearing in the February 13, 1952 edition of the *Santa Cruz Sentinel* describes Elio as suffering second degree burns about the hands and face. (It was a lot worse than that.) Later, I remember visiting him at Sisters Hospital. This poor kid (he was twelve years old at the time) was lying in a bed all bandaged up, unable to move because of the pain. The suffering must have been unbelievable.

Elio survived, but he suffered massive scarring over his legs and part of his upper body. Later when the wounds had healed, I remember going to the beach with the Rodonis. Elio would be wearing only his bathing suit. I will never forget those massive scars on his legs. Yet, I had to laugh when Elio would say in Italian to Andreina, "I'm going to take a walk down by the ocean now, so I can give a *good scare* to all those people that have been staring at me." Elio never skipped a beat. His positive attitude and good sense of humor saw him through these terrible times.

The Rodoni fire was by no means the only time that a *rancere* suffered severe burns on his body. I remember Bronco and Valentina talking about Francesco Franceschini and his near-death experience. According to his son Tony Franceschini, the accident occurred on the Marina Ranch *su per la costa* in 1940. His father was using a hand-held sprayer to kill fleas around the perimeter of a chicken coop. Francesco was using a mixture of gasoline that was being funneled to the sprayer nozzle from a tank he had strapped to his back. Nearby, there was an open fire that had been set to burn a pile of brushes and weeds. A spark from that fire caused the tank to ignite and explode. Francesco was able to free himself from the tank and then rolled on the ground to extinguish the flames on his body. Thus, he was able to save himself. Nevertheless, according to his daughter Rita, he received first, second and third degree burns over most of his body.

Francesco spent three full months at Santa Cruz Hospital and another three months in an apartment nearby. During this period, his wife Nuncia, along with special nurses cared for his every need. Francesco was so severely burned that he could not feed himself. Nuncia was constantly at his side taking care of him, talking to him and reading from the Italian newspapers and books to keep his moral up. (The reader needs to remember that there were no television sets in hospitals in those days. Suffering and boredom were the routine.) Finally, Francesco was given the green light to return to his home *su per la costa*. However, for years to come he would have to undergo painful skin grafting surgeries to help heal the wounds. In time he recovered sufficiently to take over his role as *il bosso* of the Marina Ranch.

Fire was scary, but water could also threaten body and soul. The Pacific Ocean *su per la costa* has had its fair share of stories concerning deaths, shipwrecks, and other accidents. Usually these involve a swimmer caught in the rip tides and drowned, a boat washing up on the rocks during a storm, or a fisherman falling from a bluff, or being swept off the rocks by a giant wave. *Il Mare* was always *spaventouso,* and a real threat. This was brought home to me once when the Pacific Ocean spoke to me. Well, maybe it didn't really speak to me, but it surely demonstrated its awesome and frightening power.

Remember the beach where Mario and I spied on the man and women entwined in the throes of lovers' bliss? Many a day, we kids played on this sandy beach. We often ran across the sand, played ball, or climbed on the rocks to explore the tide pools for sponges, starfish, and other creatures of the sea. The surf was always rough, with big rolling waves breaking on the shore, and forming strong undertow currents as it receded from the sloping sandbank. Our parents made us well of aware of the dangers. We never swam in that ocean and we were very careful even when we just soaked our feet in the surf. Aside from this, and the noise of the roaring ocean, we found the beach a peaceful and quite safe place to play in and explore.

But *circa* 1950, a giant rainstorm hit the coast. The rain and wind came down upon us, buffering the walls and roof of our small, fragile house. Rain hit the Coast Road in such volume that it quickly caused the drainage ditches to overflow. Water formed on the road, creating wild currents of water, which flowed past our house and down into the Gulch. Amid the sounds of rain, wind and rush of flowing water, we could hear the ocean roaring in the not-too-far-away distance.[88]

This whole scene reminded me of a film that Dante would often show us at the ranch. (I think it was a Laurel and Hardy silent feature.) The old flick was a comedy, but rather scary because it depicted an old rickety house situated on a beach. A big storm hit, and giant waves swept the house off its foundation and into the ocean. To ride out the storm, the fat man and the skinny guy sat on the roof of their house, as it bobbed about in the ocean. If the 1950 storm had continued, I imagined that we would have gotten into the same situation as those two guys. Thankfully, the rains would stop in time and we would be once again safe. However, in the background we could still hear the roar of the ocean loud and clear.

A few days later I took a stroll down to the beach. The ground was still wet, but the sun was shining and things were getting back to normal. I walked to the top of the bluff overlooking the beach at just about where the "lookout" house used to be. What greeted me was something unreal, something that you might now see in a special effects Hollywood movie. It was if I was looking at the creation of a whole new world. The surf had hit so hard that it had completely wiped out the sandy beach, exposing the bedrock beneath, and had so much force that the tide was driven up into the gulch by about 300 feet. The sides of the gulch were completely denuded of vegetation. It was as if giant bulldozers had carved out a new canyon, making it ready for development. The only difference was that the sides of this canyon were soaking wet and dripping with salt-laden kelp and seawater. As I stood looking agape at this amazing scene, *Il Mare* in the background kept roaring, its sound now reminiscent of rolling thunder. I could almost hear it saying to me: "See there, little boy. This is what I have done in the past and what I can still do in the future. Beware. Beware."

Of course, after several weeks the sand returned, the vegetation began to grow back, and we once again played on the beach. This beach, like the other ocean beaches, was inaccessible to the general public during the time I lived on the Gulch Ranch. Nowadays, because of the California Coastal Act, many people visit the beach every year, and it is a favorite spot for ocean surfers. For their sake, I close this chapter by sounding the following alarm: *Now heed me well, fellow beachcombers and riders of the wild ocean surf. Do not trust the ocean waves here, for I have seen their might and heard* Il Mare's *tumultuous roar. Therefore, in turn, I pass on to you its warning to me. Beware! Beware!*

Endnotes

[86] In their book, *Memories of the Mountain*, The Ladies of the Bonny Doon Club have included a haunting class photograph, taken at the Bald Mountain School in the 1930s. It shows a young Amerigo DeLucca, and an even younger Norma Rocchi, smiling at the camera. Also in the photo are other members of the Rocchi family. Their youthful images give no hint of the two tragedies that would come a few years later.

[87] "Driver Sought In Fatal Crash," by Jondi Gumz, *Santa Cruz Sentinel* staff writer, June 27, 2002, and her subsequent article captioned, "Highway 1 Crash Victims Mourned," dated June 29, 2002.

[88] On October 27, 1950, the headline in the *Santa Cruz Sentinel* read "Heavy Ground Swells Damage Beach." The article stated that the municipal wharf in Santa Cruz had to be evacuated ("Waves Cause Crack") and it described damage done by the storm to the boardwalk, pleasure pier, and bandstand. Winds were recorded at 52 miles per hour. A picture on the front page shows huge waves crashing over the boardwalk. Major damage throughout the county was attributed to the storm.

27. Rancio D' Bronco ~ Casa D' Valentina
(Bronco's Ranch ~ Valentina's House)

I think it is now appropriate to take the reader back to where we left off when the Comelli family was forced to leave the Gulch Ranch. As you will recall, Joe Antonetti had told my father that he did not have enough faith in him to manage the *rancio*. I am certain that this hurt my father's pride even more than Pete Rinaldi's refusal to stay on unless Bronco would leave. This ran counter to Bronco's expectations of one day having his own ranch to run, and of having my brother, John, as a partner with him. Bronco was determined to make this happen and in the process, I presume, to prove Antonetti, as well as others, wrong.

As the reader will recall, our house on the Gulch was physically removed southward to a new location on Bulb Avenue in Capitola. And for a time, the Comelli family stayed with it. In making the deal with Joe and Lina, an agreement had been reached that we could live in the reassembled house until we could relocate permanently. Therefore, we lived at 1505 Bulb Avenue for about six months. During this time my father set out to find suitable ranch property to lease. My mother, on the other hand, set out to find a suitable place in Santa Cruz for us to live. For a time it seemed that my mother's wishes would be put on hold. Ranchland property, owned by Mr. Donald Younger, a prominent Santa Cruz attorney, had become available. And so, in 1954, he leased approximately 60 acres of land, just outside the north city limits of Santa Cruz, to Bronco and my brother. The land was just east of the old Walti-Schilling Meatpacking Plant. [89]

On Mr. Younger's property, there existed (just barely) a dilapidated old house. He offered to rent this to us. Valentina, thinking she could preserve valuable capital that could be used for the ranch, was interested, on the condition that certain improvements be made to the property. At first, Mr. Younger agreed to that, but he later changed his mind. I think that the costs of improvements may have proved to be too much for Mr. Younger. In the long run, this certainly proved a blessing for my family. Who wanted to live in that crappy old place, anyway? For the first time in our lives, we were going to find a brand new house to live in.

Soon after, Valentina found an empty lot for sale in the middle of a block on Seaside Street in Santa Cruz. Having lived on a ranch all my life, I thought that the 50-foot by 100-foot lot was rather small. Valentina, on the other hand, thought it was the perfect location. Being situated behind Bay View Elementary School, on the west end of Santa Cruz, the lot was only a ten-minute drive to Bronco's ranch. My mother quickly made and offer and eventually bought the property for $1,500.

As my mother set out to employ a contractor to build a house, my father and brother set out to start up a ranch. This was no easy task. The sixty acres was barren land with no wells or irrigation pipes on the property. One of the conditions of the lease was that Mr. Younger had to dig a well and find suitable water to irrigate the sixty acres. If water was found in sufficient quantity, Bronco would plan and pay for the irrigation pipes. Subsequently, water was found and in sufficient quantity; however, test results from a laboratory showed traces of salt in the water. My father and Mr. Younger were devastated. The ranch that they had anticipated (for different reasons) was now placed in jeopardy. Brussel sprouts, or any other crop, could

La Nostra Costa (Our Coast)

not survive on salt-tainted water. After what seemed an excruciating length of time, further testing at the lab determined that the amount of salt in the water was insufficient to cause damage to the crops. Much to their delight, Bronco, John and Mr. Younger could now proceed with their ventures.

Meanwhile, Valentina contracted the Cacacci Construction Company, for the total sum of $11,500, to plan and build our house on Seaside Street. My mother decided on a single story, two bedroom, one bath house (to include a separate shower stall), with a living room and a den. Of course, she had to have a large kitchen with a combined dining area. The den was one decision that she later regretted. In retrospect, she would often say that she should have substituted a third bedroom for the den. (Indeed, a third bedroom would have come in handy, especially after my grandmother came over from Italy.) On the other hand Bronco was to become quite satisfied with her decision. He adopted this room as his own and spent many hours watching TV while relaxing in his big sofa chair. Oh, I almost forgot. There was a small utility room located at the back entrance of the new house, which was plumbed with an oversized sink. Reminiscent of her days *su per la costa*, it was here that Valentina, using her brand new electric washing machine, did all of our washing.

Is the reader asking me, "What colors did Valentina paint the new house?" Since our old house had been a gray color—which, by the way, blended in quite well with the gray skies *su per la costa*—I think my mother wanted the new house to have bright colors, to go with the sunny skies (at least, more of them) in Santa Cruz, and this new beginning for her family. Valentina painted the house an off-white with red trim. The colors were indeed bright, but not garish. The new house was beautiful. For years after, *Casa D'Valentina*, displaying all her colors, was the flagship of this block.

I must also mention that the house had an unusual feature. Inside the big two-car garage just behind the house, Valentina had an enclosed toilet built; the garage plumbed for a wash basin as well. Obviously, Valentina did not want Bronco and John, when returning home after a hard day's work, to enter the brand new house wearing their dirty clothes and muddy boots. According to her wishes, they had to first wash up and change their clothes in the garage. (Shades of the Salz Tannery days.) She also contemplated saving wear and tear on the brand new kitchen, by having the garage fitted for natural gas. She subsequently bought a second-hand stove and installed it in the garage. There she did all her deep-frying and other heavy cooking.

This garage-kitchen area was to become so popular, that often we cleaned out the garage and set up a large table with accompanying chairs. With the garage door open, Valentina would invite a large group of our friends over to enjoy her cooking. Specifically, I can remember one memorable day, *circa* 1961. It was in the summer time and I was on leave from the Army. The gathering must have numbered 14 or 15 people, including the entire Rodoni and Delgi Esposti families. My mother was at her best that day. With an outside charcoal grill and both indoor and outdoor stoves going full blast, she cooked up a huge meal of steaks, potatoes, verdura, salads, pastaciutta and tortas. It was like the old "cookahousa" days *su per la costa*. With such a meal, the reader will certainly understand why it was so difficult for me to return to "mess hall" cooking, Army style.

Bronco did not make many demands in planning for the house. He figured that if Valentina was happy with it, he would be happy with it. On the other hand, he was worried that house and the big garage would not leave him much room to garden. As it turned out, the large lot afforded plenty of room for a lawn and a moderately sized garden, just behind the garage. In the ensuing years, Bronco would be able to successfully raise a multitude of vegetables and even apples in that small patch of dirt. Thus, he became totally satisfied with the outcome of the house.

The lawn encircled the front, side, and also the immediate rear of the house, where there was a strip of lawn that ran parallel and adjacent to one side of the garage. Guess what? Valentina hired Mario Giovannoni, who lived with his wife Gloria (Esposito) on Seaside

Street, to construct two wooden poles with bolted cross sections of wood at the tops. She directed Mario to paint the poles and cross sections white and to set the two at opposite ends of that particular strip of lawn. Then Mario strung four clotheslines between the two poles, attaching them tightly to the cross sections. Mario did such a professional job, that the new addition to the yard seemed simply to be an extension of the new house. Until her dying day, Valentina used Mario's "drying apparatuses." She never did own an electric or gas clothes dryer. Once having been a "professional" laundress herself, she was of the opinion that the sun could do a much better job. (The clothes certainly smelled better.) Besides, she didn't have to worry about the wind and the smell of *pattume*. She could hang her clothes to dry and not have to worry about them. I am sure that the reader would agree with me that this must have been sheer heaven for her.

As the construction on the house commenced, Bronco and John met with civil engineers to map out how the ranch was going to be irrigated. This in itself was unusual. Most all ranches when taken over by a new *rancere* already had irrigation pipes in place. This one didn't. The fact of the matter was that Bronco's ranch had to be built up from scratch. In addition to the irrigation system, Bronco and my mother (my brother certainly didn't have anything to contribute), had to shell out further money to buy tractors, trucks, and that all-important electric sprout-cleaning machine. Nothing but the dirt, and some old shacks, were included as part of the deal.

A second-hand Willy's Jeep Truck was one of Bronco's first purchases. Bronco and John would park the truck (usually facing the wrong way) along the curb next to our new house. Phil Netto, the son of Edith and Manuel Netto, had the dubious privilege of attending Santa Cruz High School with me. Along with his parents, brother David and sister Laurie, Phil lived across the street from our house, at 722 Seaside Street. Phil often told me that he "cursed that infernal truck," for waking him up so early in the morning. Sorry, Phil. If we had had more money we could have bought a less noisy truck.[90]

Next to transplantation of the seedlings, proper irrigation is probably the single most important thing to raising a successful new crop. Of course, Bronco had known this from his *bagnatore* days on the Gulch, but it got a tad more complicated now that whirlybird sprinklers were used instead of the *shavola*. The arc and the flow of water from each successive sprinkler had to interlock, reaching and covering certain areas without leaving any dry spots. Water pressure from the well, the number and length of the water pipes, the strength and direction of the wind at various times of the day, all had to be calculated into the final equation. In planning for this venture, Bronco and my brother had considerable help from the engineers and also from Dante Rodoni, who, because of his personal experience with whirlybird sprinklers, was very adept in such matters. Intertwining their work experience with the mathematical and logistical knowledge of the engineers, Dante and Bronco (I doubt that my brother John had much experience in this at the time) finalized a plan for implementation of the irrigation system that would eventually serve the Comelli family for over twenty years. I didn't know it at the time, but this was going to be very important to me.

From 1955 through 1959 I attended San Jose State College. My summers were spent working on *Rancio D'Bronco*. As I have previously mentioned, the *shavola* method of irrigating the fields had been, by now, replaced with irrigation via long aluminum pipes and sprinklers. My main job, during the ten-hour day, was moving these pipes through the brussel sprouts fields. This was all done by hand (and feet). I wore hip boots to shield my lower body from the water that had collected on the plant leaves (from the sprinklers) and thick polyvinyl gloves to protect my hands from being grated by the aluminum pipes I carried. I learned very quickly that muddy aluminum shreds bare palms quite readily. Each pipe was 20 feet long, with a stem pipe about four feet in length affixed perpendicularly at one end. Securely screwed to the top end of the stem pipe was a "whirlybird" type sprinkler head.

The trick was to grab the 20-foot long pipe at the right spot, so it would balance in your hands. The pipe was then lifted to the waist or higher, and the stem with sprinkler head attachment was allowed to rotate to the bottom. Once this was accomplished, the first pipe was carried forward six to 20 rows, depending on which direction the wind was blowing and how strong its gusts were, and then attached to a pipe which had been previously hooked up to a valve attachment. These valve attachments, which controlled the flow of water to the fields, were set on a series of larger pipes that ran horizontally across the top of the field. (These larger pipes replaced the main ditch, which under the *shavola* method carried the water from the *dama* to the fields.) Each subsequent "whirlybird" pipe was then carried forward in the above-described manner and attached to the previously laid pipe. This routine was performed six or seven times a day. The number of attached pipes varied depending on the length of the row of brussel sprouts.

This work got harder (and wetter) as the sprout plants grew in length. This meant a walk between wet leafy plants with the pipe raised high to the chest. I remember that in the mornings when *il vento* was not blowing, I had to walk through the mud to set up the pipes. In the afternoons it was easier, because the wind blew the water away from the side where you were moving the pipes; thus you did not have to walk through that gooey, foot-sucking mud. As if to counter this advantage, *il vento* blew its gusts directly into your face. This caused resistance against the long pipes and, depending on how hard the wind was blowing, could start a backward sway, knocking you off your balance. (Nice work if you can get it, and you still can today. Moving irrigation pipes now has not changed much from my days on the *rancios*) Once the pipes were set and the end capped off, the main electric pump was turned on and the water flow through the pipes gradually built up enough pressure to shoot out of the rotating "whirlybird" sprinklers and onto the brussel sprout plants. Mission accomplished

Our first planting season on Bronco's ranch, and our first year living in Valentina's house, almost perfectly coincided. If memory serves me correctly, the first crop of brussel sprouts was planted in the spring of 1954, and our move into the brand new house was completed in the summer of that same year. Talk about momentous changes! For the first time, the Comelli family owned a brand new house as well as the land beneath it, and we had our very own ranch to run. Bronco was now *il bosso,* John was his *soto bosso* (under-boss) and, as illustrated above, I was the apprentice *bagnatore*. The truth of the matter was that I did most of the heavy lifting, but Bronco, with his watchful eye, was always there to ensure that the sprout plants received the proper amount of water. At times, he would even resort to his trusty *shavola*, building *paratas* to guide additional water to or from a particular area. Once a *shavola bagnatore*, always a *shavola bagnatore*.

The reader, being somewhat impressed, might now say, "All was now in place for a glorious future." Well yes, but not right away. The first year on Bronco's ranch was a disaster. It happened to occur in the middle of President Eisenhower's recession of 1954 to 1955. There was a glut of brussel sprouts on the market. This, plus the decrease in demand due to the economic conditions, caused a dramatic drop in the price for sprouts. Costs to grow the sprouts and to bring them to market far-exceeded revenues from sales.

I can remember a certain ten-acre parcel on the ranch that had been pastureland. Brussel sprouts had never been planted on it. It was virgin ground and it produced the most bountiful and beautiful crop of sprouts we had ever seen. (John won first prize at the Santa Cruz County Fair that year by exhibiting these particular sprouts.) I can remember Bronco throwing his hands up in despair, as the sprouts came across on the conveyer belt during the cleaning process. "Look at these sprouts!" he would shout in exasperation. "We have grown the most beautiful sprouts ever seen *su per la costa,* and nobody wants them."

Ranceri, su per la costa, have endured many of these "boom or bust" cycles. It was part of their lives. However, for the "bust" cycle to hit in the very first year of Bronco's venture was almost fatal. It meant that the Comelli family could not recoup monies spent out of their savings; it also meant that Bronco and Valentina had to shell out more monies from their personal bank accounts in order to stay in business for another year. I can remember my mother and father having these terrible arguments about "chucking it all in," or continuing on for another year. Surprisingly, it was Valentina who wavered the most and wanted to give it up. Bronco on the other hand stuck to his guns. "We have money to go on for one more year. Let's do it," he told my mother. He finally convinced Valentina and the table was set for another year on Bronco's ranch.

Meanwhile, as all this was happening during the first year, I started my senior year at Santa Cruz High School. For the first time I actually could walk to school without taking a bus. The walk from Valentina's house on Seaside Street to the school on the corner of Walnut and California Street was only about twenty minutes. I used to love these walks early in the morning, especially when the sun was shining. While I walked, I sometimes thought about all those things I would be doing as a policeman. I certainly wasn't going to be a *rancere*. Not after all that had happened to the Comelli family during the last couple of years. Being "kicked off" one ranch, and now going broke in another, was not my idea of a stable occupation. I wanted something more secure. Never once, as I will relate in the following chapter, did I ever think that this security would come with such a heavy price.

While my parents and John were having such a terrible time on the ranch, I was having a great old time at the high school. I palled around with my buddies, played football, attended all the after-game dances, and did all the other things that seniors normally do in their last year at school. Oh, yes. I also found ways to use Bronco's ranch for my own—as well as my friends'—amusement.

At various times after football and basketball games, it was quite common for my buddies—Mike Kuffel, Jerrold Kerrick, Don Binsacca, Jim Ceragioli, Jerry Mungai, Ken Olsen, Bruce Hansen, and/or others—to pile into the Old Torpedo, my parent's 1949 Chevrolet, which I was now allowed to borrow, and drive to a nearby liquor store to buy a six-pack of beer. Since I was the biggest of the lot, and probably looked the oldest, I was selected to go inside to buy it. Amazingly, even without a fake I.D., I was able to purchase the beer. One particular liquor store, situated at Mission and Bay streets, never once asked to see my I.D.—until after I had actually turned 21. (I must get younger-looking as I age, don't you think?)

Needing a safe and private place to drink, we would drive to Bronco's ranch (this was always after dark) and there in the open fields with car headlights on (turning them off when we suspected we might be spotted), we drank our beer and sometimes smoked Tiparillo cigars. We never did have enough beer with us to get seriously drunk; however, we pretended a lot. Then we would pile back into the Old Torpedo and drive back to the high school for the "sock hop" dances held in the girl's gym. Once there we strutted around for everyone (especially the girls) to see how drunk and crazy we were. Shades of those *ciuco* boys at the Laguna picnic. Only, we were not really drunk and never did get sick. Besides, we never did get caught and had a lot of fun doing this. In retrospect, it probably wasn't the smartest thing I did. A "minor procuring and possessing alcohol" on my record would not have looked too good on my résumé when applying for entry into the police field. That experience "bootlegging" for Smerigli on the Gulch Ranch had apparently "learnt me nutt'n."

Not really being impressed, the reader is probably thinking, "Buying beer? Not such a big deal. Everybody did that in high school." Okay, then how about stealing gasoline? One of my school buddies, Jerrill Kerrick, owned a 1932 Ford coupe with rumble seat.[91] Although it was green and didn't sport the same garish colors, it was similar in style to the hot-rod used in the movie "American Graffiti."[92] Along with Mike Kuffel, we drove everywhere in Santa Cruz County in Jerry's "rod." Mike even made an attempt to drive Jerry's Ford. Much to his chagrin, he failed miserably. Attempting to park on a hillside, he stepped on the clutch instead of the brake. The "rod" promptly rolled back down the hill, striking a parked Oldsmobile. So much for Drivers' Ed. classes.

As in the movie, the three of us had our misadventures with the local police. I remember one time specifically, when Jerry was cited for driving on the wrong side of the street. We were by the high school; seeing some buddies, Jerry crossed over the white line to park the car, driver side next to the curb. No too smart, since he did it in front of a cop. I will always remember the police officer's famous quote as he handed Jerry the ticket. "Do you think you guys are from England, or something?" he inquired with a smirk on his face. "No sir," Jerry answered sheepishly. "I was just trying to park." (I must confess to the reader that I would use this cop's words, with some satisfaction, once or twice myself, when doing my own ticketing. Funny, the things you learn when you are in high school.)

As the reader might expect, doing so much driving caused the car to be always wanting for gas. No problem. There was a gasoline storage tank with pump on Bronco's ranch. Again after dark and with great stealth, we drove up and into the ranch and parked the "rod" alongside the gasoline pump. There we found one small obstacle to overcome. A padlock secured the hand-pump lever, which of course activated the flow of gasoline. Since I did not have a key, we could not operate the pump freely. However, through trial and error, we discovered that the lever had enough play in it to prime the pump. It took a great deal of patience and a lot of up-and-down pumping with that lever, but we always managed to squeeze out a gallon or two of gasoline.

The inquisitive reader might now ask, "Why in the world didn't you turkeys simply buy the gasoline? It only cost about 30 cents a gallon at that time. Right?" Right. I can remember buying gas as low as 20 cents a gallon (or perhaps even lower during frequent gas station "wars"), but doing so wouldn't have been as much fun. Besides, I really thought I was putting one over on my parents and John. And, of course, we were saving money for those six packs of beer. The truth be known, I am sure my parents (and maybe even John) would have given me a key, if only I would have asked.

The first god-awful year on Bronco's ranch passed, and the uncertainties of the second year with all its anxieties and fears descended on the Comelli family. What if the recession continued? What if the price of sprouts should continued to fall? These were the thoughts sifting through my mind, while I hoed weeds and moved those aluminum irrigation pipes during the summer of 1955. My plans to go on to college might be completely disrupted. My family could be hurting really badly, and I would have to go to work in order to help out. What if we lost the house? Luckily, Valentina and Bronco had paid cash for the house; thus there were no mortgages or liens on the property. However, what if we had to sell to get some money to live? All these uncertainties were out there in those planted fields that summer. Certainly, if I was worried, Bronco and Valentina must have been doubly so.

The blessed truth of the matter is that things turned around dramatically that second year. Bronco's ranch made a nice profit that season, and it continued to produce profits for the next 20-plus years. Mercifully, we didn't have to sell our house and I got to go on to college. Yes, there were a couple of down seasons along the way, but things never got as bad as that first year. Unfortunately, as we shall see later, Bronco was not allowed to close out his career on his ranch. However, my father was given enough time here to prove, mostly to himself, that he, along with my brother John, could indeed run a *rancio* successfully. This was his dream all along and he had fulfilled it here on *Rancio D'Bronco*.

My mother, for the most part, also fulfilled her dream. Valentina continued to live in her house in Santa Cruz until her death in 1977; Bronco lived there until his death in 1983. As I have previously mentioned, the house still stands with my niece, Denise, and her family living in it at present. As a witness to those "ghosts of the coast" stories, Denise to this day swears that at times she hears unexplained noises and has seen a shadow moving surreptitiously across the hallway wall. The alarmed reader poses the obvious question, "My gosh, doesn't this frighten Denise?" At first it did, but now she believes quite strongly that it is only her grandmother's benevolent spirit coming back to make sure that everything is going well at *Casa D'Valentina*.

Endnotes

[89] In truth the meatpacking plant was more like a slaughterhouse. In an article appearing in the *Santa Cruz Sentinel*, dated October 19, 1950, reporter Peter J. Heller described it as having an improved 80 ft.-by-80 ft. "killing floor" that would enable the plant to increase its killing capacity. I can remember working the fields adjacent the plant and watching all those cows and steers, mooing and rustling about behind a wood fence, waiting for their moment to be led to the "killing floor." What could they have been thinking? Fortunately for their descendants, this plant is no longer in operation.

[90] Phil Netto was a star basketball player at Santa Cruz High School, *circa* 1956 to 1957. Credible reports have it that his father Manuel, who worked for many years at the Portland Cement Plant, had been even a better player than Phil.

[91] For many years, the Kerrick family owned and operated Kerricks Laundry. It was founded (*circa* 1919) by Jerrill's great-grandfather William O. Kerrick (a two-term mayor of Santa Cruz), and his great-grandmother May (Sargent) Kerrick. Last situated at 620 Water Street, it was sold years later to Bariteau's Laundry and Dry Cleaning. Since that time, Dr. Jerrill Kerrick has achieved prominence as a much-respected math and computer science professor. Professor? I would never have guessed it by the way he baby-sat his "Auntie Dear."

[92] "American Graffiti," Universal Pictures (1973), produced by Francis Ford Coppola, directed by George Lucas, starring Richard Dreyfuss, Ron Howard, Harrison Ford, Cindy Williams, Suzanne Sommers.

CASA D'VALENTINA

AMICI DELLA COSTA MEET AT CASA D'VALENTINA

C. 1958

28. Il Ponte E La Polizia
(The Bridge And The Police)

Throughout this book, I have given the reader glimpses of my police career. It is not my intention here to discuss at length my life as a Police Officer. That is another segment of my past and perhaps the subject for another book. However, I do believe that I should explain further, how *un figlio della costa* (son of the coast), born and raised on a brussel sprouts *rancio* became a cop for a big-city police department. More improbable, how did the grandson of a notorious smuggler make it to the "bigs"? Therefore, in this chapter I will attempt to assume the role of *pontiff* (bridge-maker), and allow the more adventurous reader to journey with me across the bridge that took me to the police, and perhaps to give him or her a peek of what lay ahead for me.

I have already discussed the influences of Carabiniere at the Hotel D'Italia, Vic Calhoun at Serafina's, Tom Leonard at the Santa Cruz Beach-Boardwalk, and Officer Charles Derby at Laurel School. There were other influences that oriented me towards a police career. Unbeknownst to me at the time, the first of these influences probably started way back in the early 1900s in my parent's hometown of Nimis, Italy.

My paternal grandfather, Giovanni Comelli, was a big man, standing six feet three inches tall (or more) and weighing well over 200 pounds. In the little town of Nimis, he was renowned for his large stature and for his ability to traverse with ease the rugged hills and mountains bordering Yugoslavia and Austria. Village lore has it that he walked through mountain passes barefooted, *sans* shoes and *sans* passport or visa. Once over these natural barriers, he then proceeded to buy or barter for food and other items that could be sold or bartered for a profit back in Italy. By making surreptitious deals directly with the producers and consumers, he avoided any sales taxes or customs duties that the governments might impose. These sorts of activities, called "contra bandiera" ("against the flag"), were, of course, illegal and most certainly frowned upon by the government.

Although his vocation was well known in the Friuli region, the local authorities either could not catch him in the act, or were induced (bribed) to look the other way. Most likely it was a combination of both. Although my grandfather was very successful in his work, apparently there was a price to pay. Someone up above must have decreed that some of my grandfather's descendants would have to atone for his malfeasance. First he chose his oldest son, then, perhaps, one of his grandsons. However, that is getting ahead of our story.

My father entered the Italian army just after World War I. Ironically, he was assigned to the *Guardia Di Finanza* [fee **nahn** zee-ah], the military arm of the Italian customs service. He was now assigned to guard the very same borders that my grandfather supposedly crossed. Bronco, by his own admission, was Italy's worst *guardia* [**gwar** dee-yah]. I don't think he ever encountered my grandfather crossing the border, but from time to time, he chose to look the other way when members of the "contra bandiera" trade came walking through.

Although Bronco did not do a very good job as a *guardia*, he did enjoy his stint in the military. Later, at our dinner table in America, he would often talk about his adventures or misadventures in the armed services, and would always end by saying that if he had not been given the opportunity to come to America in 1923, he would have most certainly re-enlisted. Hindsight being what it is, it was a good thing he didn't. He probably would have become embroiled in one of Mussolini's "little" wars in Africa or even in World War II. From my point of view, Providence had given Bronco an opportunity. To his credit he made the right decision in coming to America.

God must have thought that Bronco's time in the *Guardia* was not good enough to atone for his father's misdeeds. One of Bronco's sons had to pick up the mantel and this time he had to be serious about his work. Thus, the seeds of what I had to do were implanted in my mind at a very early age. Events came to pass which started me across the bridge to that other life.

I wasn't much of a troublemaker during my school days. However, when I was in the eight and ninth grades at Mission Hill Junior High School (1951 to 1952), I palled around with a couple of boys including Jerrill Kerrick (of hot-rod fame) and Mike Kuffel. Mike had recently come to the school from Pismo Beach, and since he was fairly new to Santa Cruz, his character and background were not well known. Mike was a dark-complexioned youth who wore glasses and scowled a lot, pretending most of the time that he was really tough. Because he often didn't go along with the program (as set down by the teachers), he soon acquired the reputation of being a troublemaker. Once we got to know him, we found out that he was a bit irreverent, but on the whole Mike was a nice guy and more importantly, he was a lot of fun to be with. Soon some of the teachers began referring to our group as "Kuffel's Gang" and Mike's reputation started to rub off on us. Those of us that hung around with Mike rather enjoyed our new-found notoriety. The only one that didn't like it was Mike himself. To this day, he will deny that there ever was a Kuffel's Gang. Although we never really got into serious trouble, the above information has some bearing on the story I am about to tell the reader.

This episode involved, of all people, Charles Derby, the police officer who had been in charge of the School Safety Patrol at Laurel

School. It appeared, for a few anxious moments, that the very man I admired most as a police officer would arrest me. That indeed would have been something—to be arrested by the man who made such a great and lasting impression on me. Since the facts of this story incriminated me as a prime suspect (there were several suspects), they are still well embedded in my mind, and I am quite certain that the *corpus delicti* of the crime was established in the following manner. (Many lay people used that term to refer to the body of the victim. This is a very loose interpretation of its meaning. The *corpus delicti* of a crime does not need to be a dead body. The term means the material evidence of a crime. Thus, a theft or a burglary also has a *corpus delicti*.)

It happened like this. Unknown to most of the students at the school, someone was stealing money and other things from lockers in the boys' gym. The school principal, Mr. Samuel Reed, called the Santa Cruz Police Department to investigate. The police came and set up a trap to catch the thief. Having garnered the cooperation of a reliable and honest student, they placed a wallet, fully dusted with florescent powder, in his gym locker. The powder was intended to get on the thief's hands and clothes when he took the wallet. Although the thief could brush off the powder, the residue, invisible to the naked eye, would remain on his hands and clothes. This invisible residue, as I was about to learn, would appear as white streaks under florescent lighting.

The trap was set by leaving the combination lock on the "victim's" locker unlocked, as if the student had forgotten to clasp it. This in itself was not uncommon. Students frequently left their locker, forgetting to clasp the lock, only to return later to find their lock duly locked in a reverse position, making it very difficult for them to work the combination. It didn't take long for the thief to spot his target of opportunity and to quickly snatch the wallet. The trap was sprung. Unfortunate for me, he chose to do his reprehensible deed during my gym class.

Hurriedly, we were told to go to the basketball court and to sit there until we were called into the coach's office. I happened to sit myself down next to a blond-haired boy who was fairly new at the school. I remember playing "grab ass" with him while we waited. We wrestled and grabbed at each other's clothes as we tried to kill time.

When I was called to the coach's office, I eagerly went without hesitation. I can assure the reader that I had done nothing wrong, and I was most confident that I would be quickly released without further inquisition. Waiting in the offices was the coach, Milo Badger. There also was Sergeant Derby, who was by then a Juvenile Officer for the Santa Cruz Police Department. Holding a lamp equipped with a florescent light bulb in his hand, Sergeant Derby briefly explained to me what they were doing and then asked if I had any knowledge about the crime. Naturally, I said, "No." Then, he switched on the handheld lamp and directed its purplish light at my clothes. The telltale white streaks were all over me. *Porca la miseria!* They had caught their thief and he was me.

The astonished reader may now wish to pose an interesting question. "Why didn't you simply tell them what had happened?" Because, I hadn't quite figured it out at the time. Further investigation by Sergeant Derby disclosed that a couple of other boys, including the real thief, also had telltale white streaks on their clothes. The real thief happened to be the blond-haired boy (name withheld to protect the living) who was playing "grab ass" with me. It was then that it hit me. The thief had discovered that the wallet was full of powder. He realized that he had been caught in a trap. In a desperate attempt to divert suspicion, he decided to contaminate other students by touching them with his hands and clothes. Neat trick, but it didn't work. Because of the superior interrogative skills possessed by Sergeant Derby, the blond-haired boy admitted committing the crime. I was released and I never did see the boy again. This incident reaffirmed the belief in my mind that the police were smarter than the crooks, and that they always got their man. I was becoming more determined than ever to become one of them.

A humorous, but nonetheless serious, aspect to the above story has recently developed. In discussing the above incident with Mike

Kuffel, he has revealed to me, for the first time, that he too had been a prime suspect in the caper. He too had the telltale powder streaks on his hands and clothes. Up until I told him recently that there were other suspects in this case, including me, he had thought he was the only one accused, and that the real culprit had never been caught. Thus, up until now, he has always believed, because of his misconceived school reputation, that he was the only suspect in this case. This has been so embarrassing to him, that he has kept what he thought was his secret, buried inside him all this time. Fear not Mike, let the truth, and this book set you free.

I was an average student during my early school years. I didn't think I was very smart. I certainly never thought I was smart enough to go on to college. I figured that I would become a *rancere* like my father and brother. Things started to change when I attended Mission Hill Junior High School (1949 to 1952). I found out that I was pretty good at some subjects. The school had a very good Spanish teacher, Miss Hulda Van, who also happened to be my homeroom teacher. Because I spoke Italian, Spanish came easily to me. I started to get A's in the subject. By studying basic Spanish grammar, I got better at English grammar and started to get A's and B's in that subject, also. Later, thanks to Mr. Evans and Miss Young, I got A's and B's in math. Finally in the ninth grade, I made Mission Hill's School Honor Roll. I had come a long way since that "F" in the fourth grade. I began to notice that many of my peers—Mike Kuffel, Jerrill Kerrick, Don Binsacca, Bruce Hansen, Ken Olsen, Esther Frizza, Dorthey Beardsley, Florence Bianco, Muriel McPherson, and Betty Aldrich, as well as Jerry Mungai, Jimmy Ceragioli, Dennis Soo Hoo, and Marvin Del Chiaro—were also doing well in school. I also became aware that they were preparing themselves to go on to college. I started to think that maybe I should also start thinking about preparing myself for college.

My parents did not exactly encourage me to do so. Valentina believed that one should have something firmly in mind before setting out to get a college degree. In her mind a person should go on to college only if he had designs on becoming a professional, such as a lawyer, a doctor, or a teacher. She certainly didn't think that you had to go on to college to become a *rancere*.[93] I told her that I was thinking about becoming a policeman. That didn't make any difference. In her mind, police work was not a profession. Most of the people I knew seemed to agree with her. You did not have to go to college to become a cop.

The time was fast approaching to make a decision. Graduation from Santa Cruz High School was soon at hand. I knew I wanted to be a police officer, but I was not old enough to join the police force. Since my friends were all going on to college, it seemed to me that I could kill some time by staying in school. As luck would have it, I found out that San Jose State College was one of the very few colleges in the United States with a police school. Its four-year curriculum was well known, and the school was held in high regard throughout the country. (At this particular time, Thor Spindler, a former Santa Cruz police officer, was starting a two-year police program at Monterey Peninsula College. If I hadn't been accepted at San Jose State, I probably would have gone there.)

The city of San Jose is only about 40 miles north by north east of Santa Cruz. I could go away to college and not be all that far away from home. I could either commute daily or return home on the weekends. (I would use these facts adroitly in trying to persuade my mother to let me go.) In four years I would earn a BA degree in Police. By that time, I would be old enough to join a police force. I had it all worked out in my mind. Now all I had to do was to convince my parents.

My father would go along with whatever my mother said, so I had to first convince Valentina. Unfortunately, she wanted to keep me down on the farm. She still didn't see the value of going to college to become a policeman. Further more, police work was dangerous. She didn't want to see her baby boy get hurt. It was Battista Lorenzi who finally won the day for me. His argument that any education was good and that in the end I would probably change my mind about becoming a cop finally convinced my mother to let me go. Battista, of course, was right about the education, but dead wrong about me changing my mind.

In truth, I probably would have gone on to the Police School, with or without my mother's permission. Being a teenager at the time, I reveled in going against my parent's wishes. However, it certainly made things easier for me to have her go along with my decision. It also helped that Marvin Del Chiaro, my boyhood friend from Laurel School, had decided to seek a degree in Accounting at San Jose State.

Marvin's mother, Effie, and my mother, teamed up and started to look for a place in San Jose where Marvin and I could stay. I remember going to San Jose in the summer of 1955, with Valentina, Effie and Marvin. At the time, San Jose was situated at the heart of one of California's most fertile agricultural valleys. It was known then as the Santa Clara Valley, and it officially bears that name today. However, for the most part it is no longer agricultural and it is now more commonly famous—or rather, infamous—as Silicon Valley. Fruit trees would ultimately be traded in for silicon chips.

Effie took us to a rooming house at 626 South Sixth Street. There we met Bud Glans and his wife Nadine. The Glans, along with their daughter Susie, lived on the bottom floor of the big Victorian-style house. The Glans had remodeled the top floor to accommodate nine students. In the beginning, the accommodations were quite comfortable. The students usually bunked two to a room, and shared a large kitchen area, where they could prepare their own meals. Later, during each summer break, the enterprising Bud Glans would remodel the top floor, cutting the bigger rooms into smaller rooms, so that he could accommodate more students. I left after two and a half years, finding that the "lodge" was becoming a bit too crowded. Marvin stayed on and by the time he left at the end of four years, Bud had managed to squeeze 14 students into that top floor.

Initially, my mother was somewhat dubious of me surviving by cooking my own meals. Effie eased her fears by suggesting that she and my mother could prepare home-cooked meals to send along with us when we returned from weekends at home. Thus we would only have to reheat the food. This became pretty much the formula for the next two and half years. On Friday, we would arrive in Santa

Cruz with a bag of dirty clothes. On Monday morning, Marvin and I would return to San Jose with an assortment of clean, freshly pressed clothes, and a box of frozen and/or pre-cooked meals. Such was life on the road.

Having found a suitable place to stay, Marvin and I had to figure out how we were going to get back and forth. Fortunately, Marvin had a 1949 Ford, and we would use this to commute between San Jose and Santa Cruz. The travel time between the San Jose State College and my house on Seaside Street was approximately one hour. At the time there was no freeway from Los Gatos to San Jose. We had to drive over the Santa Cruz Mountains, taking Highway 17 eastbound out of Santa Cruz to Los Gatos. In Los Gatos, Highway 17 turned into the Los Gatos-San Jose Road. We continued on that road to West San Carlos Street in San Jose. Turning east on San Carlos we proceeded to San Jose State College which was and still is located at Fourth and San Carlos Streets in downtown San Jose. The Glans' rooming house was within walking distance, just four blocks south of the campus.

At times, especially during the spring, we took an alternate route, driving east on Blossom Hill Road then north on Almaden Road to San Carlos Street. San Jose at the time had a population of about 150,000. This was the time before expressways and freeways traversed southern San Jose and there were very few houses in existence. On the other hand, there were many orchards, with cherry and prune trees displaying their magnificence in a sea of white blossoms. During the spring months, tourists riding in buses were transported to southern San Jose, specifically to see this awesome sight. Today, San Jose has a population in excess of 900,000, with many houses and expressways, and the sea of white blossoms is no longer there. Marvin and I probably didn't think so at the time, but we were indeed fortunate to witness this most beautiful sight. We never imagined that someday it would completely disappear.

Traveling in Marvin's Ford was always an experience. The car, which looked like a big, grayish-white metal box on wheels, had dual exhaust pipes fitted with mufflers that seemed grossly inadequate for suppressing the loud rumble of the engine. This was especially true when the car accelerated. Early, each Monday morning, I would wait for Marvin to arrive at *Casa D'Valentina*. I never had to worry that I might miss my ride. I could hear Marvin coming from blocks away, as he slowed the car for the intersections and turns, then quickly cranked up the engine as he came down the straightaways. I'm sure that the noises orchestrated by the "old box" Ford were loud enough to wake up the entire neighborhood. (Just another annoyance to rattle Phil Netto out of his sleep.)

During the trip over the hill, the inside of the car filled up with noxious fumes from the engine. On one memorable trip we rode with a mixture of engine fumes and skunk stink in the cab. Apparently, the night before a skunk had decided to assault the car while it was parked in Marvin's barn. *Sempre avanti!* We merely aired out the car by lowering the windows and kept going forward. It was a wonder we weren't asphyxiated.

During the winter of our third year (1957 to 1958), Santa Cruz was hit by a freak snowstorm. I looked out the door of our house and saw these strange white flakes coming down. Soon after, Marvin called on the phone and asked if we should cancel our trip over the hill. As it was, I had a final examination that same morning. Even though I never had driven in snow, I confidently exclaimed, "This thing isn't so bad. If we hurry up and go we can make it over, before it really gets bad."

Marvin was more cautious, however he agreed to try it. Disregarding Valentina's strenuous objections, we started up the grade. No problem. As the going got tougher, Marvin simply grabbed the manual gearshift, which was mounted on the steering column, and shifted into low gear. This caused the "old box" Ford's engine to roar louder and spew more noxious fumes. I thought we were making very good progress. I figured that as long as we could hear that engine and smell the fumes, we were all right. As we approached the summit, the snow really started to come down. The "old box" Ford started to slip and slide. "Keep going, Marv," I said. "We'll make it." As if to contradict me, the car started to slide off the roadway. With a look of concern on his face, Marv now asked the question that probably had been on his mind from the very start of our trip. "Do you think that you could take your exam some other time?"

Seeing that we were not making any headway, I reluctantly agreed to stop our adventure. Marv slowly turned the car around and very carefully guided its descent back down the hill, slipping and sliding all the way. With Marvin's careful driving we made it back to Santa Cruz. Not willing to give up, I convinced Marvin to look for some snow chains and try again. I figured that with snow chains we could easily make it. Who has snow chains in Santa Cruz, anyway? We couldn't find anyone we knew in Santa Cruz who had them. Just as well, because the summit was soon closed off to all traffic until much later that day. Much to our mothers' relief we decided to wait until the next day to go over the hill.

I think this was the only time the "old box" Ford really failed us. Oh yes. My professor at San Jose State allowed me to take the exam on another day. So, there I was in an empty classroom, taking the final all by myself. I guess the solitude and extra time for study did me some good. I remember acing the exam. Thanks for the memories, "old box" Ford.

At this point, I must beg the reader's indulgence as I diverge somewhat from my trek across *il ponte* to tell one of my favorite "believe it or not" stories. After settling in at the Glans rooming house, Marvin and I found a small neighborhood market conveniently located only a couple of blocks north of the rooming house, at Sixth and Williams. We soon learned to use the L&F (Lou & Frank) Market to supplement our food supply. The market was owned by the Moro family and there, for the first time, I met Lou and Enes Moro, and their daughters Donna and Sandy. Enes soon told me that her maiden name was Peracchi and that she was born and raised in Santa Cruz. Her mother, Velia, still lived in Santa Cruz. Now the reader might find this difficult to believe, but my mother and father knew Velia quite well. In fact, during the time (1953) that our old house was being reassembled in Capitola after being moved off the

Gulch Ranch, the Comelli family stayed at a motel near the Santa Cruz Beach. Velia owned and managed the motel. Furthermore, I knew Velia's son, Emo Peracchi, who was a Santa Cruz police officer. Even more coincidentally, I later found out that Lou's parents, Mary and Frank Moro, were originally from the Friuli region of Italy, though my mother and father did not know them at that time.

The reader has probably guessed what would happen next. Or maybe not. Just before I left for the Army in 1960, Velia made arrangements with my mother to have the Moro family meet the Comelli family for the first time, at *Casa D'Valentina*. There, Donna, then seventeen years old, was introduced to my brother John. Two years later, while still in the Army, I was informed that I was to be best man at Donna and John's wedding. They now have two daughters, Denise and Christine, and four grandchildren, Shaina, Matthew, Andrew and Ryan. Incredibly, all of this happened because of my need to supplement my food supply.

Directing the reader's attention back to where we left off, let's continue on with our journey across the bridge to the police. The Police School at San Jose State College was housed in old World War II type barracks on the south side of the campus, adjacent to San Carlos Street. The Police School administrators, headed by Willard Schmidt, Melvin Miller and Gordon Misner, assured us that these were only temporary units. A brand new Police School building would be built. Well, I found the barracks, and for the next four years I studied and learned within their "hallowed" halls. Yes, and when I graduated in 1959 with a BA degree in Police, the barracks still housed the School. It was only later, in the mid-1960s, that the new building was finally completed. It is situated on the southwest corner of 7th and San Carlos, and students now graduate from this building with degrees in the Administration of Criminal Justice. Not so ironically, the barracks are now gone, and so are the degrees in Police. Or, are they? Maybe, they just bear another name.

The four years I spent at the Police School reaffirmed the fact (at the time) that I had made the right choice. The administrators and teachers of the school were fervent in their belief (some more than others) that police work needed to be elevated to a professional status. Higher education was the means to that end, and their graduates were going to be the managers and administrators of the future. They would be in the vanguard, leading law enforcement forward to ultimately reach this lofty goal.

I bought into this—hook, line and sinker. In July of 1959, I completed my journey over *il ponte*. At the ripe old age of twenty-two I joined the San Jose Police Department, and for the next thirty years I attempted to do my part to help upgrade the police profession. I wish that I could say for certain that I did a good job. The very nature of police work and the restraints of an ever-controlling bureaucracy often made the task difficult. I must admit to the reader that one event, above all, tended to jade my attitude about police professionalism in its purest form.

August 6, 1970, is a date forever ingrained in the annals of the San Jose Police Department. On that date, my best friend and one-time roommate, Officer Richard Eugene Huerta, was assassinated by a lone gunman. He was only thirty-six years old. The incident occurred during that turbulent period of our history when it was common for radicals advocating "black power" to extol the virtues of killing a "pig." [94] Apparently (though no one will know for certain) one black male, Emile Thompson, then in his early twenties, took that message literally. As Richard sat in his police vehicle, writing a citation to a third party (not involved in the crime), the lone assassin crept up from behind the car, and suddenly shot the unsuspecting officer in back of the head. This brutal and cowardly act killed Richard almost instantly.

Still in the early morning hours, I was awakened from a sound sleep by a telephone call. On the other end of the line was Officer Jim Emmons, a friend, who also happened to be a former roommate of Richard's. Jim, who was on duty at the time of the shooting, delivered the message that haunts me to this day. "Richard has been shot."

Still half asleep, I asked Jim if Richard was all right. Jim responded in an unemotional and very controlled manner, which is very typical of a professional police officer under stress. "No. I think he is dead. I thought you'd like to know."

In a state of shocked amazement, I quickly put on some civilian clothes, grabbed my off duty revolver, and drove myself (I was living in Scotts Valley at the time) to the San Jose Police Station. Once there and still in off-duty clothes, I hooked up with on-duty Sgt. Phil Norton. Together we joined the search for the assassin. It wasn't long before Norton received a radio call informing him that the killer had been found hiding in a back yard, in the 500 block of North Thirteen. Sgt. Norton quickly responded to the scene and both he and I were present when the assassin was dragged from his hiding place and placed in handcuffs.

I guess you might say that I, as well as Sgt. Norton and the officers who actually made the arrest, acted professionally in not shooting Thompson in the head. This thought certainly crossed my mind and, at the time, I actually had my finger on the trigger of my snub-nose "38." Not committing the act certainly didn't make me feel any better or more professional. (Probably the only one who wasn't restrained by "police professional behavior" was the police dog on the scene. Without asking permission, he promptly took a bite out of the killer.) The murderer is now in his fifties, serving out his life sentence. I doubt if he spends much of his time thinking about the consequences of his act. Richard's death left two young children without a father. Marie Huerta was left alone to raise Leanne and Richard Jr.[95]

Probably the most frequently untold story about a policeman's death, is the impact it has, not only on the slain officer's immediate family, but also on the families of other police officers. I can tell the reader now, that Richard's death affected my mother quite severely. Prior to his death, Richard on several occasions would join the Comelli family for dinner at *Casa D'Valentina*. Both Bronco and Valentina took a deep liking to Richard. In addition to being a police officer, Richard was an accomplished accordionist and music

La Nostra Costa (Our Coast)

teacher. It was well known at the San Jose Police Department that on weekends, Richard augmented his police pay by giving music lessons to young children.

At *Casa D'Valentina* after dinner, Richard often serenaded us with his accordion. This particularly delighted Bronco, who continually urged him to play more Italian songs. Richard would reply that he was not familiar with many of the songs requested; but next time around he would know the songs well enough to play them. Unfortunately, for all of us, time ran out.

Richard's death hit Bronco and Valentina hard, but it was my mother who took it the hardest. Valentina was so distraught after hearing of Richard's death that she went into a deep depression. She was unable to bring herself to attend his funeral. I am sure that she was relating Richard's death with the heightened possibility of the death in the line of duty of her youngest son. Although this did not happen, I am certain that the thought was constantly on her mind. After my mother's death I discovered various saved newspaper clippings. Some were in regards to my police career; but the majority were about other police officers, throughout the country, who had been killed in the line of duty. Surely, Valentina was empathizing with those other mothers, in their grief for the lost of their loved ones, while also worrying about my unpredictable future.

One of the greatest experiences in my lifetime was being a police officer at a relatively young age. The thought that the job was dangerous and that harm could happen to a fellow police officer or me was deeply recessed in back of my mind. It was all part of the excitement of being a police officer. Richard's death changed all that. I am sure that I speak for other San Jose police officers of my generation when I say that after Richard's assassination, reality set in. I know that at about that time, the *ultimate* goal in my mind was not police professionalism; rather, it was *survival*. Survival for me and the men I supervised became a very serious business. No matter how careful a police officer is, he will often be placed in harm's way. In my mind, I formed the following "short list" for survival, which helped me get out of some sticky situations. Thinking back,

I probably had formulated these rules long before Richard's death, but his murder certainly solidified them in my mind. At times, when put into action, they may have conflicted with what is considered to be "true professional" behavior. In various quarters nowadays, a police officer articulating some of these rules might be considered "politically incorrect." So be it.

1. *Crooks do not play fair.* Never trust them. Don't give them a break, unless it is to your advantage.

2. *Always watch your back.* Crooks and/or cowards will always take advantage of your blind side.

3. *Watch their hands and eyes.* Furtive movements and/or fleeting glances will often convey what a crook is about to do.

4. *At all times, be aware of and protect your gun side* Do not, under any circumstances, allow a crook to grab your gun.

5. *Be quick.* Restrain and subdue a crook before he has a chance to act. Rely on your instincts of self-preservation and act accordingly.

6. *Hesitation and indecision when in harm's way may cost you your life, or the life of a fellow officer.* Use your weapon as a last resort, but be sure ahead of time (as best you can) that you are willing and capable of shooting another human being.

Of course, depending on the circumstances, the rules as stated above may also apply when making contact with the ordinary, up-till-then law-abiding citizen. A police officer never knows what is going on in the mind of a person simply stopped for a traffic violation, or being interviewed during a family disturbance call. He must be constantly on guard for the unexpected.

For the most part, rules five and six are those that, when put into action, will most likely get a police officer in trouble. As the reader is probably well aware, through reading the newspapers or watching the evening news on television, "Monday morning quarterbacks" tend to criticize the police for acting too quickly or with too much force. Acting too quickly and with a measure of force, no matter how necessary, often evokes cries of police brutality or unprofessional behavior. A recent article appearing in the *San Jose Mercury News* illustrates this very point quite clearly, while giving the reader a quick "look, see" into the murky world inhabited by police officers.[96]

According to the article, officers responding to a call of an unsupervised child, shot and killed a twenty-five-year-old Vietnamese-American mother of two, who allegedly was wielding a knife. Again according to the article, the shooting occurred after the officers entered the house. As often occurs in this kind of incident, some citizens in the community questioned whether the victim had posed any threat at all to the officers, and whether the officers had acted too quickly and with excessive force. The community members claimed that the victim had held an Asian vegetable peeler in her hand; conversely, the police claimed that it was a cleaver with a six-inch blade. Investigation of this incident will probably never determine for certain what actually happened inside the house. What the police officers actually saw and what danger they perceived is only known to them. Consequently, they will have to live with their decision, right or wrong, for the rest of their lives. Even if exonerated of any wrongdoing, I am sure that the officers will wish they had never received this call. Thus is the life of a police officer. In the blink of an eye, it can be transformed (usually for the worse) for ever. (Later, a grand jury failed to indict the two officers, exonerating them from any wrongdoing.)

The afore-mentioned incident notwithstanding, I personally think that it is much better for a police officer to be quick and forceful when making an arrest, chancing the complaints that most certainly will come, rather than be too slow and restrained, chancing serious personal injury that may occur. To the young reader that perhaps aspires to become a police officer, this rule, and the others I have written above, were never intended to be all-inclusive. Experienced police officers worth their salt will have their own personal short lists (held in their minds, at least) to augment survival techniques taught during their training. Having said all this, I still must admit I truly believe the ultimate determiner of survival to be just plain luck. In retrospect, I was very lucky; regrettably, Richard was not.

As promised, I have now given the reader a peek at what lay ahead for me once I had crossed *il ponte*. As I have stated before, once across the bridge to the police, my whole life and way of thinking changed. The memories I had previously accumulated on the coast seemed to fade and become more and more like figments of my imagination. It was not until I had retired from police work years later that I began to think more and more about my life *su per la costa*. What is certainly true is that both phases of my life were indeed real and that I was very fortunate to have experienced the former while surviving the latter.

Endnotes

[93] My brother John, along with some of our boyhood friends—Donald Bargiacchi, Natalino Marchi, Elio and Mario Rodoni—did in fact become successful farmers without going on to college.

[94] "Pig" was a disparaging word use by these radicals and others to refer to the police. Much to their consternation, the police turned it into a verbal badge of honor by taking the word as an acronym: "Pride, Integrity and Guts."

[95] In the July 2004, publication of *The Vanguard*, the official publication of the San Jose Police Officers' Association, Officer Jaime Saldivar writes a poignant and emotional article about attending Thompson's last parole hearing on April 21, 2004. At that hearing, Thompson was denied parole. His next parole hearing is scheduled for the year 2008.

[96] "S. J. Police Defend Officer's Action," by Rodney Foo, appearing in the *San Jose Mercury News*, dated July 16, 2003. Website: www.bayarea.com/mld/mercurynews

THE CONTRA BANDIERA BANDIT

GIOVANNI COMELLI – C. 1946

ACROSS IL PONTE – 1959

FALLEN OFFICER RICHARD HUERTA

1970

THE LAST TRUMPET – 1989
SILVA–SIMPSON FUNERAL

29. Si Ritorna A La Costa
(Let Us Return To The Coast)

In the course of writing this book, I took several trips up the Coast Road, hoping to locate some of the places I was writing about, thus jogging my memory about things that had occurred in the past. None was more profitable or enjoyable than the trip I took with Reno Cantarutti and his wife, Franca.

Reno requested that we first attempt a visit with Augie Gemignani in Santa Cruz. Augie is the only Gemignani brother still living. Reno told me that his father had worked with Augie, and that the latter had even contemplated going to Richmond, California with him to work for the Richmond Sanitary Service. I eagerly agreed to this visit, hoping we would find Augie at home. We drove past *Casa D'Valentina* on Seaside Street, where my family had once lived and where Richard had serenaded us with his accordion. The house is painted a different color now, but still in very good shape. Valentina had had it built to last. She made sure it would be there for her family, as needed, far into the future.

We proceeded to Bay Street and as luck would have it, found Augie and his wife, Sista, at home. At the time Augie was eighty-six years old, but his mind was (and is) still sharp as a tack. We had a wonderful reunion, and Augie reminisced about *Il Golce* and about working with my father. Although they were partners, Bronco and Augie hadn't really got along all that well. With mellowing, caused by the passing of time, they had learned to tolerate each other. On the other hand, he had got along famously with Valentina, and remembered quite vividly working with her in the packing shed in *il buco*. He told Reno a wonderful story of how Reno's younger brother had happened to get his name. In 1940, Aladina, Augie and Sista's first daughter, was born at Sister's Hospital in Santa Cruz. As luck would have it, Evelina, Reno's mother, was at the same hospital at the time, also having a baby. Apparently Evelina was not quite sure what to name her newborn son. Augie suggested Lido, the name of his younger brother. After thinking it over, Evelina decided it was a beautiful name. Thus, a future Honors Graduate of the University of California, and present Director of the Italian Film Festival, was forever named Lido Cantarutti.[97]

After our visit with Augie, we proceeded north on Highway 1. At the northern-most city limits of Santa Cruz, just west of the intersection of the Coast Road and Shaffer Avenue, we found *Rancio D'Bronco*. The ranch where I had worked during my summer vacations, moving all those irrigation pipes, was still under cultivation growing brussel sprouts. As I gazed upon the green planted fields, I began telling Reno the strangely ironic story of why my father and brother, years later had been once again forced to pack up and leave yet another ranch. I explained why my father had left the Gulch Ranch after his dispute with Pete Rinaldi, and how, with my brother, he had formed his own company

Circa 1957, Julio Rinaldi, Pete's only son, in a joint venture with other partners, leased land near where the University of California Santa Cruz now has its Marine Science campus. As Providence would have it, the dirt road to that piece of property cut through Bronco's ranch. Pete Rinaldi often drove down this road to visit his son. Bronco would grit his teeth every time he saw Pete driving through his ranch. He still held Pete Rinaldi personally responsible for him having to leave the Gulch Ranch. He considered Pete's reappearance into his life to be a very bad omen.

La Nostra Costa (Our Coast)

It took several years to come to pass, but Bronco's forebodings proved correct. In 1973, Donald Younger, the attorney who owned the land, informed my father and brother that he was not going to renew their lease. It was later learned that he had in fact made arrangements to lease the land to Julio Rinaldi and his partners. According to my brother, this was strictly a business deal. Although my brother doesn't know for sure who really initiated the process, it was obvious to him that *Rancio D' Bronco* was used, somehow, as an inducement to seal the deal.

After nearly 20 years of leasing the land and faithfully paying the rent, my brother and father, as well as my mother, were shocked that they were not afforded the time or opportunity to renegotiate the terms of the lease. Once again Bronco and my brother, with very little warning, were sent packing. Of course, my father blamed the Rinaldis. However, Valentina thought the attorney was more to blame, because he had not given them an opportunity to stay. In fact, in a chance encounter at a local grocery store, my mother, who was still very upset about the matter, approached Younger and told him exactly what she thought of him. Using pretty good English, Valentina with some anger in her voice said, "Mr. Younger, you are no gentleman." She then turned her back on the astonished attorney and walked away.

I told Reno that many years later, I happened to have a conversation with Pete Rinaldi. By then "Il Bosso", who had outlived both my parents, was in his nineties. He began by telling me that he had been carrying something on his mind for several years and that he wanted to talk to me about it. Not hesitating a bit, he told me that he had advised his son Julio against taking over my father's ranch. He proceeded to tell me that he had always felt badly about what had happened on the Gulch Ranch, and that he didn't want to create any more problems for my family. Pete said that he was very troubled by the eventual take-over.

Out of the blue, Pete then remembered a chance encounter he once had with me when I was working on my father's ranch *circa* 1958. As he was driving by in his pickup truck (going to visit Julio), he saw me working in the fields near the dirt road. As he approached where I was standing (probably with a hoe in my hand), he was surprised to see me give him a slight wave of the hand. This encouraged him to stop his truck and to start a conversation with me. As I recall it, the conversation was short but amicable. We mainly discussed my desire to become a policeman. Like Bronco, Pete thought that any occupation was better than that of the *rancere*. That conversation with me at that particular time, according to Pete, gave him some hope that eventually things would get better between our two families. I can assure the reader that Pete spoke with such conviction on this latter occasion, that he left me with no reason to doubt his sincerity. Of course, any chance of reconciliation with my father and mother ended when Julio and his partners took over Bronco's ranch. "Il Bosso" died not long after having this conversation with me. He had lived to be ninety-eight years old. He and his wife, Rina, are buried at Holy Cross Cemetery in Santa Cruz, not too far from Bronco and Valentina.

Leaving Bronco's ranch, Reno, Franca, and I proceeded north to the Rodoni Ranch. The ranch compound looked pretty much the same, although the "big gravel yard" seemed a lot smaller than I remembered it. The house were Dante showed us all those movies is still there, as is the barn where we played "Rubber Guns." Mario Rodoni and his family still manage the Rodoni Ranch and now, also, the Gulch Ranch (except for *il buco*). They also own the land and houses off Dimeo Lane, where the Fambrini family once lived and farmed. As much as things seem to change, some things stay almost the same.

Continuing on, we drove past the spot where our house used to be (or at least where I thought it was) and proceeded down what would have been a big dip in the road. There is not much of a dip now. Those cement trucks certainly would have had a much easier time on this kind of road, but I don't think Fernando would have had as much fun riding his motorcycle here. There to our right, just off the road, was *il buco*. We turned right and descended into "The Hole." We parked near the old barn where my mother once cleaned sprouts and where I had once played "I Spy" in the sprout leaves. I told Reno this was the place where my father had had his faithful argument with Pete Rinaldi. What's that old saying? If walls could only talk! A lot of Comelli family history was recorded in that barn.

Looking straight ahead we saw the "cookahousa." Now that I got a closer look at it, it seemed smaller then I had remembered it. It appeared that someone was living there now. But absent were all those throat-tightening, saliva-producing "quando si mangia" smells created by Valentina's cooking. Ironically, the cookhouse was shut down shortly after we left the ranch. The *ranceri* had gotten a twenty-five cent an hour raise, but their hot, cooked meals were taken away. The reader asks, "Who got the better deal?" Depends on who was doing the cooking.

Reno turned the car around, and we proceeded back towards the Coast Road. Looking to my left, I spotted a place where we used to play as kids. I asked Reno if he remembered the hornet's nest incident. He said that he did. I pointed out that it happened at that spot just off to his immediate left, just below the Coast Road. At the time it was mostly vacant land covered with shrubs, fallen Eucalyptus trees, and abandoned farm equipment. As kids, we used to play cowboys and Indians, chasing each other over the fallen trunks. We even climbed up on some of the old abandoned farm equipment, pretending that they were covered wagons. (Westward, Ho!) Unbeknown to us, a group of hornets had decided to hitch a ride, by building a hive underneath one of the wagons. On one particular occasion, our play disturbed them, and they commenced a pre-emptive strike! We all panicked and started running. I got stung on top of my head. My brother got stung on the lip. The others suffered minor stings. After the attack my brother's lip became so swollen and deformed that we naturally nicknamed him, "Ubangi." Well, Ubangi was stinging mad. I guess he didn't like me kidding him about his fat lip, because he started chasing me all over the house. I don't think he ever caught me. I was young and fast; Ubangi was old and slow.

We reached the Coast Road and proceeded north, passing the Red, White and Blue Beach, where the Scaroni family once had lived, and reached the Lorenzi Ranch. I told Reno to turn left onto the Old Coast Road. There they all stood as before: first, the house where the Cerris had lived, then the Lorenzi house, then the Ceragioli house. They looked a little worn, but all still standing. I became a little sad when I told Reno that "Glo Glo", who kept us informed of all the happenings *su per la costa*, had died so young. These coastal houses seem to find a way to outlive their owners.

I asked Reno to stop at 5420 Old Coast Road. This was Serafina's. I got out of the car and took a really long look. I couldn't believe this was the same building where my mother had had her party, and where I had waited impatiently for all those police officers to come in. It seemed we couldn't have had so many good times in that small house. I resisted the impulse to knock on the door and see whether the people living there would let me come inside and look. Naw! Better to preserve the memories I have in my mind. Besides, the jukebox is no longer there. It wouldn't be the same without hearing it play the lively "Beer Barrel Polk," or hearing that guy melodiously tell that certain lady to "Lay That Pistol Down."

Giving a wave good-bye to the old building, I got back in the car and we proceeded north along the new Coast Road. We didn't have to go too far, for there on our right we spotted the sunken enclave. Even though it was denuded of trees, Reno immediately recognized Laguna. We turned right off the road onto what surely must have been part of the old Laguna curve. Although there was no fog, Reno, like my father, drove the car very carefully down to the bottom of the hill. As I have previously written, the old Laguna Inn building was still standing, but no one was around. Now we parked for a while and talked about all the good times we had enjoyed during those festive picnics. The attentive reader asks, "Did you find the spot where those *ciuco* boys from Davenport vomited all over their car?" No way. The old barn-like building was gone, thus my point of reference was also gone. All that's left is the memory.

At about this time, Reno and I broke out singing "Quel Mazzolin di Fiori," in tribute to the "Cantatori di Laguna." Franca broke out laughing. I was glad to see her having such a good time. After

La Nostra Costa (Our Coast)

finishing our song, Reno turned the car around and we chugged up the hill. Reaching the top, we turned right on the Coast Road and headed for Davenport.

At Davenport, we made a right turn where the New Cash Store stands today (at Coast Road and Davenport Avenue). I recounted to Reno all the times my father drove us to this location to buy groceries at the Old Cash Store. Reno said he still remembered the savory smells of dry salami, cheese, and ground coffee beans, which permeated inside the building. Guess what? Just thinking about it caused my throat to tighten and my mouth to fill with that sweet watery liquid. Tony Marcucci's favorite snack of cheese, salami, fresh French bread, and a glass of red wine would have tasted really good.

The reader now asks with some annoyance, "Why didn't you two turkeys just go in and get some food?" Alas, I don't believe that the proprietors of the cafe in the new building would cater much to the culinary tastes of two *figli della costa*. Sons of the coast or not, the *chiacciera* would be missing. The "chatter and gossip" among the storekeepers and the patrons, which were so much a part of the ambiance of the earlier store, had now gone silent.

We proceeded down the hill, along what was once the Old Coast Road, and turned right on Fair Avenue. Reno pointed to the house where he and his family had once lived. To my surprise, it was directly across from the spot where my godmother, Pina Micossi, had moved her family after the Hotel D'Italia burned down. As we were standing outside our car looking at the houses, Reno struck up a conversation with a woman living next-door. She told him that she and her family had been living in the Davenport area for about 50 years. She pointed to the house where Silvio and Elena Moro once lived, on the corner of San Vincente at the intersection of Martin and the Old Coast Road. She said she still remembered Fernando Moro riding his motorcycle to the end of Fair Street, making a u-turn, and roaring back up the street. Reno, of course, couldn't resist telling her his favorite Davenport story, regarding the ice cream cone and the Fascist salute. Leaving her with a quizzical look on her face (which said, "Could that really have happened right here in Davenport?") we said our good-byes and headed down the hill, to the place where the Hotel D'Italia used to be.

As the reader already knows, trees and shrubbery cover the area now. Unfortunately, there was no evidence—which I could see—that the hotel had ever been there. I guess we will have to rely on historical writings, old pictures, and our memories to preserve its very existence. On the other hand, wouldn't it be something if some young entrepreneur (perhaps the reader) came along and built a replica of the old hotel, complete with a *bocce* ball court? Maybe a descendant of one of those Native American tribes could purchase the land and build a gambling casino with lots and lots of slot machines. Why not here—where all those cement workers and *ranceri* once lived and socialized? Just some thoughts from an old *figlio*.

In the old days the road continued up and around the Hotel D'Italia, in a semi-circular manner, much like the Laguna Curve. The road is now blocked off, so Reno had to turn the car around and head back in the same direction we'd come. As we passed the parking lot where Charlie Bella's Ocean View Hotel used to stand, a vision of that *ciuco* with the fat belly, telling me not to look at him, flashed across my mind. I wondered what ever had happened to him? It doesn't really matter. I am sure he never did realize how his behavior that day, so many years ago, affected a little boy from *la costa*.

With this thought still in my mind, I asked Reno to stop at the Whale City Bakery Bar and Grill, on the southeast corner of the Coast Road and Ocean Avenue. We went inside to get a couple of Cokes and refresh ourselves. Today the store caters mainly to tourists, bicyclists, and whale watchers. In the "good old days," this once had been the Miramar Cafe, which was owned by Gilbert and Mary Caiocca, who also owned the Davenport Bakery. As I remember it then, the building had a bar section along one side and a store section in the front where bread and other items were sold. As the reader might remember, after the Hotel D'Italia burned down, Pina Micossi took her liquor license with her, and continued in her occupation as a cook at this location. Instead of visiting my godmother at the Hotel, we would have visited her here.

I can still remember going into the kitchen in the back to see her. While Pina cooked, she and my father would converse in Friulano. Soon, getting bored, I would wander to the front of the store and look at all the items for sale. Then I would engage in my favorite pastime of watching the men drinking and talking at the bar. With the Hotel D'Italia gone, the bar at Ocean View Hotel, and the bar here, became the two main watering holes in Davenport. Since this was a smaller bar than the one at the Ocean View Hotel, most of the patrons here, knew then that I was the son of *Bronco della Costa*. I don't remember ever being told not to look at them while they were drinking.

Later, the building was remodeled. The store section was eliminated and the bar was installed in the front section of the building. As we looked around, I remembered a Friulano named Louie, who had bartended right where the front counter is today. I told Reno that Louie had been a notorious *ciuco* who didn't last too long. As Pina soon found out, it had been like putting the fox in the henhouse. Louie liked to drink behind the bar, but not pay. Thinking about this reminded me of a humorous story about Bronco giving Louie a lift, which then I told to Reno and Franca. It went like this.

One evening, Bronco offered to drive Louie back to Davenport. (Louie had probably conned someone else to bring him to our house.) With John and I seated in the back, and Louie in the front passenger seat, Bronco shifted the Old Carrettone into high gear and proceeded north on the Coast Road. On the way up, my brother and I found it quite amusing to hear Louie, who always had a few belts in him, giving my father advice—on when to dim the lights, and how to "steer the curves." Thinking that my father was driving too fast, Louie kept demanding that he "slow down." This was very funny to us, because Bronco was not known to drive very fast. After delivering Louie to the Ocean View Hotel, presumably to have a nightcap, Bronco turned the old car around and sarcastically commented to us in Italian: "Figli, that's the last time I will give him a ride. I will never again listen to him telling me how to 'drivar la macchina.' If I would have listened to that old *ciuco*, we would have gotten to Davenport *domani sera*." Personally, I thought that Bronco's estimated arrival time of tomorrow night, might have been a bit optimistic. (Later, of course, I was to learn that it is typical of older "drinking drivers" to drive very slowly, unknowingly making themselves easy marks for any police officer on the prowl.)

Having refreshed ourselves at the Whale City Bakery Bar and Grill, we turned to leave. "Wait a minute!" Reno exclaimed, pointing. "Didn't the Gregory's have a service station on that corner over there?" I replied, "They certainly did."[98]

"Well," Reno said, "there's where I was offered the ice cream if I gave the Fascist salute. There used to be a building in the back. The meeting was held there." Indeed, we could see there was a small building in the back, though Reno was not sure it was the same one.

Unable to decide whether or not the building was the same, we continued on with our journey, driving past the Cement Plant, and turning right into New Town. There on First Street, Reno pointed out where the Brovias lived. Reno recalled that Pete wasn't too happy that Pino was spending an inordinate amount of time playing ball on this street. Reno remembers that he and his dad often visited the Brovia household. Pete would pour a couple of glasses of wine at the kitchen table, and then, peering over his eyeglasses and speaking in his deep baritone voice, he would say to Guido, "I have two daughters and one crazy son. Look at him out there! Gioca [**joh** kah] sempre con con quella palla!" Not knowing too much about the game of baseball himself, Pete did not quite understand why Pino was always playing with that ball. (Sometimes I get the same feeling nowadays, as I watch my young grandsons, Wyatt, Cole, Willie, Michael, and Kristian, standing in an open field, all the while enduring the hot rays of the afternoon sun, just to play with that ball. Just like Pino, they love the game.)

La Nostra Costa (Our Coast)

Later, when Pino played professional ball, Pete became a thoroughly knowledgeable and devoted baseball fan. When my family visited the Brovias at their new home in Santa Cruz *circa* 1953, Pete would station me or my brother in front of a small radio set. As the baseball game came on he would interrupt his conversation with my parents and ask me, "Who is hitting clean up?" Using my best baseball-announcer voice, I would reply, "Joooe **Broo**-vee-yah!" A big smile would come across Pete's face and he would say, "That's good, that's good. Let me know when Pino comes to bat." Then he would pick up the conversation just were he'd left off.

Reno pointed to the house at 19 Third Street, which he believed was where the Comelli family had lived. However, Pino's sister, Virginia, told me, at a recent Coast Road reunion, that our family had lived on First Street, not Third. First or Third, I know that I can lay claim to having once lived in this historic section of Davenport, even though I don't remember anything about it. So much for being too young.

We left New Town and proceeded northbound up the Coast Road, inspecting Davenport Landing, where it had all begun. There, near the intersection of Davenport Landing Road and Highway 1, Reno pointed out the very first school he ever attended. It looked a bit dilapidated now, but if I am correct in my thinking, this was the school building mentioned in Margaret Koch's book, *Santa Cruz County, Parade Of The Past*, as once having been moved in its entirety, under stealth of night, from Scotts Creek to here—by unknown persons. Apparently, those who'd done it (presumably adult males from Davenport Landing) didn't like the fact that the kids living at Davenport Landing had to travel all the way to Scotts Creek to attend school. Therefore on one memorable night *circa* 1908, they simply hitched their horses to the building, and towed it to its present location. I guess that was how things were done in those days. If you didn't like things as they were, you simply changed them. No need for a referendum. (On a subsequent trip in 2004, I noticed that the building had been torn down. Even *su per la costa*, some things don't last forever.)

As we drove down Davenport Landing Road, I saw a very nice sandy beach near where Captain Davenport had built his pier. This was probably a place of great excitement in those old whale-hunting days. A thought suddenly came to mind. I ask the reader to take a moment to imagine with me: *ranceri* coming out of the planted fields with harpoons in hand, running across that beach to get to their boats, all the while shouting, *Ecco la soffiata* [so **fyah** tah] *va! Ecco la soffiata va!* which very loosely translates as "Thar she blows! Thar she blows!" It could have happened—don't you think?

Laughing at this humorous notion, I urged Reno to proceed north on the Coast Road. Approximately four miles north of Davenport Landing, Reno pulled over to the west side of the road. "Here," he said. "Here is where the old Cantarutti house was located." We got out of the car and looked towards the ocean. The house (or shack) is no longer there, but I could still see why my mother was afraid that I would fall in the ocean. About 500 or so feet from where Reno said the house used to be, there is a cliff that drops straight down into the Pacific Ocean. My gosh! *Il vento* could have blown us right over. Given the hard times experienced in those years, the *ranceri* had to live somewhere, but this was certainly no place for kids. (I think $5 per month was outrageous rent for such a place.) After taking some pictures of the place, we continued northward, then turned right onto the northern-most connection with Swanton Road. This road at first runs in an easterly direction up a steep grade, and then down into a valley. Then in a semi-circular fashion it cuts back through the valley (for about seven and a half miles) and rejoins the Coast Road roughly two miles north of Davenport. According to Margaret Koch's book, this area in the 1800s was known as Laurel Grove. It was later renamed for Fred Swanton, who in 1896 had established here the Big Creek Power Company, which was the first to service Santa Cruz and Watsonville with electricity.

Interestingly enough, it was also Swanton's idea to build a "Coney Island" type resort on the beach in Santa Cruz. This is now the location of the famous Santa Cruz Boardwalk. As attested to by banner headlines in the May 4, 1927 edition of the *Santa Cruz Evening News*, this amazing man was elected Mayor of Santa Cruz.

The paper described his "sweeping" victory. Wow! I must confess to the reader that, as a boy, I thought this area was called Swampton, because, to my way of thinking, it had a big swamp with "quicksand" hidden deep in its interior. My sincere apologies to His Honor, the Mayor.

As we started up the steep incline of Swanton Road (I believe this is identified by Margaret Koch as Gianone Hill), a sudden thought came to my mind. I told Reno that I believed this was where Bronco was almost killed in a traffic accident. The incident must have occurred some time before my father's return to Italy in 1931. I remember Bronco telling the story many times. He was a passenger in a vehicle driven by a friend. As they were coming down the hill, his friend took the curve too fast. The car went over the side and rolled down the hill. Bronco was knocked unconscious. When he came to his senses, he found himself lying face down on the ground. The only injury he had sustained was a badly bruised knee. He quickly got up and limped to the wrecked car to see if his friend was all right. To his dismay, he found his friend dead, still seated inside the car. Apparently he had died from a broken neck. It was too late for his friend. However, Bronco was able to climb to the top of the hill and find help. He never could figure out how he was thrown clear of the wreckage without being killed. Lucky for me he wasn't. Otherwise, I would not be here today writing this story.

I later learned from Thelma Gill, that my father had been working for Vittorio Basso at the Belvedere (Beautiful View) Ranch.[99] He and this friend, who she could identify only as Guerino, were on their way to a wedding that day, when the accident happened. The year was 1927 (my father would have been twenty-seven years old at the time). The Belvedere Ranch was in the area. Could it be that my father had mentioned this to me, or were those "ghosts of the coast" playing games with me?

Reaching the top of the hill, we started our descent into the valley. At the bottom of the hill, Reno was able to find yet another one of his old schools. The building is still there. It is a red building and bears a sign over the door: "Old Seaside School." It has been remodeled and apparently a family is living there now. The amazing story here is that Reno had to walk to this school from that "shack" where he lived on the coast—about six miles. Reno said it was all right when the weather was nice, but that when it rained, the forest he had to walk through got wet and muddy. This made it kind of rough going. I guess so! And I had complained about walking to the Rodoni Ranch to catch the bus! I never knew I had it so good.

As we proceeded southward on Swanton Road, another flashback memory came to me. I asked Reno if he remembered Johnny Modolo. "Sure," he said. "His family had a ranch in this valley. I think he was killed when he was thrown off a bull. There was a big funeral. The whole coast must have been there."

At this point the reader might think it a bit incredible that, at the time, I did not know Johnny Modolo's family had a ranch in the Swanton Valley. All I knew was that Johnny Modolo had lived up the coast near Davenport. As I have said before, those "ghosts of the coast" have a strange way of talking to me. I do have memories of Johnny Modolo from when we rode the school bus that took us to Santa Cruz. I was still in elementary school and he was attending the high school. (Johnny was a 1946 graduate of Santa Cruz High School.) I remembered him as being tall and very good-looking. He was always smiling and it seemed that everybody on the bus liked him. He even took time out to say a few kind words to me, only a small fry at the time.

According to a very short article appearing in the *Santa Cruz Sentinel*, dated Monday, May 3, 1948, Johnny died on that date, at a local hospital, from injuries sustained on the previous Tuesday (April 26), after being thrown from a cow. In a much more recent article, it was stated that Johnny "had been bucked off a cow while fooling around with a couple of his friends..."[100] When he fell, he apparently sustained internal injuries which led to his untimely death. He was only twenty years old. The whole coast mourned his loss. Although I had only known him a short time, I felt I had lost a friend.

We proceeded onward and finally arrived at the southern-most intersection of Swanton and the Coast Road. As we were about to pull out onto the Coast Road, I told Reno to stop the car. I asked him if he remembered *The Accident*. "How can anyone forget?" he replied. "I think it involved a fire truck." Indeed, this was probably the most infamous intersection in Davenport traffic history. This was where the DeLucca car smashed into the Forestry Fire Truck—all those people killed and maimed here, more than 55 years ago.

I got out of the car and made a visual inspection of the intersection. Standing on Swanton Road and looking southward down the Coast Road, I tried to visualize the DeLucca car approaching the intersection. As Swanton Road approaches the Coast Road, it makes a noticeable dip as it comes off a downhill grade. The high ground on the left side (the driver-side approaching the Coast Road) of the roadway obstructs the view of oncoming traffic traveling north. However, the stop sign on the right-hand side of the intersection where I now stood is forward of that high ground. I had a clear view of oncoming traffic. Under present conditions, the driver of the CDF truck should have had decent visibility from where I was standing, at least enough to see the car approaching from the south. On the other hand, Amerigo DeLucca should have had enough time to see the CDF truck pulling out onto the roadway. The article in the *Santa Cruz Sentinel*, dated August 3, 1947, stated that Highway Patrol officers believed that the truck was traveling at a low rate of speed and that the sedan was traveling at a high rate of speed. Was speed the only factor here? What about impaired visibility? Perhaps the roadways were later improved to provide for better visibility. Or perhaps, with all those people in the DeLucca car, some distraction was involved? Just the thoughts of an "old cop" here. I don't think it matters much anymore. People died here so long ago and nothing will ever change that.

Still weighing these considerations in my mind, I returned to the car and we proceeded southward along the Coast Road. We passed Davenport, passed Laguna, passed Serafina's, passed the Gulch and Rodoni Ranches, and finally passed *Rancio D'Bronco*. Just like *that*, my earlier year's *su per la costa* had flown by—or so it appeared to me. But before leaving the coast, I knew I had one more thing to do. I had to retrace the steps of my father. Those "ghosts of the coast" would not let me go in peace.

Endnotes

[97] The Italian Film Festival, featuring newly released Italian films, is held annually in San Rafael, California. Website: www.italianfilm.com.

[98] For many years, the Gregory family owned and operated a service station and small grocery store on the northeast corner of Highway 1 and Ocean Avenue. Brothers Alvin and Francis later sold the store and, like many inhabitants of Davenport, moved to Santa Cruz.

[99] Vittorio Basso, also known *su per la costa as Vittorio del Belvedere*, was a Friulano who for many years worked on the coastal rancios, mostly for Pino Phyffer. A life-long bachelor, he was renowned (at least during the time I knew him) for his silver-white hair and his skill at smoothly gliding, with a female companion well in hand, over a ballroom dance floor. Later, at John's Confirmation, he would be my brother's padrino.

[100] "If These Walls Could Talk," by Peggy Townsend, *Santa Cruz Sentinel*, July 9, 2000.

30. Da Solo (Alone)

This time I went alone—to the spot where our house and the Gemignani house had stood side-by-side along the Coast Road, so long ago. I parked my truck off Dimeo Lane where it intersects the Coast Road—just about where the Gulch Ranch *dama* used to be. I walked the short route (though on the opposite side of the road) which I had once walked every day with my brother, to and from the bus stop at the Rodoni Ranch, until I came to where I thought the two houses had once been.

Of course, nothing seemed the same anymore. It appears that a segment of the new Coast Road actually cuts across the site were the two houses once stood. Also, as I have previously mentioned, when the new Coast Road was built, the steep grade that descended into the Gulch was leveled off. Now there is only a slight downward slope to the road. I tried to locate the approximate site of the houses. I looked off towards the Pacific Ocean and found a dirt road running in a westerly direction off the Coast Road. It appeared to be in roughly the same location as the one that the Coast Guard and their security dog used to take on their evening marches to the "lookout house". As I recall, our house was just to the left of that road as you faced the ocean. I was pretty sure that I had located the general area where my family once walked and where Joe Gemignani cursed his defiant motorcycle.

Turning myself around, I looked to the east towards the foothills and tried to locate the "road course" that my brother and I had used with the Old Carrettone. The dirt road is no longer there, however, I still could visualize the two of us coming down that hill at breakneck speed: the Old Carrettone, right-side wheels off the ground, left-side wheels digging deep into the dirt, making its sharp turn at the bottom, at just about where I was now standing.[101]

After a few moments of solitude, I turned to the north and began walking towards *il buco*. The path that my father actually took to work each day, is probably no longer there, because of the construction of the new Coast Road. However, the direction and the distance are the same. As I walked, I tried to imagine my father starting his morning walk to the "cookahousa," dressed in an old, faded brown work shirt, and blue Levi pants with the legs securely tied to his ankle-top leather boots. Yes, I now could see him—his *cappllo* slightly pulled at an angle over his right eye—walking along while singing, in his deep resonant voice, the words of an old Italian song:

"Sul Ponte di Bassano,

Noi si darem la mano,

Noi si darem la mano,

E un bacin da mor,

E un bacin da mor,

E un bacin -daaa MORRR"[102]

On the Bassano Bridge

We will give each other our hand

We will give each other our hand

And a kiss of love

And a kiss of love

AND A KISS OF LOVE!

Before I knew it, I had reached the top of the Gulch. I looked down and there, for the first time since my family left the ranch, many years ago, I saw *il buco* from the top of the Gulch, just as my father would have seen it on a normal work day. There at the bottom of the incline was the old cookhouse where my mother cooked and where my father had his daily meals. It is still hard to believe that all those men used to eat and/or live in that small building. Unknown to me at the time, this was the last opportunity that I would ever have to see the "cookahousa" standing.

Later, on March 30, 2002, while driving on the Coast Road I noticed the charred remains of the old cookhouse. Quickly, I drove my car down into *il buco* to get a better look at the ashes and rubble that remained. Perhaps I could find a clue as to what had happened. There I met, Mr. Lee Yen, who informed me that the cookhouse had accidentally burned down the month previous. Mr. Yen was of the opinion that the fire was caused by faulty electrical wiring.[103]

Seeking more information about the fire, I found an article appearing in *The Santa Cruz Sentinel*, dated February 8, 2002, which reported that firefighters had responded to 3050 Coast Road on the evening of February 7 at approximately 8:45 p.m. According to the story, nine farm workers and a two-month-old child had lived in the structure. Thank God, no one was reported killed or injured. It just would not have been fitting for the old "cookahousa" to go out that way. On the other hand, a "Viking Funeral" was not a bad way to go. Imagine all those memories rising up in smoke, to circulate the Earth forever and ever.

Yet as I stood now at the top of the Gulch looking down, unaware of the misfortune to come upon the old "cookahousa," I tried to visualize *il buco* as it once had been. I noticed that the sheds, where the men used to wash up and where the wine was stored, were now gone. Many of the other sheds and garages were also gone or moved to different locations. I also noticed that only a single building that had housed the Filipino workers was still standing. As I have previously written, the big barn where Valentina used to clean sprouts was still there, but gone was the corral where Charlie and Prince used to romp and stomp. A house (probably where the foremen used to live) stood in its place.

For some reason, I hesitated and did not actually descend into *il buco*. Instead I turned and slowly retraced my father's old steps, back to where our old house had been. Once on the spot, I turned and looked at the Pacific Ocean. I decided I had to take one last walk to *Il Mare*. I walked back to my truck and drove to the main access road to the beach, which still turns off the Coast Road just west of *il buco*. This is the way taken by the ocean surfers of today.

I walked down (only farm vehicles are allowed) this dirt road and arrived at the Southern Pacific railroad tracks. There, still running parallel to the tracks, was that infamous dirt road where I had learned to drive the Old Carrettone. Oh, how many times had I driven up and down this dusty road, trying to master the intricacies of stepping on the clutch and shifting the gears without killing the engine? As I said, Bronco must have had a lot of patience. At least I was better at it than my brother.

I continued on towards the beach. Just to the west of the tracks was a barren field. I paused and took a long look at the ground. It was then that I remembered the airplane crash and my father's impromptu burial of human remains. In memory of the two fallen pilots, I bowed my head and silently said an "Our Father." Then using the two fingers of my right hand, I made the sign of the cross over the field and said out loud, "Dominus Vobiscum. In Nomine Patris, et Filii, et Spiritus Sancti, Amen." Today, at least *one* visitor to the beach would remember what had happened here on that day so long ago. The "ghosts of the coast" did not let me forget.

I proceeded to the bluff where the "lookout house" used to be. There I gazed again on "The Beach" for the first time since I care to remember. To my surprise the water was calm. So much so, that would-be surfers were leaving in disgust. There were very few waves to speak of. Could it be that *Il Mare* had calmed itself after all these years? And where was *il vento?* There was very little wind blowing. No smell of *pattume,* either. This was definitely not how I remembered *la costa.* I walked closer to the edge and took a good look at the gulch where on that memorable day, the ocean with such vengeance had completely ripped things apart. This time it still had all its green vegetation and looked undisturbed. This was further evidence that the ocean had been behaving itself. In the background *Il Mare* was emitting a low moan, rather than a roar. It looked even inviting enough to take a swim. Then I remembered. This is how it lulls you into thinking it is safe. "Come on in, little boy. Nothing is going to happen. It's safe, and you can have so much fun!" It was then that I remembered my mother's warning: "Il mare e traditore [trrah **dee** torreh]." Her meaning was clear. "The ocean is a traitor. It will turn on you."

Remembering Valentina's warning caused a very frightening vision to cross my mind. In the early 1990s I had taken my grandson Andrew, then about four years old, to Carmel Beach. The surf that day was rather rough, but Andrew begged me to take him wading. I gave in and took him into the water with me, but kept him away from the breaking surf. I watched him very closely as he stood by a sandbar waiting for the water to come up to his feet. Time and again the surf came up and the water gently caressed his feet. I kept a cautious eye on Andrew, but I had my back to the ocean. All of a sudden, a big wave crashed down behind me. The surf rushed past me, hitting the sandbar. The impact caused the water to violently splash upward and then curve back towards the sea, creating a forceful undertow. Andrew, caught in the whiplash motion of this current, was being swept off his feet. Fortunately, I was standing next to him. In one quick movement, I grabbed him and carried him out of harm's way. *Damn you, Mare! Valentina was right! You are a traditore! From thee I snatch this innocent soul. Damn you!*

Now, standing on the bluff, I shook this vision from my mind, and walked to the spot where I believed Mario and I had stood watch over the two lovers grappling in the sand. Because the rock formations on the beach itself were pretty much as I remembered them, I was able to find the spot with some degree of accuracy. (The hole that Mario had dug to get a better look was no longer there.) Looking over the edge, I could see what a precarious spot it really was. The drop to the sand below must be at least 100 feet, or more. Whoa! What if we had gotten really excited and leaned way over the edge to get a better look? It could have been more than an empty sprout crate falling on those two below. That certainly would have gotten their attention.

Laughing to myself as I recalled Mario's dirt-filled eye, I suddenly remembered that I, too, had enticed a young lady to this beach. It was during my college years, and I had fallen in love with a Mexican girl. Rosie Linda Reyes was tall and slender, with light brown skin, long black hair, shining white teeth, and dark brown eyes. Remembering what I had seen on this beach as a boy, I thought that I might have similar success with her; thus did I lure her to this very spot. I must confess that I did make some progress, though Rosie stopped me from fulfilling my boyhood fantasy. It was not to be.

As fate would have it, nothing was to be. Just before I entered the Army in 1960, Rosie and I decided to break up. When I returned to San Jose in 1962, I was dealt a crushing blow. Rosie had been diagnosed with cancer. A year later she was dead. Rosie Linda Reyes was only twenty-four years old. Still thinking about her, I looked out over the Pacific Ocean. From way out there a familiar tune came to my mind. Quietly, I began singing the lyrics: "Out in the West Town of El Paso, I fell in Love with a Mexican Girl." Marty Robbins' 1959 hit record "El Paso" will forever remind me of that time, this place, and a beautiful Mexican girl. Just as in the song, this story ended with a sudden and tragic death.

Now that the State of California, by law, has granted beach access, everybody has an opportunity to see and use this beach, which I once called my own. Maybe that's as it should be. The only thing I don't understand is why, when we were young, my mother always took us to the beaches in Santa Cruz. We seldom came to this beach to sunbathe. It was often cold and the water too rough to swim in. I guess the advent of the wet suit has changed all that. The surfer is king here now.

Perhaps trying to get a glimpse of the past, I took one last look, as the golden rays of the afternoon sun reflected off the blue green hue of the Pacific Ocean. Wouldn't it be wonderful, I thought, if somewhere out there, memories of the past *did* coincide with the realities of the present. Wouldn't it be wonderful if the old could join with the new, to once again roam the open fields *su per la costa*. With a touch of sadness in my heart, I turned and slowly walked back from whence I came. *No ci son pui i ranceri; no ci son pui i amici della costa lunga passata.* Yes, it was true. The ranchers were gone and so were the coastal friends of long ago. With them went the stage on which they played out their lives. *La Nostra Costa* is the name I have chosen to give to their stage; and to the faithful reader who has been with me on my journey to and from *la costa*, I most assertively, and with great sincerity, give the following assurance. Their actions on that platform were live, vivid, and above all, real. Hopefully, this book, in some small way, will help preserve their performance for others who follow. *Adio, ranceri mi! Adio amici della Nostra Costa!*

Endnotes

[101] Come to think of it, things haven't changed much now. My seventeen-year-old grandson Christopher recently wrecked his second-hand Jetta by driving too fast on his own "road course." Coming down a hill at breakneck speed, he quickly zipped up a steep embankment on the opposite side (shades of Fernando and his motorcycle at *Il Golce*) and found himself airborne (100 feet) at the top. He wasn't hurt. However, his car wasn't the Old Carrettone. Its undercarriage was completely wiped out.

[102] Il Ponte di Bassano is an ancient bridge in Italy that crosses the river Brenta in the province of Vicenzo. It has been destroyed and reconstructed eleven times and is the subject of much folklore. It is also known as Il Ponte di Alpini. Websites: www.vecio.it/bassano.htm .

[103] Interesting enough, I was to learn from Mr. Yen that *Il Buco* was now privately owned. Mr. Yen, a mushroom farmer, said he had purchased the parcel from Al Rossi, a local rancher and landowner. Apparently, when the State of California, in an attempt to preserve the coastlands, purchased many of the coastal ranches in the 1960s, 16 acres that included Il Buco were partitioned for private ownership. Al Rossi, apparently, purchased the property and subsequently sold it to Mr. Yen. This was probably the same Albie Rossi of Joe Gemignani's *Figli di Ferro* fame.

31. Dopo La Costa
(After The Coast)

In 1973, Bronco, Valentina, and my brother John, for the first time in their lives ventured off the coast to work a new *rancio*. Having to leave *Rancio D'Bronco*, they negotiated a lease with Mr. John DeBenedetti for approximately 100 acres of farmland near Manresa Beach, not too far from Watsonville, an agricultural town just south of Santa Cruz. By this time, John was *il bosso*, having taken over most of the responsibilities for managing the G. Comelli and Son Partnership. There they continued to grow and harvest brussel sprouts, the crop that had provided them with so much success *su per la costa*. As for me, I continued on with my career as a San Jose police officer.[104]

In 1976, Valentina was suddenly stricken with stomach cancer. Despite our determined efforts to save her, using conventional as well as unconventional means, my mother died in April 1977. She was only sixty-four years old. A large number of *ranceri* and *amici della la costa* attended her funeral. Many condolences were expressed that day; however, one woman, without saying a word, expressed above all, what the death of my mother meant to her *amici su per la costa*. I was standing by my mother's coffin when I saw this woman, dressed entirely in black, walking alone, completely overcome with grief. As she passed the casket, this woman looked at me with tears in her eyes, and then bowing her head, slowly waved the palm of her open right hand close to the side of her face. Serafina's gesture said it all: *Your mother's love and friendship meant everything to me. I will miss her more than you will ever know.*

My mother's death, of course, devastated us all, but Bronco took it the hardest. At the time of Valentina's death, he was seventy-seven years old. Being thirteen years older than Valentina, he had always expected to go before her. After forty-five years of marriage, through good times and bad times, he now felt completely lost without her. Life, for Bronco, had lost its meaning.

Shortly after my mother passed away, I took Bronco back to Nimis, Italy. There, where his journey to *la costa* had begun, I was hoping to revive his spirits. Together we visited places that brought back memories of when a young Bronco first met Valentina. My grandfather's "bar" was no longer operational, though my mother's younger brother, Tita Bressani (he who had escaped from the Nazis in 1944), his wife, Teresina, and their young son Sandro, were still living on the premise. There, as we dined *al fresco* in my uncle's courtyard, Bronco recounted how he would bring his phonograph here, to entertain the beautiful teen-age Valentina. Then, Bronco with a touch of amusement in his voice, revealed how my grandfather, growing wary of his intentions, had chased him off with a brusque "Via di qui! E tardi!" ("Get out here! It's late!")

According to Bronco, it was much easier persuading Valentina to marry him, than getting my grandfather's permission to let her go. My grandfather was no fool. Valentina was a valuable asset to his household. On the plus side, there would be one less mouth to feed; on the minus side he would lose a diligent worker and also his main attraction at the "bar." Valentina would be of little use to him in America. Bronco still didn't know how he did it. "Tu nono era duro," Bronco told me, meaning that my grandfather was a hard man to deal with.

Although the Friuli region had just been hit with a major earthquake a year earlier, in 1976, the house of my grandfather

(Bronco's father), although damaged, was still standing. Bronco's brother Giovanni, and his wife, Laura, were living there now. Also standing, and still in reasonably good condition, was the second-story addition Bronco had built way back in 1931 with his hard-earned American dollars. Bronco was able to use it as his sleeping quarters during our stay. "Isn't it amazing, Ivano?" Bronco said to me in Italian. "After all those years *su per la costa*, I am once again back here in Nimis, sleeping in the very same room where your mother and I spent our wedding night." He added, in a very sad tone of voice, "But this time, I will be all alone."

The visit with his family in Nimis did seem to raise Bronco's spirits to some extent. Upon retuning to the United States, he remained in reasonably good health, and was still able to do some work on the *rancio*. He even made a return trip to Italy in 1979. This time he went by himself and stayed for six months. Upon his return, he continued to live at *Casa D'Valentina*.

In 1980, Bronco's extended family gathered together with old *ranceri* and *amici della costa* at Adolph's, that venerable Italian restaurant in Santa Cruz. There we celebrated my father's eightieth birthday. I was privileged to be the master of ceremonies that day. I gave a synopsis of Bronco and Valentina's journey to and from *la costa*, which encouraged many of the *amici* present to chime in with stories of their own personal experiences with my parents. Afterwards, much to the delight of the gathering, Bronco, accompanied by an accordion, entertained us with many of the Italian songs he used to sing *su per la costa*. Unfortunately, this would be the last time that Bronco would sing for his *amici*.

After his eightieth birthday, Bronco's health commenced to decline. Unexplained intestinal bleeding subjected him to constant blood transfusions. In 1983, several months after a major abdominal operation to control the bleeding, my father died. He lived to be eighty-three years old.

Although their deaths were six years apart, Bronco and Valentina both died in the same town (Santa Cruz), in the same hospital

(Dominican), and astonishingly, in the very same room. They are "buried" side-by-side, at the Holy Cross Cemetery in Santa Cruz. Hard work, perseverance, and above all, their unmitigated love for their two sons, gained them enough time, before their deaths, to realized their hopes and dreams of a better life for John and me, and consequently, also for our families. Bronco and Valentina's journey to and from *la costa* was now over.

Endnotes

[104] In 1977, my brother John and I purchased the land from the DeBenedetti family. John managed the ranch until 1997. He is now semi-retired, living with his wife Donna in Santa Cruz. I retired from the San Jose Police Department in 1989, with the permanent rank of Captain. I am currently living in Monterey County with my wife, Mildred.

Il Ultimo Ponte (The Last Bridge)

Suddenly, the *rancere* found himself at the foot of a wooden bridge, spanning a deep, dark chasm. He could not see to the other side, because of the dense fog that engulfed everything. Shivering from the cold and dampness about him, he tried to step forward, but his bent body, now old and crippled by infirmities, would not respond. The *rancere* felt confused, bewildered, and somewhat frightened. What was he doing here, in the midst of all this infernal fog? Because of his age and maladies, it had been years since he was able to walk the fields on his own. Doctors, nurses, and hospital beds were now his constant companions. This could not be—standing here alone, with this bridge that only seemed to lead deeper into the blur, before him.

As he continued to stare into the fog, he soon realized that the thick mist was starting to lift, but only on the other side of the bridge. This mystical occurrence was by no means new to the *rancere*. Numerous times, when working the fields *su per la costa*, he had found himself surrounded by fog, while *il vento*, blowing the eerie mist from land to sea, created a clearing before him. It was as if he was witnessing the world creating itself anew, while he remained, just for a moment, steadfast in the fog's obscurity.

In the clearing, the *rancere* could now see that the bridge led to a lush field of green, bathed in glorious sunlight and speckled with flowers of lavender and gold. There, amidst this floral spectrum, he thought he saw a gathering of young people. Yes, he could clearly see them now. There they were, waving to him, laughing and singing old Italian songs. Again, the *rancere* tried to move forward, but his feeble body would not respond. He tried to cry out, "Aiuto![**ai** yuto] Aiuto!" but the distraught *rancere* found himself completely helpless. No words came forth from his mouth. He couldn't even shout for help.

Miraculously, as if someone had heard his muted cry, the rancere saw what seemed to be the figure of a young woman starting to cross the bridge. Focusing his old eyes on her, he noticed the fog mysteriously receding before her, as she slowly advanced towards him. At the center of the bridge, the *rancere* could clearly see that the woman was indeed young—and so very beautiful. As the young woman stepped ever closer to the rancere, the fog released its grip on him, taking flight on the soft, gentle breeze of the wind.

The young woman now stood beside him. The *rancere's* eyes began to well up with tears of joy, as he recognized this beautiful lady to be his young wife of so long ago. The *rancere* tried to speak words of love and true endearment, but once again, no words came forth. Then without saying a word, his young wife kissed the rancere on the cheek and, taking him by the hand, urged him to walk with her, back across the bridge. With trepidation, the rancere attempted to take his first step. To his amazement, he found that he now could move his old body forward with relative ease.

Slowly at first, then with an ever-increasing pace, the *rancere* and his young wife crossed the bridge, and approached the gathering of young people. As he set foot on the other side, the *rancere* suddenly realized that his body was no longer bent over, crippled by age and infirmities. Like the others in the gathering, he once again was young and strong. In but a moment, he recognized the young people around him. His family, *ranceri* and *amici della costa*, all were there, singing and laughing, celebrating his very presence.

Finding that he once again could speak, the *rancere* turned to his beautiful wife, and asked in a voice filled with emotion and wonderment, "Oh, my dear, sweet wife! How can this be? I was old and sick, shadowy death constantly by my side. Now, by you I stand, young and able, so glad to be alive!"

His young wife smiled and looked up at the *rancere*.

"*O rancere mi,*" she replied in a soft and gentle voice. "*Don't you know? Now you are in Heaven.*"

Riconoscimenti
(Acknowledgements)

During the course of writing this book, I had great help from many friends who lived *su per la costa* during my boyhood years. Some, such as Andreina Rodoni, Diana Dinelli, John Battistini, Fred Dimeo, and Fred Moro passed away during the time I was writing. It is because of such extraordinary people, and those that had gone before them that I felt compelled to complete this book. Their contribution to the history of Santa Cruz's North Coast should not be forgotten. Fortunately, some had recorded their memories for the "Davenport Oral History Project." That fine undertaking inspired me to dig deep into my own memory and to set down in writing what I could remember.

I must thank Evelina Cantarutti and her sons Reno and Lido, whose collective memories of our families' days *su per la costa* contributed greatly to the writing of this book. A special thanks to Reno, for spending time with me "on the coast," as we relived those adventures of yesteryear. He re-affirmed many memories I had about *la costa* which, otherwise, I might have thought to be only figments of my imagination. Now, if he would only tell me if he ever got that ice cream cone for giving that stupid salute.

On the same note, I am eternally gratefully to my father's goddaughter, Thelma (Micossi) Gill, for spending so much time with me on the internet, not only exchanging information about the Hotel D'Italia, but also sharing her memories of her mother (Pina), of my father (a young Bronco), of Carabiniere, and of all those Friulanos who once worked and lived *su per la costa*. Reading her e-mails sent me back in time, to a place where I could actually see the places and people of that bygone era. Also, I must thank her cousin, Rina Micossi, for sharing her memories of her family, of Pescadero, and of the Elkhorn Restaurant.

I must not forget to thank Norma (Dinelli) Wilson and her friend Patty Morelli, for sharing their memories of Davenport and the Coast Road and for sending me information about the Lorenzi Ranch, of the DeLucca accident in Davenport, and of Johnny Modolo's premature death. Norma was only a young girl at the time, but I could see that these events affected her deeply and are indelibly etched in her mind. *La Nostra Costa* could indeed be s*paventosa*.

Marvin Del Chiaro, my old college roommate, has a memory second to none. He still can recall those drives over the hill to San Jose, and the Glans' rooming house, as if it were yesterday. He was indeed helpful in coming up with names, by which I could accurately identify many of the people I have described in this book. Still, I think that if he had been a better driver, the "old box" Ford would have made it over the hill on that snowy day in '58.

My aunt, Lina (Bressani) Gemignani, was most gracious in allowing me to use her very private memories as recorded in her book, *My Yesterdays*. After first reading it many years ago, the thought would always be in the back of my mind, of one-day doing the same. I only wish she would allow others to share her experiences, by publishing this book. I found it fascinating and well worth reading.

Alverda Orlando, who has been in the forefront in the preservation of the history of Davenport, and who is the current television moderator for the "Davenport Oral History Project," was indeed helpful in reading my original manuscript and offering useful suggestions for the improvement of its content.

I am most appreciative of the welcome afforded me by Cathy Brovia, who allowed me to use the photos of her late husband Joe "Pino" Brovia.

I am indebted to Brian Bianchini, who spent many long hours editing the manuscript. His suggestions and changes greatly improved the presentation of the story.

A very special thanks to my lovely wife, Mildred, who endured many hours of my virtual absence, as my mind wandered *su per la costa* to another time and another place. It was her approval of the final manuscript (she liked it) that encouraged me to publish the book.

Finally, a most grateful thank-you to all the *ranceri* and *amici della costa* who lived and worked "on the coast." Their lives made the story of *La Nostra Costa* possible.

— Ivano Franco Comelli

CPSIA information can be obtained
at www.ICGtesting.com
Printed in the USA
FSHW011947230320
68415FS

9 781420 879766